A CATECHUMEN'S COMPANION

A Guide to Praying with the Lectionary

Edited By

ROBERT M. HAMMA

and

DONNA M. CRILLY

Paulist Press • *New York / Mahwah, N.J.*

Text design by Cynthia Dunne
Interior art by Stella DeVenuta

Library of Congress Cataloging-in-Publication Data

A Catechumen's companion: a guide to praying with the lectionary /edited by Robert M. Hamma and Donna M. Crilly.

    p. cm.
    ISBN 0-8091-3920-0 (alk. paper)
  1. Catechumens Prayer-books and devotions—English. 2. Catholic Church—Liturgy. 3. Bible—Devotional use. 4. Church year.
I. Hamma, Robert M. II. Crilly, Donna M.
BX2170.C38C38
264'.02034—dc21   99-36228
                                    CIP

Published by Paulist Press
997 Macarthur Blvd.
Mahwah, N.J. 07430

www.paulistpress.com

Printed and bound in the United States of America

Contents

Preface

A Catechumen's Lectionary has been an important and favorite resource of RCIA participants throughout the United States during its twelve-year history in print. However, with the revision of the *Lectionary for Mass* by the National Conference of Catholic Bishops, the readings in *A Catechumen's Lectionary* no longer exactly match what its users hear at the Sunday eucharist.

A Catechumen's Companion has its roots in *A Catechumen's Lectionary*, edited by Robert Hamma. It was our desire to update *A Catechumen's Lectionary* by incorporating the revised texts, but this proved impractical. Rather than allow a well-loved resource to become outdated, we have not only excerpted the reflections and guides to prayer and journal writing from *A Catechumen's Lectionary* but have also revised them in light of the new Lectionary text. We have also updated all the Scripture references to reflect the refinements and additions in the new Lectionary.

Instead of being restricted to the Lectionary alone, now readers can take advantage of the wide range of scripture translations available in bookstores and on the Internet. Users of the *Companion* will be able to see where the readings fit within the context of the Scriptures. Bibles with commentary and notes can be used as well to unfold the richness of meaning of the Word of God. The *Companion* can also be used with a missal or other worship aids and can help catechumens as well as the Catholic Christian faithful understand the structure of the liturgical year and the rhythm of the seasons as they flow from Advent through the end of Ordinary Time.

The design has been updated and the type reset, but apart from this, it very much echoes the language and spirit of the book that Bob Hamma and his colleagues produced twelve years ago. Our thanks go to them for giving the church a still-valuable, classic resource for its new members as well as for anyone who wishes to reflect on the Scriptures in the context of the liturgical year.

Donna M. Crilly
Editor, *A Catechumen's Companion*

Introduction

The Rite of Becoming a Catechumen describes the time of the catechumenate as a journey. As a catechumen, you are invited to walk on the road of faith, following Christ, your loving guide. Having come to know God through the wonder of creation, now the way of the Gospel opens before you. Signed with the cross, you enter the church as the presider says, "We welcome you to the church to share with us at the table of God's word." Then the Gospels are presented to you with these words: "Receive the Gospel, the good news of Jesus Christ, the Son of God." The catechumenate is a journey made with the Scriptures in hand.

Each Sunday you will celebrate the liturgy of the word with the entire community. At the conclusion of this first part of the Mass, you will be sent with the other catechumens to reflect on the meaning of the Scriptures you have just heard. This session is the time when you will deepen your understanding of the Scriptures. The Bible is the basis of our faith and you will come to understand the meaning of Catholic faith and tradition through the Scriptures and the liturgy. But most importantly, it is a time when you will hear God calling you personally, inviting you to share more deeply in God's own life and sending you out to share the Gospel with others.

Living the Gospel is not simply a matter of the head. It involves a transformation of the heart, a modeling of oneself after Christ. This conversion happens through prayer. The period of the catechumenate is a time of prayer. For some, it may involve learning how to pray. For others it will involve a deepening of a life of prayer already begun. The reflections and suggestions in this book are designed to help you pray, whether you are a beginner or more experienced. Many people find the use of a journal to be a helpful tool. It offers a way of focusing new insights and allows one to see patterns of growth or persistent calls to change. For this reason, suggestions for journal keeping have been included for each week. Prayerful reflection on the Sunday Scriptures, both before and after the catechumenal session, will enrich the time of the session and make you more receptive to God's call.

The contributors to this book are all people of prayer. Out of their experience of praying with the Scriptures, their experience of struggle and growth, they share their faith with you. They are also people committed to the catechumenate. Having worked with catechumens, they share with you what they have found most helpful. Their reflections and suggestions spring from their experience of teaching many others how to pray, of sharing the Catholic tradition of liturgical prayer with other catechumens. Although they are speaking first to catechumens, sponsors and catechumenal ministers, all Christians will find their suggestions useful.

I would like to express my gratitude to all the contributors. Their enthusiasm and willingness to work under a tight schedule have made it possible to bring out this book. Thanks, too, to Karen Hinman Powell and Joseph P. Sinwell, editors of the three volumes of *Breaking Open the Word of God.* Their helpful suggestions and support enabled me to locate many of the fine contributors to this book. Hopefully it will serve as a resource that enables many to be nourished at the table of God's word.

Robert M. Hamma

Praying with the Lectionary

The Lectionary is one of those books we come in contact with most often. For many, its selections from the Old and New Testaments are the only access they have to the Bible. The Lectionary, along with the Sacramentary with its eucharistic prayers and other special prayers, and the Bible itself, is one of our very special books, one of those shared by Catholics all over the world, and one largely shared by Episcopal and Protestant churches as well. And yet, most Catholics have never had a chance to examine it and become personally familiar with it.

THE LECTIONARY

The Lectionary includes all the readings from the Old and New Testaments that we use in the eucharistic liturgy. It has readings for important seasons such as Advent, Christmas, Lent, and Easter, for the Sundays throughout the year, and for solemnities such as the feasts of All Saints and the Immaculate Conception, as well as the readings for the daily celebration of the Eucharist.

For Sundays, including some of our greatest feasts, such as Easter and Pentecost, the Lectionary includes three great cycles, A, B and C, each responding to an entire liturgical year, and each drawing its Gospel readings from Matthew, Mark, and Luke, respectively. We read John primarily during Eastertide and during the year of Mark (Cycle B), since Mark is a much shorter Gospel than Matthew and Luke.

For weekdays, the Lectionary contains only two readings, but on Sundays and feasts there are three. Usually the first is from the Old Testament and is chosen to prepare us to hear and appreciate the Gospel reading. The second reading is picked independently of the other two. It provides a fairly continuous reading of one of Paul's letters. That way, over the span of three years, we become familiar with much of the Bible or at least with a very good sampling of it.

PRAYING WITH THE LECTIONARY

The liturgical reading of the most important Scripture passages in the eucharistic assembly, especially when accompanied by a good homily, is one of the great formative forces in Christian life. No one assumes, however, that it is enough. Beyond reading and hearing the word of God, and beyond homiletic reflection on it, we need to pray with it, and an excellent way of doing so is to pray with the readings selected for the liturgy that Sunday or that day, as the case may be.

Praying with the Lectionary should normally begin with the Gospel reading, since the Gospel text is what governed the choice of the first reading, that from the Old Testament, and the responsorial psalm which moves us beyond stories of faith, prophetic announcements and wisdom instructions directly into prayer. The same is true of the Alleluia and its verse. After the Gospel, one can then take up the first reading, the psalm and the second reading, in that order. That way we follow the order that governed the formation of the liturgy of the word for each celebration. The second time around, someone may prefer to start with the first reading and follow the order of the liturgy of the word as it is actually celebrated.

In praying with the Lectionary for a particular Sunday, it often proves helpful to recall the previous Sunday's readings and even to glance at those for the Sunday that follows. That way the Gospel text will be seen in biblical context as well as in liturgical context. This is especially helpful when the reading is the continuation of a long discourse of Jesus and such as we find in the Gospel of John. It is good to recall the concrete setting in which Jesus gave the discourse. Otherwise, the reading appears too abstract, even in the case of something as familiar as the Sermon on the Mount. Sometimes one has to go back several Sundays to find the setting.

In seasons such as Advent and Lent, when the Gospel readings for each Sunday are meant to form one continuous Advent Gospel and Lenten Gospel, it is even more helpful to place each Sunday's Gospel reading in the context of the entire season. For example, it is much easier to pray with the Gospel for the First Sunday of Advent, which looks to the final return of Christ, when we know that it forms the introduction for the Advent Gospel. With it, the Church wants us to situate ourselves squarely in our own moment of history. Jesus' life, teaching and miracles, as well as his passion, resurrection and ascension, all are behind us. We are in the era of the Church, looking ahead to the final coming of Christ, his second and definitive advent. Then on the second Sunday, for all three cycles, a Gospel story about John the Baptist and his mission models how we are to prepare the way for Christ's final coming.

PRAYERFUL READING

Prayerful reading is, first, a close attentive reading, open to what the Gospel and the other lessons say to us. This requires that we respect the Gospel's literary form. We do this easiest in the case of actual prayers, such as the Lord's Prayer, the Psalms, and the Magnificat, Mary's great song of praise. All of these were meant to be prayed. Even so, a prayer of supplication is not the same as one of repentance or praise, and our prayer must respect the difference. Our attitude should be attuned to the nature of each prayer.

In praying with the little stories told by Jesus, his parables, respecting the literary form includes taking note of the context in which the story was told, to whom Jesus told it, and what occasioned his telling it. The story of the prodigal son, for example, is well understood when we note that it came in response to the complaint of Pharisees and their scribes that Jesus was welcoming tax collectors and others who failed to observe the law and that he was actually eating with them. Only then does it become clear that its principal focus is on the older brother who refused to celebrate the return of his younger brother who had gone astray but had now returned home (Lk 15:1–32). We are never told what the older brother did. Did he persist in resisting his father's pleading? Did he finally overcome his anger and hurt feelings and join in the reconciliation banquet? We do not know. The reading invites us to provide our own feelings and answer those questions based on what we would do. It provides an excellent launching pad for prayer.

Prophetic texts and the letters of Paul speak to us directly in the second person. We need to listen to them, meditate on how they apply to us and ask the strength to hear their message and live by it. Like some of Jesus' own prophetic statements, which ask that we reform our lives and believe the Gospel, they can be extremely challenging. Even to hear what they ask of us is a difficult and purifying experience.

Then, of course, there are the stories, usually written in the third person. There are stories of Abraham and Sarah, stories of Moses and the exodus, stories of judges, warriors and kings, as well as stories of Jesus, his disciples and the apostolic community. These require special attention.

ENGAGING THE IMAGINATION

In every case, but especially in that of stories, it is most important to engage the imagination. This means we have to resist the temptation to rest satisfied with finding the point of the story. We need to enter the story, that is, think of ourselves among its personages, listening and responding with them to what Jesus and others say. We need to enter eager to join in the dialogue.

There is no engaging the imagination without taking time to picture the place where the event in the story takes place. We need also to pay attention to the time at which it occurs. Being in Jerusalem for Passover is not like being anywhere else at Passover, and eating Passover away from Jerusalem is not the same as eating it in the ancient city of David, Israel's great symbol of freedom, of the Lord's presence, and of every blessed hope.

Only when the imagination is engaged can we follow the contours of the story as participants, attentive to those moments when it invites prayer. The moments of invitation include the sayings and other teachings of Jesus. Sometimes no one in the story responds to them. This silence calls for our response. Other moments consist in questions, such as Jesus' questions to the disciples: "Who do people say that I am? Who do you say that I am?" We know how the disciples and Peter answered. How shall we answer?

The biblical stories are filled with great images: the garden in Eden, the tower of Babel, Mount Sinai, the desert of the exodus, the Jordan crossing, the ascent to Jerusalem, the shores of the Sea of Galilee, Simon's fishing boat, the loaves, the fishes, drinking the cup Jesus drinks—all of these must lodge in our imagination. Then when we leave formal prayer they accompany us throughout the day. What was it like to cross the Sea of Galilee in a little boat when a storm suddenly descended? Does that ever happen to us? Where is the Lord Jesus at those moments? Is he sleeping in the bow of the boat? And what are we to think when Jesus chides his disciples for having so little faith?

The readings in the Lectionary ask many questions of us. We too must be able to ask many questions of them. Why does Mark call his Gospel "The beginning of the gospel of Jesus Christ, Son of God"? Was this story of passion and death really a beginning? What does this say to us of moments in our lives that seem to be the end? Might they not, like Mark's Gospel, be new beginnings? Passion and resurrection are over and over again. Ah, yes, Lord! That we may see!

Eugene LaVerdiere, S.S.S.

FIVE STEPS FOR PRAYING WITH THE
LECTIONARY

1. Begin with the Gospel, then the first reading, the responsorial psalm and the second reading.

2. Look back and ahead at the Gospels of surrounding weeks to get the concrete setting of this Gospel.

3. Remember the liturgical season (e.g., Advent)

and relate this Gospel to the meaning of the season.

4. Look for the literary form that the reading takes. Is it a prayer, a parable, a prophecy, a story? Understanding the kind of reading this is will help you respond appropriately to it.

5. Use your imagination to enter into the scene, to create the characters. Be there in the world of the reading.

Choosing a Bible

Over the last thirty years, Catholics have had the opportunity to choose from a variety of Bible translations. Formerly, the only official Catholic translation in English was the Douay-Rheims, from the Latin Vulgate—a translation of a translation that is inaccurate in places.

Today we are fortunate to have Bibles translated from the original Greek and Hebrew. Especially since the nineteenth century, many ancient manuscripts of scriptural and other texts have been discovered: the Dead Sea Scrolls are just one example. Scholars can compare differences and discover the meanings of "lost" or obscure words by finding them in the context of other writings from the biblical period. As a result, the newer Bible translations are probably closer than ever to the original meanings of the texts.

There are three major Catholic Bibles in use today. The choice of which to use is a matter of

personal taste. The **Revised New American Bible** was done under the auspices of the National Conference of Catholic Bishops for use by American Catholics. It has been widely used for liturgical proclamation and is the version closest to the text in the new Lectionary. The Revised New American Bible brings biblical texts into current American English and is sensitive to inclusive language while remaining true to the literal meaning of the original text. It is available in a variety of formats from several publishers.

The **New Jerusalem Bible** is a free translation with greater attention paid to beauty of language rather than literalness. It is known for its excellent notes. Doubleday publishes two versions, a Regular Edition, and the Readers Edition, from which some of the notes have been dropped.

The **New Revised Standard Version** is an ecumenical translation available in a Catholic edition. It is the descendant of the King James

Version and the Revised Standard Version, and retains the elegance and dignity of these classic translations without being archaic. It is reputed to be the most literal of modern Bible translations and, like the Revised New American Bible, is available in several editions.

In addition to the above, there are many other translations of the Scriptures such as the *Good News Bible* (Today's English Version), which is in very simple English. If you opt for a Bible that does not say "Catholic edition" on the cover, be sure to get one that includes the Deuterocanonical Books—books such as the Letter of James, the Book of Sirach and parts of the books of Esther and Daniel that the Catholic Church considers part of the biblical canon and uses in the liturgy. They are often omitted in Bibles widely used by non-Catholics.

You may want to use alternate versions from time to time. Different nuances are emphasized by different translations—a single word does not always convey the entire meaning of the original. The variety can bring new life to your understanding of the text.

Whatever translation or missal you choose, *enjoy* your Scripture reading. There is something in the Bible for everyone, regardless of education or experience. As St. Augustine said, it is deep enough for an elephant to swim. . . and shallow enough for a baby to wade.

CALENDAR OF CELEBRATIONS IN THE LITURGICAL YEAR
2000–2025

Year	Lectionary Cycle	First Sunday of Advent	Ash Wednesday	Easter	Ascension Thursday	Pentecost	Body and Blood of Christ
2000	B	November 28 *1999*	March 8	April 23	June 1	June 11	June 25
2001	C	December 3 *2000*	February 28	April 15	May 24	June 3	June 17
2002	A	December 2 *2001*	February 13	March 31	May 9	May 19	June 2
2003	B	December 1 *02*	March 5	April 20	May 29	June 8	June 22
2004	C	November 30 *03*	February 25	April 11	May 20	May 30	June 13
2005	A	November 28 *04*	February 9	March 27	May 5	May 15	May 29
2006	B	November 27 *05*	March 1	April 16	May 25	June 4	June 18
2007	C	December 3 *06*	February 21	April 8	May 17	May 27	June 10
2008	A	December 2 *07*	February 6	March 23	May 1	May 11	May 25
2009	B	November 30 *08*	February 25	April 12	May 21	May 31	June 14
2010	C	November 29 *09*	February 17	April 4	May 13	May 23	June 6
2011	A	November 28 *10*	March 9	April 24	June 2	June 12	June 26
2012	B	November 27	February 22	April 8	May 17	May 27	June 10
2013	C	December 2	February 13	March 31	May 9	May 19	June 2
2014	A	December 1	March 5	April 20	May 29	June 8	June 22
2015	B	November 30	February 18	April 5	May 14	May 24	June 7
2016	C	November 29	February 10	March 27	May 5	May 15	May 29
2017	A	November 27	March 1	April 16	May 25	June 4	June 18
2018	B	December 3	February 14	April 1	May 10	May 20	June 3
2019	C	December 2	March 6	April 21	May 30	June 9	June 23
2020	A	December 1	February 26	April 12	May 21	May 31	June 14
2021	B	November 29	February 17	April 4	May 13	May 23	June 6
2022	C	November 28	March 2	April 17	May 26	June 5	June 19
2023	A	November 27	February 22	April 9	May 18	May 28	June 11
2024	B	December 3	February 14	March 31	May 9	May 19	June 2
2025	C	December 1	March 5	April 20	May 29	June 8	June 22

Abbreviations of the Books of the Bible

Acts	Acts of the Apostles	Jas	James
Am	Amos	Jb	Job
Bar	Baruch	Jdt	Judith
1 Chr	1 Chronicles	Jer	Jeremiah
2 Chr	2 Chronicles	Jgs	Judges
Col	Colossians	Jl	Joel
1 Cor	1 Corinthians	Jn	John
2 Cor	2 Corinthians	1 Jn	1 John
Dn	Daniel	2 Jn	2 John
Dt	Deuteronomy	3 Jn	3 John
Eccl	Ecclesiastes	Jon	Jonah
Eph	Ephesians	Jos	Joshua
Est	Esther	Jude	Jude
Ex	Exodus	1 Kgs	1 Kings
Ez	Ezekiel	2 Kgs	2 Kings
Ezr	Ezra	Lam	Lamentations
Gal	Galatians	Lk	Luke
Gn	Genesis	Lv	Leviticus
Hab	Habakkuk	Mal	Malachi
Heb	Hebrews	1 Mc	1 Maccabees
Hg	Haggai	2 Mc	2 Maccabees
Hos	Hosea	Mi	Micah
Is	Isaiah	Mk	Mark

Mt	Matthew	Sg	Song of Songs
Na	Nahum	Sir	Sirach
Neh	Nehemiah	1 Sm	1 Samuel
Nm	Numbers	2 Sm	2 Samuel
Ob	Obadiah	Tb	Tobit
Phil	Philippians	1 Thes	1 Thessalonians
Phlm	Philemon	2 Thes	2 Thessalonians
Prv	Proverbs	Ti	Titus
Ps(s)	Psalms	1 Tm	1 Timothy
1 Pt	1 Peter	2 Tm	2 Timothy
2 Pt	2 Peter	Wis	Wisdom
Rom	Romans	Zec	Zechariah
Ru	Ruth	Zep	Zephanaiah
Rv	Revelation		

LET US WALK IN THE LIGHT OF THE LORD

ADVENT

First Sunday of Advent [A]

READING I	*Is 2:1–5*
Responsorial Psalm	*Ps 122:1–2, 3–4, 4–5, 6–7, 8–9*
READING II	*Rom 13:11–14*
GOSPEL	*Mt 24:37–44*

Reflection on the Readings

Stay awake; be prepared; you cannot know the day your Lord is coming.

Jesus reminds the disciples to be vigilant and to prepare themselves for the Lord's coming. No one knows when the Lord shall come. For Matthew and the early Christian community, the return of the Lord was anticipated daily. For we who live at the dawn of the twenty-first century, is our anticipation as vigilant? How tragic it would be for the Lord's coming to find us unconcerned. Was not that the fate of those of Noah's time, going about their life without regard for tomorrow?

But you who have put on the armor of the light are indeed ready. To put on Jesus and to take on the cross speaks of preparation, a making ready of oneself. Those deeds done in darkness are cast aside by the light of Christ.

This preparation that we make daily is done for salvation's sake so that we will be among those called into the reign of God. As Isaiah reminds us, if we turn to the Lord, if we pursue the Lord, if we climb the Lord's mountain, if we listen to the Lord and would be instructed by God's word, if we walk in the path of the Lord, we would receive the promise of fulfillment to dwell in the house of the Lord; a house of peace, a house of joy.

O house of Jacob, come,
Let us walk in the light of the LORD.

Suggestions for Prayer

1. Isaiah 2:3 invites a meditation prayer. In a relaxed position, close your eyes and with your imagination place yourself in the presence of the Lord. Picture yourself receiving instruction from the Lord. What does the Lord wish to teach you today? Allow yourself to hear this instruction repeatedly in your mind.

2. What are the deeds of darkness in your life that must be cast off as you put on the armor of light?

3. Read Psalm 119:33–40 each day this week as a morning and evening reflection.

Suggestion for Journal Keeping

How have you already prepared yourself for the Lord's coming?

What preparation do you now discern is still needed in your life?

John T. Butler

First Sunday of Advent [B]

READING I	*Is 63:16b–17, 19b; 64:2–7*
Responsorial Psalm	*Ps 80:2–3, 15–16, 18–19*
READING II	*2 Cor 1:3–9*
GOSPEL	*Mk 13:33–37*

Reflection on the Readings

As anxious pilgrims we are called to *watch*. "Be *watchful!* Be alert! . . . Watch!" (Mark) How are we to understand these words? With *alarm?* (Isaiah: "Behold, you are angry and we are sinful.") With *secrecy?* (Isaiah: "Would that you might meet us doing right.") With *diligence?* (Isaiah: "Why do you let us wander, O LORD, from your ways?") With *anticipation?* (Isaiah: "No ear has ever heard, no eye ever seen, any God but you doing such deeds for those who wait for him.") With *longing?* (Isaiah: "We are the clay you are the potter; we are all the work of your hands.")

Most of Chapter 13 of Mark speaks of the second coming and also the destruction of Jerusalem. The tone is certainly ominous. Mark's audience may well have been expecting the "end times," but when the end did not take place, those early listeners had to ask the same questions that we ask today. How shall we *watch?*

We must be on *watch* day by day as we look for the Lord. If we harbor unrepented sin, certainly the meeting of the Lord is alarming. If we have failed to do the good that we ought, we will be fearful that the Lord will find us out. However, if we have strayed from the path, we will be watching anxiously, with outstretched hand, for the Lord to show us the way. And if we are "ready to go" to follow in his footsteps, we can hardly wait for him to come! And if we know that we love him, and are first loved by him, the *watch* will be much too long as we await the caress of the potter Lord.

"Be watchful!"

Suggestions for Prayer

1. Close your eyes. Take a few deep breaths. Place yourself in God's presence. Imagine the caress of the potter Lord. Sit quietly and experience "being loved." Don't worry about words.

2. Pray for unrepentant sinners, especially those who are close to death. Ask the Lord to give them another chance, as he did so often when he walked this earth. Pray for those who are "lost." Ask the Holy Spirit to open their eyes to God's love and goodness. Pray for those who have no one to pray for them.

3. St. Joseph, the foster father of Jesus, is called the Patron of a Happy Death because he had both Jesus and Mary at his side when he died. Ask St. Joseph to pray with you for those who will die today. Pray that their death will be a joyful step into the wondrous life that "no ear has heard, and no eye has seen" (Isaiah). Ask God for the blessing of a happy death for yourself.

Suggestion for Journal Keeping

Describe your own watch as a pilgrim. Describe your watch as it is today. If today you meet the Lord, face to face, are you ready? What is today's message for you?

Joanna Case

First Sunday of Advent [C]

READING I	*Jer 33:14–16*
Responsorial Psalm	*Ps 25:4–5, 8–9, 10, 14*
READING II	*1 Thes 3:12—4:2*
GOSPEL	*Lk 21:25–28, 34–36*

Reflection on the Readings

Advent highlights waiting and expectation. When we wait for a person to come or an event to happen, we prepare. Advent provides a time for each of us to renew the spirit of expecting God. The message of the Gospel says, "Be vigilant. . . be on watch." One of the challenges of expectation is to become more conscious of how God comes to us in our everyday life.

God is present in creation in the beauty of the flowers, rivers and mountains, and in the changing of the seasons. Our relationships at home, work and play can reveal the presence of God. In the events of our ordinary life, we can discover God. We may need to spend time reflecting and allowing God to become present to us. This waiting will need energy, attention, patience and time. In finding the presence of God, surprises may happen. We may discover the vast richness of God's mercy, the immensity of God's love and the demands of God's justice.

God's presence offers hope.

Each of us is challenged to let God's presence enter our lives and become a living symbol of God's presence to each other. How do we invite God into our lives? How do we prepare for the coming of God?

Suggestions for Prayer

1. Reflect on people, events and things that you could offer to God, and complete the responsorial psalm:
"To you, O Lord, I lift up _____."
2. In the first reading, God is called "the Lord our justice." Reflect on the injustices that exist in your life, community and the world. And ask God to free us. As a response, you could use this form: "From (name injustices), O God, deliver us."
3. Recall people and events today. How was God present in the people and events? Respond to God's presence with your own thoughts or words.

Suggestion for Journal Keeping

God's presence in our lives offers hope. What does hope in God mean for you? How do you offer hope in God to others?

Joseph P. Sinwell

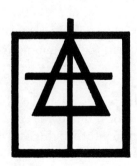

Second Sunday of Advent [A]

READING I	*Is 11:1–10*
Responsorial Psalm	*Ps 72:1–2, 7–8, 12–13, 17*
READING II	*Rom 15:4–9*
GOSPEL	*Mt 3:1–12*

Reflection on the Readings

Repent, for the kingdom of heaven is at hand.

John the Baptist appears to speak a harsh word, calling the Pharisees and Sadducees who were coming forward to be baptized "brood of vipers" and admonishing them to give some proof that they intended to reform their lives. Repentance, change, turning from evil to God is what John preached. It is likely that those whom he addressed felt themselves to be ready. John's challenge invites them to see that something more radical is needed than just the rigid adherence to the law.

How much are we like the Pharisees and Sadducees, assuming that all is well since we follow the law not realizing that more is required of us? Today's Gospel invites us to take seriously our preparation, to take responsibility for the faith we have been given. It invites us to see the deep-rooted change that needs to take place if we are truly to be made ready for the Lord's coming.

Isaiah's vision, in which the wolf shall be a guest of the lamb, is a testimony to the radical nature of the change that is required on our part. The very core of our being must be affected by the peace and love of Christ, if we are to truly reform our lives. Paul's prayer in Romans 15:5–6 affirms this call to perfect peace in Christ.

Suggestions for Prayer

1. If confronted by John the Baptist, what would be the signs of reform evident in your life?
2. The vision of peace that Isaiah reflects on calls for profound change. What prevents you from living in perfect harmony with those around you?
3. Reflect on Psalm 25:4–5 by reciting these verses throughout each day of this week.

Suggestion for Journal Keeping

John the Baptist warned that every tree that does not bear good fruit will be cut down and thrown into the fire.

What fruit has been born by you?

John T. Butler

Second Sunday of Advent [B]

READING I	*Is 40:1–5, 9–11*
Responsorial Psalm	*Ps 85:9–10, 11–12, 13–14*
READING II	*2 Pt 3:8–14*
GOSPEL	*Mk 1:1–8*

Reflection on the Readings

Over and over in Scripture, the term "kingdom of God" or "reign of God" is used. We learn that it is "at hand," "within us" and in our "midst." It is a way of "seeing" the world in God's terms; it is a process of living and responding to life with goodness and mercy and justice; it is "now" because the Lord is in our midst calling us to life as God intends it; it is "not yet" because God's reign is not perfect in us; it is a *being* and a *becoming*: "Thy kingdom come, thy will be done on earth as it is in heaven."

Today's readings have a lot of good news about the kingdom! However, if you read *carefully* there is a very insistent theme that is revealed about the kingdom: a change of heart is required. Isaiah says: "Every valley shall be filled in. . . .Then the glory of the LORD shall be revealed." Peter says that the Lord wants "all to come to repentance." Mark says that John the Baptist proclaimed "a baptism of repentance for the forgiveness of sins." Repent. Change your heart. Turn around the other way (conversion). All of these words define the Greek term *metanoia*.

As with the chicken and the egg conundrum, repentance occurs when a person is touched by the reign of God, yet God cannot reign in an unrepentant heart. Conversion of life, *metanoia*, goes on and on and on.

Suggestions for Prayer
1. If possible, get a recording of Handel's Messiah and listen to the Isaiah reading set to music. Keep the written words before you as you listen. What words and phrases seem to "jump out" at you? How does it make you feel about God? About yourself? Listen again. Play the recording in your car as you travel the highways (making them straight, of course). Don't forget to praise God for Handel's beautiful music!
2. Read the verses of Psalm 85 that are selected for today's responsorial psalm. Look for the words "justice" and "peace." Remember that Peter spoke of the new heavens and new earth where "righteousness dwells." Think about the relationship of righteousness, justice and the kingdom of God. Ask yourself what you are doing to promote peace and

justice. What might you do? "If you want peace, work for justice" (Pope Paul VI).
3. The color of Advent is the color of the sky right before the dawn: blue tinged with a little purple. It is a moment of anticipation as the darkness is expelled. Watch the dawn one morning soon. Then you will know how to feel as the kingdom comes upon us.

Suggestion for Journal Keeping
Chronicle some of the *metanoia* in your own life. How has the Lord called you to change?

Joanna Case

Second Sunday of Advent [C]

READING I	*Bar 5:1–9*
Responsorial Psalm	*Ps 126:1–2, 2–3, 4–5, 6*
READING II	*Phil 1:4–6, 8–11*
GOSPEL	*Lk 3:1–6*

Reflection on the Readings
The Gospel centers on announcing the ministry of John the Baptist. John's message is important. He speaks directly to us, saying "Repent." The challenge is to change your life; believing in the risen Christ demands personal conversion. What actions, attitudes and values need your attention?

John the Baptist's message implies that preparing to receive the Lord Jesus makes a difference in one's life. The difference lies in turning to God. Who is the God you look for? The first reading describes a God who is powerfully merciful, just and caring. How does this description compare with your image and experience of God?

John the Baptist proclaimed forgiveness of sins. God forgives us when we fail. Each person must be willing to seek and ask. The forgiveness of God will enable us to be free from the bonds of sin and to grow in love of God and others.

Suggestions for Prayer

1. "The Lord has done great things for us." What are the great things God had done for you? Give thanks to God for each person, event and object.

2. *Reflect on the following questions:* How do you experience the forgiveness of God? How does my forgiveness of others reflect the forgiveness of God?

3. We need to be open to the call of God in our lives. Pray slowly this prayer of St. Ignatius:

Take, Lord, and receive all my liberty, my memory, my understanding, and my entire will, all that I have and possess.
You have given all to me.
To you, Lord, I return it. All is yours. Dispose of it wholly according to your will. Give me your love and your grace, for this is enough for me.

Suggestion for Journal Keeping

Describe a personal conversion experience. What was God calling you to change? In light of this Sunday's Gospel reading, what is God calling you to change now?

Joseph P. Sinwell

Third Sunday of Advent [A]

READING I	*Is 35:1–6a, 10*
Responsorial Psalm	*Ps 146:6–7, 8–9, 9–10*
READING II	*Jas 5:7–10*
GOSPEL	*Mt 11:2–11*

Reflection on the Readings

Are you the one who is to come or should we look for another?

This question put to Jesus on behalf of John the Baptist offers a point of reflection for us today. Having awaited the Messiah with such anticipation, Jesus does not meet the expectations of those of his day. John the Baptist, who pulls no punches, may have expected Jesus to bring about the destruction of all those who did not remain faithful. Yet, Jesus appears preaching love, healing those who were sick and reconciling sinners.

The question that we might ask is: What kind of Messiah are we looking for? What is it that we expect Jesus to do in our lives and in the world? What kind of Savior do we want? For the Savior who comes gives sight, so that those who fail to see might now see. The Savior who comes empowers and strengthens so that those who are weak are made strong in the ways of the Lord. The Savior who comes brings healing to a world sick with sin. The Savior who comes calls to new life all who are willing to die in faith.

If this is the Savior whom you seek, then steady your heart because the coming of the Lord is at hand.

Here is your God who comes with vindication,
with divine recompense, who comes to save you.

Suggestions for Prayer
1. *Reflect on the following:* What are the signs of Christ's presence in the world today? What are the signs of Jesus' presence in your life?
2. Reflect prayerfully on Psalm 146:6–10 as a morning and evening prayer this week.
3. In a relaxed position, meditate for several minutes on Isaiah 35:4 by personalizing and repeating this verse to yourself:

   Here is my God, who comes to defend and
   make divine amends for me.
   Here is my God, who comes to save me.

Suggestion for Journal Keeping
Describe an experience of radical change that has already taken place in your life.

John T. Butler

Third Sunday of Advent   [B]

READING I	*Is 61:1–2a, 10–11*
Responsorial Psalm	*Lk 1:46–48, 49–50, 53–54*
READING II	*1 Thes 5:16–24*
GOSPEL	*Jn 1:6–8, 19–28*

Reflection on the Readings
For the past two Sundays we have traveled with Isaiah and John, Peter and Paul, and today Mary joins us, singing her joyful canticle (Responsorial). Kingdom persons, all of them! Today's readings give an apt description of those who belong to the Kingdom.

How to be a kingdom person:

Isaiah	God calls, "The Spirit of the Lord is upon me."
Isaiah	We respond, "I rejoice heartily in the Lord."
Isaiah	God gives a mission, "He has sent me to bring. . . . "
Paul	We respond, "Rejoice always, never cease praying."
Paul	God calls, "Do not quench the Spirit. . . . He who calls us is trustworthy. . . . "
Mary	We respond, "My being proclaims the greatness of the Lord, my spirit finds joy in God my Savior."
John	God gives a mission, "There was a man named John sent by God who came as a witness. . . . "
Mary	We respond, "God who is mighty has done great things for me. Holy is his name."
You	God calls *you*, "The Spirit of the Lord is upon *me*."
You	You respond, "God who is mighty has done great things for me."
You	God gives *you* a mission, "There was *I*, sent by God to _____."
You	*You* respond, "_____."

Read all the readings again. Fill in the blanks in your heart.

Suggestions for Prayer
1. Last Sunday Peter spoke of the new heavens and new earth where "righteousness dwells." Last Sunday we reflected on the Kingdom of God. Today Isaiah says: "He has. . . wrapped me in a mantle of justice." Today we reflect on those who respond to the kingdom call. Justice again. Read Isaiah's list again from the point of view of justice. Pray for the

brokenhearted, the captives, those who have no glad tidings today.

2. John the Baptist was a prophet, a truth-sayer of God's word. Think about the people in your own experience who have been truth-sayers for you (even the ones you did not want to hear). How did these prophetic voices affect you? Did you change anything in your life? Who are the prophets in the Church? In the world? Has the Lord called you to be a prophet? Pray today for more prophets, more truth-sayers and for more truth-listeners.

3. The Canticle of Mary in today's Responsorial is also known as the Magnificat (from the Latin). This is often set to music, as is the Ave Maria (Latin for "Hail Mary"). These are often included with Christmas collections of music. Try to find one to listen to this week. (Keep it handy for next week too.)

Suggestion for Journal Keeping

Describe a "kingdom person" that you know (it doesn't have to be one who is already perfect). Is this person also a prophet? Which words from today's Scripture apply to this person?

Joanna Case

Third Sunday of Advent [C]

READING I	Zep 3:14–18a
Responsorial Psalm	Is 12:2–3, 4, 5–6
READING II	Phil 4:4–7
GOSPEL	Lk 3:10–18

Reflection on the Readings

The message of the first reading and the Gospel is that God who saves draws close to us. When God is near, how do we react? Do we hesitate because of uncertainty or avoid because of fear? Do we refuse to meet God because of apathy? God comes to us out of love. God comes to us whether we are ready or not. Advent centers on expecting God to come.

Our response to this coming may be joy. We can experience the nearness of God through the actions of others, nature, prayer or reflection. The smile of a friend, the listening of another, the presence of a loved one, the beauty of a sunset or the comfort of silence can reveal God. We may be able to "cry out with joy and gladness."

After this response of joy or gladness, we ask the question of the crowd to John the Baptist: "Teacher, what should we do?" The response in the Gospel to a variety of people, e.g., rich person, tax collector and soldier, is straightforward: be generous and honest, as well as just and fair to others, be conscious of who you are and what are your responsibilities, and perform them with care and unselfishness.

Each of us plays a variety of roles: citizen, worker, professional, laity, clergy, religious, mother, father, sister, etc. We can serve others in these roles. Our challenge is to bring the "good news to the people" and to enable others to share the good news of a God who is near and cares for each person.

Suggestions for Prayer

1. God is present when we experience joy. Remember a time when you were full of joy or happiness.

   What happened? Who was present? Praise God for the events, people and time by repeating slowly these words of the second reading, "Rejoice in the Lord always. I shall say it again: rejoice."

2. The Magnificat or Canticle of Mary in the Gospel of Luke announces joy at the nearness and greatness of God. Read Luke 1:46–55 and pray this prayer of the Church.

3. Imagine that God comes to you and speaks. To each phrase below you may respond. God says to you the following:

I am near to you.
Dismiss all anxiety.
Present your needs to me.
My peace is beyond understanding.

Suggestion for Journal Keeping

Remember a time when you wanted or felt that God was near to you. Describe the experience. How did God come to us? Describe God. What happened after the experience? How did the experience change you? How does the nearness of God affect you today?

Joseph P. Sinwell

Fourth Sunday of Advent   [A]

READING I   *Is 7:10–14*

Responsial Psalm   *Ps 24:1–2, 3–4, 5–6*

READING II   *Rom 1:1–7*

GOSPEL   *Mt 1:18–24*

Reflection on the Readings
   Emmanuel, "God is with us."

The promise of God's presence is the promise of salvation. The sign that was sought since before the days of Isaiah is now given to the world through the power of the Holy Spirit and the obedient response of Mary and Joseph.

Our inclination might be to view this story of Jesus' birth from one dimension, to focus exclusively on the virgin birth. Were we to do this, we would miss the perspective that Jewish faith brought to this moment. For the Jewish faith saw the Spirit as the source of God's action in the world. It was the Spirit that taught the prophet what to say and brought God's truth to the people of Israel. It was the Spirit that enabled God's people to recognize the word of God when they heard it and the hand of God when they saw it.

In Jesus, the Holy Spirit was so present as to manifest God to the world. It is Jesus who now brings God's truth to all who open their hearts. This truth, once received, would transform us as it transformed Mary who conceived the child Jesus, and Joseph her faith-filled husband. Thus transformed, Paul reminds us that we are favored with apostleship, so that we might spread his name and bring to obedient faith all who have been called to belong to Jesus Christ.

Suggestions for Prayer

1. The Magnificat, Luke 1:46–55, is a traditional canticle sung at evening prayer. Pray this canticle of Mary each evening of this week.

2. Pray Psalm 111:1–10 daily this week by reading the psalm both quietly and aloud as a morning prayer.

3. Set aside 30–45 minutes to spend in prayerful devotion to the Blessed Virgin Mary reciting the joyful mysteries of the rosary. Ask your sponsor or spiritual guide for help if you do not know how to pray the rosary.

Suggestion for Journal Keeping

Describe an experience when you felt God's presence in a special way in your life.

John T. Butler

Fourth Sunday of Advent   [B]

READING I	*2 Sm 7:1–5, 8b–11, 14a, 16*
Responsorial Psalm	*Ps 89:2–3, 4–5, 27, 29*
READING II	*Rom 16:25–27*
GOSPEL	*Lk 1:26–38*

Reflection on the Readings

More good news today! "Nothing will be impossible for God!" A young Jewish virgin, by the power of the Holy Spirit, conceives the Son of the Most High God. Nothing is impossible for God. A Jewish woman in her old age also conceives a son. Nothing is impossible for God. God intervenes in history, and nothing will ever be the same. Nothing is impossible for God. The long-awaited one is God-Man. Nothing is impossible for God.

Mary must have been a woman of prayer because she did not seem to be amazed at receiving a message from God. She did seem a bit perplexed about the message itself: "How can this be…?" With little further explanation, she replied "May it be done to me according to your word." Mary has become the mother of God. Nothing is impossible for God. Mary is the best example of a kingdom person: God called, she responded, God gave her a special role, she said yes!

When we remain faithful in prayer, listening for God's call in our hearts, watching carefully for opportunities to meet and serve the Lord in each other, then we are eager to say "yes" to God too. Can we really do it? Yes! Nothing is impossible for God.

Suggestions for Prayer

1. Try to imagine the scene described in the Gospel. Try to hear the angel's message and Mary's reply. Then say aloud the last line of Mary's response. Yes! "May it be done to me according to your word." This would be a good way to end all our own prayers too!

2. If you have one, play a recording of an Ave Maria, which is the Latin translation of the beautiful prayer of the Church, the Hail Mary. Notice that most of this prayer is directly from Luke's account. Sing or say this prayer slowly today.

   Hail Mary, full of grace, the
   Lord is with thee.
   Blessed art thou among women,
   and blessed is the fruit of
   thy womb, Jesus.
   Holy Mary, mother of God, pray
   for us sinners,
   now and at the hour of our
   death. Amen.

3. Mary was a very young woman, most likely what we would call a teenager. Young people today are really excited when they discover that the most highly-favored person in God's plan was so young. Praise God today for the many wonderful teenagers who respond so lovingly to life on this earth. Pray especially for the ones who need help to turn their lives around.

Suggestion for Journal Keeping

Describe a time when you experienced an "impossible" situation. Did you pray? How did you handle it? Who came to your assistance? Was it really impossible? Is there something in your life now that needs fervent prayer? Nothing is impossible for God.

Joanna Case

Fourth Sunday of Advent [C]

READING I	*Mi 5:1–4a*
Responsorial Psalm	*Ps 80:2–3, 15–16, 18–19*
READING II	*Heb 10:5–10*
GOSPEL	*Lk 1:39–45*

Reflection on the Readings

God is present to each of us in a variety of ways. The Gospel story points out how Elizabeth is aware of the presence of God in Mary, the mother of Jesus; her response is full of praise, joy and humility. Her response offers the challenge of becoming aware of the presence of God in our own lives.

How do we recognize the presence of God in everyday events? In the hectic pace of modern life, the presence of God can be drowned out by other demands. There's a popular saying: "Stop and smell the roses along the way." Recognizing the presence of God in creation, people and events demands that we stop and reflect. God comes to each of us: each of us can find God in our daily lives.

Recognizing God's presence is a first step. Elizabeth welcomes God's presence. She responds. God's presence in our lives demands a personal response. The beauty of nature, experiencing the kindness of a friend or the joy of a child, can reveal the presence of God. Like Elizabeth, we can respond to God. The presence of God can also urge us to deepen our relationship with God and others. Our own actions and words can bear the presence of God to others.

Suggestions for Prayer

1. Say each phrase of the traditional prayer, the Hail Mary. Respond to each phrase with silent reflection or with your words, or pray the joyful mysteries of the rosary.

2. The responsorial psalm expresses a desire for the presence of God: "Lord, make us turn to you; let us see your face and we shall be saved." Another prayer that expresses this desire is:

> *Day by Day*
> *Thank you, Lord Jesus Christ,*
> *For all the benefits and blessings*
>   *which you have given me,*
> *For all the pains and insults*
>   *which you have borne for me.*
> *Merciful Friend, Brother and Redeemer,*
> *May I know you more clearly,*
> *Love you more dearly,*
> *And follow you more nearly,*
> *Day by day.*
>
> St. Richard of Chichester
> (twelfth century)

3. Allow yourself to become relaxed. Try to put all thoughts out of your mind. Ask yourself: How is God present to me now? Can you picture or name God's presence? Respond to the presence of God.

Suggestion for Journal Keeping

Review significant events/moments in your life. What was the presence of God to you at that time? How did you respond to the presence of God at those moments?

Joseph P. Sinwell

December 25
Christmas Vigil   [A B C]

READING I	*Is 62:1–5*
Responsorial Psalm	*Ps 89:4–5, 16–17, 27, 29*
READING II	*Acts 13:16–17, 22–25*
GOSPEL	*Mt 1:1–25 or 1:18–25*

Reflection on the Readings

Keeping vigil. A night watch. Awake and waiting. Waiting for the first light of dawn. The Church is keeping vigil during this holy night, waiting, eager to celebrate the light of the world, Jesus the Christ. Again we gather to tell the ancient story "how the birth of Jesus Christ came about." The Church remembers and celebrates.

> *The virgin shall be with child and give birth to a son, and they shall call him Emmanuel, a name which means "God is with us."*

That is the part of the story we need to remember: God is with us! That is the part of the story we gather to celebrate: God is with us! This the real CHRIST-MASS!

Suggestions for Prayer

1. Make an effort to stay awake through the night and watch for the first light of dawn. Feel the holiness of the night, the silence of the night. Watch the color of the sky change and the light of the daystar come upon you. Anticipation and arrival: God is with us. Jesus. Emmanuel.

2. Look again at the list of names in the family record of Jesus in the Gospel account. Now think of the generations and generations in your own family history. Ask all those "saints of old" to gather with you tonight in praising God for Jesus. Ask them to help you to be a light for the world, just as they were in their own lifetimes. Remember them. This is a night for remembering and celebrating.

3. If you have a nativity scene, spend a few minutes gazing. What a wonderful human story unfolds. How wonderful is the mystery that the Word is made flesh and dwells among us! Holy, holy, holy night!

Suggestion for Journal Keeping

This is a holy night. Describe a moment in your life that was holy, a moment when you experienced God-with-you. Is this a holy moment right now?

Joanna Case

Mass at Midnight [A B C]

READING I	*Is 9:1–6*
Responsorial Psalm	*Ps 96:1–2, 2–3, 11–12, 13*
READING II	*Ti 2:11–14*
GOSPEL	*Lk 2:1–14*

Reflection on the Readings

"Do not be afraid; for behold, I proclaim to you good news of great joy that will be for all the people."

Our joy is that a Savior has been given to us, one who would walk among us, one who would experience what we experience, one who would not receive special favor but would even suffer and die for the sake of all. How fitting it is that Jesus is born in a common courtyard, that he is adorned in simple cloth and laid to rest in a manger. For there was no room in the inn just as there would be no room in the hearts of many who would fail to recognize him as Lord.

How are we to insure that our hearts will always be open to this Savior? How will we guarantee lodging for the one who frees, reconciles and heals us? If we never allow ourselves to be poor, to be empty, if we fill our hearts with earthly desires, if we surround ourselves with distractions and comforts, if we avoid touching the poverty of our hearts and that of the world, then we will fail to see the vacancy into which

we would invite this Lord. For it was in poverty that Jesus was born, and it is in the poverty of our hearts that we find space for this Savior to take rest.

The grace of God has appeared, saving all.

Suggestions for Prayer

1. Pray Psalm 96:1–13 as a morning prayer each day of this week.
2. *Reflect on the following:* Isaiah proclaimed, "The people who walked in darkness have seen a great light." In what darkness have you walked? How was the light of the Lord mediated to you?
3. Of what must you empty yourself so that there will be more room for the Lord in your life?

Suggestion for Journal Keeping

How could you be even more open to the Lord than you are now?

John T. Butler

Mass at Dawn [A B C]

READING I	*Is 62:11–12*
Responsorial Psalm	*Ps 97:1, 6, 11–12*
READING II	*Ti 3:4–7*
GOSPEL	*Lk 2:15–20*

Reflection on the Readings

The shepherds returned, glorifying and praising God.

The angels appeared to the shepherds to give the good news of Christ's birth. How fitting it was that the shepherds would be among the first to receive this announcement of God.

Shepherds were frequently looked down on by the religious leaders of the day, since they were unable to keep the strict ritual practice of the Jews. Those who lived a simple life, tending the lambs that might be sacrificed to God, were among the first to see Jesus, the lamb of God, who is to be sacrificed for the sins of many.

This encounter with Jesus leaves the shepherds glorifying and praising God, and Mary holding these moments in her heart. We, who have come to find Jesus in our lives, are filled with joy and as Mary, likewise reflect and treasure these wonders in our hearts. For how profound it is, Paul reminds us, that God our Savior appeared to save us, not because of any righteous deed we have done, but because of God's mercy. This is why our hearts are filled and why we glorify and praise God.

Suggestions for Prayer
1. Pray Psalm 96:1–13 as a morning and evening reflection each day of this week.
2. *Reflect on the following:* What are some of the moments in your faith journey that you treasure? Why are these moments special ones in your life? What do they say about God? What do they say about you?
3. Designate some specific time for meditative prayer this week. After relaxing by reflecting on your breathing for several minutes, allow yourself to feel God's love, kindness and mercy by recalling a special moment you treasure and repeatedly playing this moment over in your mind.

Suggestion for Journal Keeping
Describe one of your most joyful experiences in life.

How was God present in that experience?

John T. Butler

Mass During the Day [A B C]

READING I	*Is 52:7–10*
Responsorial Psalm	*Ps 98:1, 2–3, 3–4, 5–6*
READING II	*Heb 1:1–6*
GOSPEL	*Jn 1:1–18 or 1:1–5, 9–14*

Reflections on the Readings
In celebrating the event of the birth of Jesus, most people localize the time and place: Bethlehem two thousand years ago. And certainly they celebrate that event in the present in their own cities and homes. But in today's Scripture readings, the authors stretch our minds and hearts to consider a great cosmic view, maybe a God's-eye view of salvation. Imagine a camera starting with a wide-angle lens, zooming in for a close-up and returning to the larger picture. John starts with the widest possible frame, "In the beginning was the Word; and the Word was with God, and the Word was God." Then God chooses to localize, "The Word became flesh and made his dwelling among us." Isaiah broadens the lens to remind us, "All the ends of the earth will behold the salvation of our God." And the Letter to Hebrews returns us to the opening scene, "When the Son had cleansed us from our sins, he took his seat at the right hand of the Majesty on high. . . . "

As much as we like to personalize Christmas, we need to remember that our most loving God intervened in history to call everyone to himself through Jesus. "God so loved the world that he sent his only begotten Son, that whoever believes in him may not die, but may have life eternal" (Jn 3:16).

That is good news for sure! Pass it on!

"How beautiful upon the mountains are the feet of the one who brings glad tidings, announcing peace, bearing good news, announcing salvation, and saying to Zion, 'Your God is King!'"

Suggestions for Prayer

1. If indeed "all the ends of the earth have seen the salvation of our God," we would not hear of so many global conflicts and wars. Peace on earth requires peacemakers. Pray today for peace. Pray today for peacemakers. Pray that you yourself will "bring glad tidings, announcing peace, bearing good news. . ." in your own little corner of the earth. Make a resolution that you will be a peacemaker.

2. Christmas is a twelve-day feast. The custom of gift giving may vary from culture to culture, but it certainly is an essential of the Christmas celebration. Ask your family and/or friends what *spiritual* gift they would most like to have (e.g., wisdom, humility, courage, faith, prudence, patience, etc.) and tell them you will pray for them, asking God to bestow the requested gift. Pray this way each day of the twelve days (or longer).

3. Christmastime is very difficult for those who are alone. Watch for the lonely and try to share some time with them. Pray for all those who are distressed, or homeless or lonely.

Suggestion for Journal Keeping

If someone asked you to list the spiritual gifts that you have received from God, what would you say? Write a list in your journal. Don't forget to include a thank-you note.

Joanna Case

Sunday in the Octave of Christmas Holy Family

[A B C]

READING I	*Sir 3:2–7, 12–14*
Responsorial Psalm	*Ps 128:1–2, 3, 4–5*
READING II	*Col 3:12–21 or 3:12–17*
GOSPEL A	*Mt 2:13–15, 19–23*
GOSPEL B	*Lk 2:22–40 or 2:22, 39–40*
GOSPEL C	*Lk 2:41–52*

Reflection on the Readings

You who honor your father atone for sins, you who revere your mother store up riches.

On this feast of the Holy Family, the invitation is extended for us to see family as the ground on which the reality of love and virtuous living must be rooted. Sirach recounts some traditional wisdom regarding relations between parents and children, which if taken to heart must challenge us who live in a society that practically warehouses the elderly. Where is the

honor for those aging who die quietly and lonely in inner-city apartments and suburban homes for the elderly?

Often we resist Paul's exhortation to bear with one another. Have we not clothed ourselves with heartfelt compassion, with kindness, humility, gentleness and patience? Above all, have we not put on love that binds the rest together and makes perfect our Christ-like response? Only then can we truly be open to the Lord's guidance as was Joseph (Mt 2:13–15, 19–23) who sought to protect his family from those who would destroy them (Cycle A). Only then can we live in hope as did Simeon and Anna (Lk 2:22–40), standing firm on God's promise to send a Savior (Cycle B). Only then can we in obedient faith grow in knowledge and understanding of what the Lord has in store for us as did Jesus (Lk 2:41–52, Cycle C).

If we would allow the Holy Family to be the model for us in our struggle to be open, faithful and obedient to the Lord, then we might find healing for the fragmented, fractured and disintegrated families in our midst.

Suggestions for Prayer

1. *Reflect on the following:* Which relationships in your family are most comfortable? Why? Which relationships in your family are most difficult? Why?
2. How might you show more fully Christ-like love in your family?
3. Pray the prayer of St. Francis as a morning and evening prayer each day this week.

Suggestion for Journal Keeping

After reflecting on the readings and prayer suggestions, what would you want to say to any member of your family?

John T. Butler

January 1—Octave of Christmas Solemnity of Mary, Mother of God [A B C]

READING I	*Nm 6:22–27*
Responsorial Psalm	*Ps 67:2–3, 5, 6, 8*
READING II	*Gal 4:4–7*
GOSPEL	*Lk 2:16–21*

Reflection on the Readings
   You are no longer slaves, but sons and daughters.
   Mary's free acceptance of the responsibility of motherhood resulted in blessings that stretch beyond our imagination. Her *yes* not only fulfills the Old Testament prophecy but wins for her and for us a privileged place in God's salvific plan. Paul reminds us that we are slaves no more. Because of Christ, we now claim the intimacy that God intended for us, that we would be children of God.

The use of the term *Abba* expresses God as Father, not only to Jesus, but also to us who respond to him as openly and willingly as did Mary. Our sonship (daughtership) is rooted in this radical obedience and fidelity to God's will. Therefore, as true sons and daughters of God, we confidently invoke God's name and call forth blessings from the Lord—blessings promised to Moses, Abraham and Sarah, blessings always fulfilled throughout the whole of salvation history.

Suggestions for Prayer
1. *Reflect on the following:* How has the Lord blessed you? How has the Lord kept you?

2. Place yourself in a relaxed position and reflect on the peace the only Christ can give. Spend several minutes each day this week reflecting on this peace.
3. Pray Psalm 67:2–8 as a morning and evening prayer each day this week.

Suggestion for Journal Keeping
Describe what it means for you to be a child of God.

What does God as Father expect from you and/or provide for you?

What does God as Mother expect from you and/or provide for you?

John T. Butler

Epiphany [A B C]

READING I	*Is 60:1–6*
Responsorial Psalm	*Ps 72:1–2, 7–8, 10–11, 12–13*
READING II	*Eph 3:2–3a, 5–6*
GOSPEL	*Mt 2:1–12*

Reflection on the Readings
The Gospel narrates a wonderful story. Magi. Star. King. Conflict. Intrigue. Gifts. Warnings. Return. A great story. But a closer look might reveal a hidden story. The magi set out on a spiritual journey, prompted by the stirrings of their souls through ancient writings and a wondrous star. They were not certain of what they would find, but they were resolute in their intention to pay homage to the newborn king of the Jews. They found him, and we can imagine that the Isaiah line described them perfectly: "Then you shall be radiant at what you see, your heart shall throb and overflow. . . . " One encounter with the Lord and they were never again the same. They couldn't even go back the same way; their journey took a different turn.

We, too, are pilgrims on a journey, seeking the One who will make our hearts "throb and overflow." Each time we meet the Lord we come away changed, our path pointing in a new direction. Without benefit of star and message in dreams, we continue seeking the Lord in likely and unlikely places. We look for him in prayer, in good people, in good deeds, but sometimes he arrives in silence, in distressing disguises, in emptiness. But we have set out on our own journey and we must be resolute. There is no turning back, only going ahead, and, as Isaiah puts it, "Then shall you be radiant at what you see, your heart shall throb and overflow."

Suggestions for Prayer
1. The sun is the daystar for the earth. It lights the world. As soon as it is dark, see if you can see other stars and the earth's moon. The sun, the moon, the stars, the galaxy, the universe. Amazing. Overwhelming. Mind-boggling. "We saw his star at its rising and have come to do him homage." Praise God.
2. This is "twelfth night," the traditional end of the Christmas celebration. Have you noticed that on a spiritual journey, each ending only introduces you to another beginning? This is going to be a holy year for you. Watch for stars that lead you to holy places.

Suggestion for Journal Keeping
The Magi brought gold, frankincense and myrrh. The Little Drummer Boy played his drum. What is your gift? What is your most *precious* gift that you have to give to the Lord?

Joanna Case

Baptism of the Lord   [A B C]

READING I	*Is 42:1–4, 6–7*
Responsorial Psalm	*Ps 29:1–2, 3–4, 3, 9–10*
READING II	*Acts 10:34–38*
GOSPEL A	*Mt 3:13–17*
GOSPEL B	*Mk 1:7–11*
GOSPEL C	*Lk 3:15–16, 21–22*

Reflection on the Readings

To make a discovery about someone we know or to gain a fresh insight into ourselves is a threshold, a turning point. The deeper our new knowledge, the more we are changed. Once we have passed that threshold, we are never quite the same again.

What is happening in the readings of the recent Sundays and feasts is a progression in the story of the manifestation of Jesus as the Chosen One of God. John the Baptist is the one who has gone before, preparing the way, the hearts of people. John proclaims conversion. Jesus' decision to be baptized indicates his choice—he has passed a threshold, come upon a turning point in his life, as he responds to an inner call. He is making a public statement about his life and his beliefs.

The reading from Isaiah depicting the Servant of God, the Chosen One, is applied by Peter (in the reading from Acts) and by the evangelists to Jesus, identifying him as the beloved servant. The mission of Jesus is that of the servant—to bring forth justice, to be merciful, to heal and to free those in darkness and bondage. Peter's proclamation assures the early Christian community—and us—that Jesus is indeed this servant, the Chosen One of God.

We look first at John, whose whole life of simplicity, preaching and teaching called people to conversion, to a life of holiness and openness to God. We look at Jesus, responding to his call to live as the chosen servant of God. We look then at our own lives, at the call we may be hearing now to follow Jesus. We must respond, as best we can, according to our personal circumstances in life, our gifts. Your response will become visible in your faith life and in your lifestyle.

In our Church community, our individual response to the call to holiness is affirmed and celebrated in many different ways. Your journey as a catechumen will provide opportunities for support, reflection, questioning, affirmation. You will continue to meet and learn from others who have gone before to prepare their own hearts and lives, who have followed their call to holiness.

Suggestions for Prayer

1. Prepare for this prayer time by becoming comfortable, perhaps with pen and paper nearby. You may want some quiet instrumental music in the background. Move away from the distractions of noise, worry and tension.

   Think of one central, pivotal decision you have made in your life. Name it. Who or what helped prepare you for that decision or brought you to the point of wanting to make a choice? What changes result from that decision?

2. Choose and listen to a song that focuses on a theme of conversion, of call and response. Some suggestions may be available from the parish catechumenate team or music leaders, many with scriptural themes. As you listen a second time to the song you choose, become aware of a message being given to you—a reassurance of God's love, forgiveness, a renewed call to holiness or prayer, a deeper sense of God's presence in your life.

Suggestion for Journal Keeping

Take time to write a few paragraphs on today's readings and prayer. Ask yourself: What have today's Scripture readings meant to me? What insight has come to me? As you spend time in prayer, write briefly your reflections and thoughts. You may feel comfortable in writing your thoughts as a prayer: "Jesus, as I read about your baptism today and thought about your life and my own, I am coming to realize even more that. . . . "

Clare M. Colella

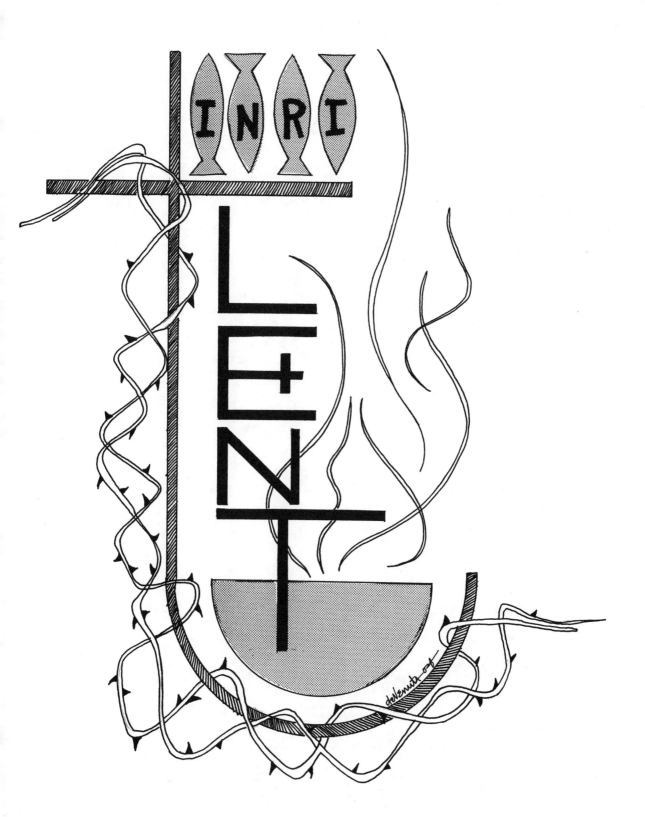

Ash Wednesday

READING I	*Jl 2:12–18*
Responsorial Psalm	*Ps 51:3–4, 5–6, 12–13, 14, 17*
READING II	*2 Cor 5:20—6:2*
GOSPEL	*Mt 6:1–6, 16–18*

Reflection on the Readings

Two themes emerge from today's liturgy. The more obvious one is the lesson that we are dust, ashes, from which we came and to which we will return. Ashes, blessed as they are, serve to remind us of our humble origins and fragile nature. The sign placed on our foreheads is a sign for our entire selves, and our hearts and minds. We are a people set aside, called to become faithful and holy, a redeemed people called to conversion.

Conversion serves as the second theme for today and the setting for the season of Lent. Each of the readings, the same ones proclaimed every year, speaks of conversion. Joel, a prophet, calls his people to renew their efforts to live a holy and pleasing life, turning to the Lord as central in their lives. His people, and we, are reminded of the Lord's goodness and mercy; the last line in today's first reading speaks of the ancient covenant: "You will be my people and I will be your God."

Living as the people of God is a process of converting our lives to the Lord. As Paul reminds the Christian community at Corinth: "We are ambassadors for Christ." Therefore our very lives are to be evidence of the grace of God active and fruitful within us. How do we do this? In the Gospel, we hear from Jesus the admonition to give alms, to pray and to fast. What is particularly striking and wonderful about Jesus' message is that we are to do so in simplicity, in our ordinary lives, looking only to God. Three times we hear that it is the Father who sees what is in our hearts.

As we prepare for this day we reflect on our lives, examining our values and lifestyle in comparison with Gospel values. To be signed with ashes, to hear the prayers of the liturgy, is to renew personally our covenant with God. It is to recognize in our own lives the need for continuing conversion, for a deeper understanding of our call to healthy holiness and to strengthen our commitment to live as the redeemed, chosen people of God.

Suggestions for Prayer

1. If possible, participate in the liturgy of the Church today. The ashes are made by burning last year's blessed palms. The ashes link us with the death and resurrection of the Lord. If you cannot be in church, but want to reflect on these prayers more thoroughly, a missal will be of help.

2. The opening prayers of today's liturgy ask for protection in our struggle against evil throughout this season and, in the alternate prayer, for forgiveness and the gift of light. Reflect on your life as it is right now. Recognizing the presence of God in your heart, pray for the light of faith and wisdom to live more faithfully as a follower of Christ.

3. Psalm 51 serves as the responsorial psalm today. Acknowledging our sinfulness, we pray for a clean heart and the joy of salvation. With a spirit of willingness and praise, we pray for a sign of our belonging to the Lord. As you pray this psalm, again let your heart and mind become glad and secure in the knowledge that you are forgiven and loved. How, during this Lenten season, will you live out your praise for God?

Suggestion for Journal Keeping

In a quiet setting reflect on those aspects of your life that are central in your faith journey: a spirit of prayer, service to others, simplicity or other qualities. What needs to be changed? What needs to be strengthened? Formulate a personal prayer of resolution—a sort of covenant—to grow in the spirit of Christ.

Clare M. Colella

First Sunday of Lent   [A]

READING I	*Gn 2:7–9; 3:1–7*
Responsorial Psalm	*Ps 51:3–4, 5–6, 12–13, 17*
READING II	*Rom 5:12–19 or 5:12, 17–19*
GOSPEL	*Mt 4:1–11*

Reflection on the Readings

In today's Gospel, Jesus goes into the dessert to be alone: to honestly struggle with all the dimensions of himself. While in the desert, he is confronted with three fundamental temptations: power (turn bread into stones), influence and control (throw himself off the temple), and false glory and idolatry (these kingdoms can be yours). Yet Jesus makes responsible choices. He chooses to live from his inner truth, from his relationship with the Father, rather than allowing the attraction of the temptations to control him.

Jesus' choices are choices we can make. The Genesis text affirms our created goodness: God breathes into Adam's nostril the "breath of life," thus giving Adam life rooted in God. At the center of each of us is this very breath of God that gives life to us. Yet, like Adam and Eve, we can choose to distrust this life of God within us that empowers us for the good and the valuable. When we begin to distrust this breath of God, we begin to make irresponsible and selfish choices (sin), choices that reflect a false center within us, choices similar to those Jesus struggled with in the desert.

But all is not lost. St. Paul reminds us that we are not destined to a life of sin. The obedience of Jesus to his relationship with the Father liberates all of us to share in that new way of life. We can live from our true center: the breath of God within.

Suggestions for Prayer

1. Slowly reread the opening sentence of the Genesis text. Ponder the meaning of the "breath of life" for you and what it means to be a "living being."
2. Find some desert time and space for yourself—time to be alone in silence. Ask God to help you come to an awareness of your own struggles that keep you from living from your true center.
3. Pray Psalm 51 slowly, making explicit for yourself how you have experienced God's mercy (i.e., the abundance of God's love and forgiveness).

Suggestion for Journal Keeping

Reflect on the last week and the choices you made. List for yourself some of these choices. What do these choices say about your sense of self, sense of relationship with others, sense of God? What do you need from God to help you make choices that are more authentic?

Thomas H. Morris

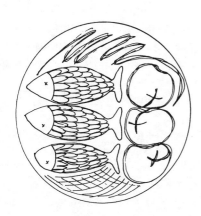

First Sunday of Lent [B]

READING I	Gn 9:8–15
Responsorial Psalm	Ps 25:4–5, 6–7, 8–9
READING II	1 Pt 3:18–22
GOSPEL	Mk 1:12–15

Reflection on the Readings

On the day when the Rite of Election takes place, how appropriate that the readings are centered on the symbolism of water and God's establishment of a covenant relationship with us.

In the story of Noah, the floodwaters that destroy are the same waters of salvation. They cleanse and purify. God offers salvation to those who live by his law. As this relationship is formed between God and his people, we pray for the grace to keep our part of the covenant. We respond to his endless love.

Today the Rite of Election reminds us of the challenge and meaning of Lent in our lives. For those fully initiated it can be a time of reflection on the past. If it has been a time of self-glorification and falling into temptation, Lent is our time of another conversion. For catechumens journeying toward the font, it is a time of reflecting on the deserts of their lives, the helplessness and lifelessness of the past. Now it is time to listen and respond to the good news. We begin this season of Lent with hope and encouraged in knowing the continued presence of God in our life.

Suggestions for Prayer

1. God has made a covenant with us that is unbreakable. He will always be our God. He always loves us. Reflect on an area of your

spiritual life this week with which you are dissatisfied. What response will you make to God's love in order to grow in that area?

2. Water can be a symbol of God's power, his gentleness, his cleansing. Take time to refresh yourself by walking near a creek, lake or sea. Reflect on these attributes of God in your own life.

3. Write a letter to God in which you respond to his presence in your life. Prayerfully petition him for continued guidance as you learn his ways.

Suggestion for Journal Keeping

Satan tempted Jesus in order to glorify himself. Instead, Jesus chose to glorify God. Describe a time when you fostered a situation in order to receive self-glorification. What was the outcome? How did you feel about receiving the glory? How could you have acted in a more humble way?

Mary Kay Meier

First Sunday of Lent [C]

READING I	Dt 26:4–10
Responsorial Psalm	Ps 91:1–2, 10–11, 12–13, 14–15
READING II	Rom 10:8–13
GOSPEL	Lk 4:1–13

Reflection on the Readings

With the beginning of the Lenten season, we take time to reflect on what it is we really believe—our faith gives direction and motivation to our Lenten search for holiness.

In the first reading from Deuteronomy, Moses tells his people the story of their origins as the people of God. This story was retold each year at the Hebrew thanksgiving or harvest festival because it capsulizes God's continuing presence and care for his people, even from the time of Abraham. We connect again with our forebears in faith and strengthen our own spiritual roots.

The responsorial psalm gives voice to our prayer for the protection and support of the Lord and the assurance that we are "delivered" by the Lord because we strive to be faithful. Paul's Letter to the Romans extends to us as well. Our belief in Jesus Christ as the Lord, risen from the dead, leads us to salvation. Our profession of faith affirms our direction toward holiness, a life according to Gospel values.

It is the Gospel that serves as the crowning profession of faith. Each year on this Sunday the church gives us the story of the temptations of Jesus as he begins his public life. Right after his baptism in the Jordan River, Jesus spent time alone fasting and praying—a soul-searching time during which he faced temptations. These temptations are present in our lives as well: to make material comforts foremost in our lives, to seek power and influence for our own use, to be reckless or thoughtless in our self-sufficiency and pride.

Our efforts in the weeks ahead will focus, to some extent, on our purification as individuals and as a community, our efforts to know ourselves better and to be more attentive in our growth toward holiness.

Suggestions for Prayer

1. Use a missal to read again the opening prayer and other prayers, asking for help in our spiritual growth. For us in the catechumenate process, there should be special attentiveness

to our efforts to grow in faith, hope and love. In your own words, formulate a prayer that focuses your Lenten efforts for spiritual growth.

2. In the catechumenate process, some catechumens will be experiencing the Rite of Election at this time. Whether you are participating in the Rite, or are present in support for others in your parish, listen particularly to the prayers of the Rite. They affirm our response to the call to holiness and assure us of the support of the community in our faith journey. Really pray the prayers and reflect on their meaning.

3. The Catholic community professes a summary of our beliefs in a Creed. Familiar to us are two different formulations of our faith: the Apostles' Creed (often prayed in the rosary) and the Nicene Creed, which is proclaimed at Mass. If you do not yet have a copy of the Creed, you may want to ask your sponsor to help you find one. Spend time praying with these statements of belief.

Suggestion for Journal Keeping

Write your own personal creed. Express in it your faith in God, in Jesus, in the Church and in yourself.

Clare M. Colella

Second Sunday of Lent [A]

READING I	*Gn 12:1–4a*
Responsorial Psalm	*Ps 33:4–5, 18–19, 20, 22*
READING II	*2 Tm 1:8b–10*
GOSPEL	*Mt 17:1–9*

Reflection on the Readings

Our Gospel today relates a rather extraordinary occurrence: the transfiguration of Jesus. This transfiguration is a change in Jesus' appearance that allows the apostles to experience Jesus as he truly was—honest, vulnerable, in his glory. More importantly, however, the apostles experience a particular call from God. The message of the voice from the cloud ends up with an active command: Listen to Jesus. The invitation is to trust the way of life of Jesus, to risk following Jesus.

The other readings today continue this message of God's call. In the Genesis reading, we hear God's call to Abraham to leave all his securities—his homeland, his heritage—in order to enter into a deeper relationship with God. In return for his trust, God promises Abraham a blessed future. In the letter to Timothy, we are reminded again of God's call to lives that are holy. But, like Abraham, we can only respond in trust to this call because of God's presence within us, God's grace.

The transfiguration of Jesus is about our call to a blessed future. When we can trust God's call to follow Jesus, we can let go of all that we hold onto for security (such as prestige, honors and money) and begin to see the various transfigurations happening all around us whenever women and men embrace honest, vulnerable and authentic lives patterned on the Gospel way of life.

Suggestions for Prayer
1. Reflect on God's call in your life. How is God calling you, and to what is God calling you? Ask God for what you need in order to respond faithfully to God's call in your life.
2. Pray Psalm 33, a psalm of trust. What images and feelings emerge while you pray the psalm?
3. Bring to prayer an experience of your own brokenness that needs to be embraced by the love of God so that it can be transfigured, so that the true glory of God can shine forth.

Suggestion for Journal Keeping
As we learn to trust, we begin to see more and more transfigurations all around us: people embracing life more fully. Reflect on your own experiences and the experiences of family and friends when life was embraced, such as in the recovery of an alcoholic, or the rebuilding of a life after divorce or the new life of an infant. How did you meet God in these events?

Thomas H. Morris

Second Sunday of Lent [B]

READING I	*Gn 22:1–2, 9a, 10–13, 15–18*
Responsorial Psalm	*Ps 116:10, 15, 16–17, 18–19*
READING II	*Rom 8:31b–34*
GOSPEL	*Mk 9:2–10*

Reflection on the Readings
We are confronted this Sunday with the difficulties as well as the blessings we encounter when we answer "yes" to God's call. Abraham says yes and is willing to sacrifice his only son because God has asked it of him. In response to Abraham's obedience God says: "Because you acted as you did, I will bless you abundantly. . . all this because you obeyed my command." Abraham is our example of complete obedience to the will of God. Are we willing to do the same?

The Gospel accounts tell us of Peter, James and John being allowed to share in seeing Christ glorified. However, they are confused by his strict request "not to relate what they had seen to anyone, except when the Son of Man had risen from the dead." What does "had risen from the dead" mean? They fail to comprehend his words. They failed to see that in order to be followers of Christ one must enter into suffering and, perhaps, even death in order to share in his resurrection. For those preparing for initiation as well as for those fully initiated, the good news of today's liturgy reminds us how like Peter, James and John we are. How often do we fail to comprehend Christ's words to us?

Suggestions for Prayer
1. Mark tells us that Christ is glorified before Peter, James and John. From the cloud they hear: "This is my beloved Son. Listen to him." Take time this week and meditate on these words. Clear your mind. Be quiet. Take time to listen.
2. Abraham made a difficult and painful decision. He put his faith in the Lord and the Lord then promised him abundant blessings. Consider a difficult situation in your life right now. How have you handled it so far? Has it gotten less difficult as a result of your

actions? Are you able to follow the example of Abraham and strive to put your faith in God for strength to make the decision?

3. Choose a quiet time and place where you will be undisturbed. Spend a minimum of five minutes in giving thanks and praise to God for blessings received.

Suggestion for Journal Keeping

The faith of Abraham is our example of listening and loving our God above our wants or needs. What still hinders you from doing the same? What are some struggles you have in letting go of controlling the situation? What is preventing you from surrendering to God's will for you?

Mary Kay Meier

Second Sunday of Lent [C]

READING I	*Gn 15:5–12, 17–18*
Responsorial Psalm	*Ps 27:1 7–8, 8–9, 13–14*
READING II	*Phil 3:17—4:1 or 3:20—4:1*
GOSPEL	*Lk 9:28b–36*

Reflection on the Readings

Each year on this Sunday the readings connect the covenant between God and Abram (Abraham) with the transfiguration of Jesus. Having faced our vulnerability with the temptations episode the previous week, we are now assured that we are rooted in the long-standing covenant of God's presence and care. Abraham is our ancestor in faith. His relationship with God is a model for us, an example of deep trust and fidelity that gives us strength. It is the "standing firm in the Lord" of which Paul speaks in the Letter to the Philippians.

When we are strong in the Lord, faithful to our covenant, we experience a continuing conversion. The event of the transfiguration of Jesus is, in a sense, a promise to his followers. Through Jesus we are called to prayer, to a deeper relationship with God and our spiritual forbears. Our reflection on the transfiguration of Jesus is also a call to a process of transformation in our lives. This is a reminder of our continuing Lenten resolve to grow in holiness, to withstand the temptations of pride and selfishness, to become more like Jesus in our lives.

Our lives will become recognizably different—the spiritual energy and growth we experience will make our faith shine. The transfiguration will become real in our lives. The promise from ancient times is renewed through us today.

Suggestions for Prayer

1. Psalm 27 serves as the responsorial psalm, in which we plead for the Lord to be our light and salvation. We pray to recognize the Lord's care and we seek God's encouragement to be strong and persevere in growing in faith. As you pray this psalm slowly, reflect on *your* own conversion to the Lord. What do you ask of him? Do you truly believe in his presence and care? Create your own personalized prayer springing from the psalm.

2. Transformation of our lives is an outcome of a process of spiritual growth. Take time to envision aspects of your life that are becoming changed as you develop your spiritual life. Pray about your growth, asking the guidance and strength of the Lord. Reflect

on ways that care and encouragement come into your life.

3. Just as Jesus spoke with Moses and Elijah, we too have persons in our lives who have given us spiritual roots and spiritual wisdom. Spend time in quiet reflective prayer. Think about those who have helped shape your spiritual life. How are you becoming more transformed to live as a follower of Jesus?

Suggestion for Journal Keeping

As you reflect on the readings and spend time in prayer, track your thoughts in your journal. Reaffirm your resolve to transform your life. We have been calling it your journey of faith, the process of conversion. Your journal is a way for you to make concrete and visible for yourself your on-going spiritual growth.

Clare M. Colella

Third Sunday of Lent [A]

READING I   *Ex 17:3–7*

Responsorial Psalm   *Ps 95:1–2, 6–7, 8–9*

READING II   *Rom 5:1–2, 5–8*

GOSPEL   *Jn 4:5–42 or 4:5–15, 19b–26, 39a, 40–42*

Reflection on the Readings

In today's Gospel, we experience the tenderness and compassion of Jesus as he encounters the Samaritan woman. Jesus helps her come to an awareness of her needs, of her true thirst. We, too, are invited to accept Jesus in order to quench our interior thirst for life, for meaning. It is only in God that we can experience the liv-

ing waters that can satisfy. This wellspring within us is beautifully described in the text from Romans: the love of God has been poured out into our hearts. The very source of our life, and hence that which can quench our thirst for meaningful life, is God within us.

We see a different response to this thirst in the reading from Exodus. Israel has failed to trust the God who has saved her, the God who has saved her, the God who has led Israel to freedom. Israel desires to serve herself—and thus threatens violence in order to have her thirst quenched. The Samaritan woman, on the other hand, trusts her experience of Jesus and is freely given living waters. She is then able to witness to God's life within her, thereby bringing others to experience God's gifts of love and life.

Suggestions for Prayer

1. Lead yourself through a guided imagery prayer. Visualize yourself as a well. What is the well made of? What is in the well? What do I need from God to drink more fully from the well of life?

2. Reflect on your thirsts for power, acceptance, relationships, freedom from suffering, etc. Now pray for a deeper awareness of your thirst for God. How is this thirst for God similar to or different from your other thirsts?

3. Slowly and prayerfully, chant the responsorial psalm for today, Psalm 95. At the completion of the psalm, allow yourself to sit in the silence to hear the voice of God.

Suggestion for Journal Keeping

Suggestion for Journal Keeping

The text from Romans proclaims: The love of God has been poured out in our hearts through the Holy Spirit. What does this mean to you? How do you block this gift of love? What does this text from Romans tell you about yourself?

Thomas H. Morris

Third Sunday of Lent [B]

READING I   *Ex 20:1–17 or 20:1–3, 7–8, 12–17*

Responsorial Psalm   *Ps 19:8, 9, 10, 11*

READING II   *1 Cor 1:22–25*

GOSPEL   *Jn 2:13–25*

Reflection on the Readings

By the cleansing of the temple Jesus foretells his death followed three days later by his resurrection. In anger he drives the merchants and moneychangers from the temple, his Father's house. In doing so, he indicates that worship through him, the new temple, will eliminate the need for those elements of sacrifice. The Jewish leaders ask for a sign of his authority. They do not understand his answer to them: "Destroy this temple and in three days I will raise it up." How can you tear down something that took forty-six years to build and rebuild it in three days?

Jesus initiates something new. No longer was worship a matter of offering sacrifice in the temple, nor was fidelity simply a matter of obeying the law. As Jesus says to the Samaritan woman, "The hour. . . is now here, when true worshipers will worship the Father in Spirit and truth." This message can be as difficult for us as it was for Jesus' hearers. We too want to rely on signs to give us certainty, or worldly wisdom to resolve our questions. Yet the only sign we have is a sign of contradiction, the crucified Jesus. He is the wisdom and power of God on whom we rely.

Suggestions for Prayer

1. In what ways do you base your faith on external signs, obedience to the law, or worldly wisdom? Has there been a time when you discovered that God's folly was wiser than you, or God's weakness stronger than you?

2. Be a sign of Christ's presence in the world today by offering your presence to someone in need. Remember, it is not words or actions, but sometimes our physical presence that is the gift.

3. Take time before retiring to reflect on your day. Have you kept the commandment of Christ this day to love one another? Ask the Lord to continue to show you his way of living and loving.

Suggestion for Journal Keeping

What presently enables you to follow Jesus: the law, his signs, his words? Why? What makes it difficult for you to follow Jesus: the law, his signs, his words? Why?

Mary Kay Meier

Third Sunday of Lent [C]

READING I	*Ex 3:1–8a, 13–15*
Responsorial Psalm	*Ps 103:1–2, 3–4, 6–7, 8, 11*
READING II	*1 Cor 10:1–6. 10–12*
GOSPEL	*Lk 13:1–9*

Reflection on the Readings

Throughout the prayers and readings today, we are reminded of the need for ongoing reform in our lives. Persistence and patience are key in a true formation according to the teachings of both Hebrew and Christian Scripture.

In parishes celebrating the rite of Christian Initiation, this is the Sunday of the first scrutiny. That rite serves to focus our reflections today—what are we doing to shape our actions and lives to the Christian values and teachings? As we examine ("scrutinize") our lives, can we affirm areas of growth while we also acknowledge our weaknesses and failures? Where is God in our lives? How central is our relationship with God in the formation of our values?

The first Scripture reading, from the Book of Exodus, has two wonderful insights for those of us consciously endeavoring to grow in faith. First, while shepherding his flock Moses encounters God through a burning bush. It is in the midst of ordinary tasks that we come to recognize the presence and voice of God. Second, God gives himself the name I AM. From ancient times on through all generations, God *is*—is present, is close to us, is covenanted with us as our God. He is not distant or unfamiliar. He is compassionate, aware of the suffering of his people. Yet we are often unaware of God. Like the fig tree in the

Gospel, we can go on year after year without bearing fruit. But eventually there comes a time when the owner of the tree cuts it down if it is fruitless. Lent is for us a time of reckoning. We must look at our lives and ask what fruit we are bearing. Are we responsive to God in our ordinary life, to God who is always with us?

Suggestions for Prayer

1. One task of spiritual growth is to move prayerfully through our ordinary surroundings—to see God in and through our daily lives. Like Moses we are to remove our shoes (habitual ways of seeing and doing) and experience all of life as holy ground. Take time to review the persons and events of the last day or so—pray about them, seeing them as "holy ground." Where do you see God?

2. In the spirit of reforming our lives, we look at, "scrutinize," ourselves, our actions and values. Picture yourself together with Jesus talking about your life. Where are the greatest weaknesses? What needs special care before you "bear fruit"? Where are your strengths as a follower of Jesus? How regular is your life of prayer, fasting or works of mercy? Because you and Jesus are together, you know you will have strength to be faithful. Let your reflection on your life become a prayer.

3. The catechumenate is a time of particular attention to our spiritual growth and way of life. Some qualities of holiness are spoken of in today's responsorial psalm—kindness, mercy, compassion, justice, graciousness, forgiveness, being slow to anger. As you pray the psalm again, ponder these qualities.

Suggestion for Journal Keeping

Picture yourself as Moses before the burning bush. Center your attention on your presence with God, however you picture God. God has a message for you. As you hear God's words to you, what is your response? Use your journal to reflect on this time with God.

Clare M. Colella

Fourth Sunday of Lent [A]

READING I	*1 Sm 16:1b, 6–7, 10–13a*
Responsorial Psalm	*Ps 23:1–3a, 3b–4, 5, 6*
READING II	*Eph 5:8–14*
GOSPEL	*Jn 9:1–41 or 9:1, 6–9, 13–17, 34–38*

Reflection on the Readings

Today's readings are filled with images of sight, light, correct vision. Jesus gives glory to God by giving sight to the man born blind. More importantly, Jesus helps the man to gain interior sight—insight—and thus empowers him to accept Jesus and his way of life. Jesus' proclamation—I am the light of the world— helps us realize that we live by an interior guide: the promptings of the heart.

The text from 1 Samuel helps us understand this. God does not see as we see. Our vision is blurred by our prejudices, our own darkness and blindness. Rather, God sees into the heart, the center of our person. Our actions may do one thing, our words may say another, but our heart is living testimony to how we truly live: by the light of God or by our interior darkness. Jesus' invitation today is to be freed from the darkness that keeps us blind, and, as St. Paul

tells us, live as children of the light. Living out of our heart, guided by the light of the world, will demand honesty and courage. As the man born blind, we may experience the abuse of those who claim to see, but whose vision has really been blurred by their self-righteousness and sin.

Suggestions for Prayer

1. Return to the Gospel story. Imagine yourself as the person born blind. Hear Jesus ask you: What is your blindness? Respond. Then hear Jesus ask you if you want to recover from this blindness. Respond. Hear Jesus' prayer for you.
2. Pray Psalm 23. Pause between verses and express in your own words what the verse means for you at this moment in your life.
3. In a spirit of repentance, reflect on areas of blindness in your own life. Ask God for what you need to be healed from this blindness.

Suggestion for Journal Keeping

Recall the insight from 1 Samuel: God sees not as we see, but God sees the heart. Write a letter to yourself from God, telling you the quality of your heart, of your authentic center. Describe how you are faithful in your lifestyle to the insights gleaned from the letter.

Thomas H. Morris

Fourth Sunday of Lent   [B]

READING I	2 Chr 36:14–16, 19–23
Responsorial Psalm	Ps 137:1–2, 3, 4–5, 6
READING II	Eph 2:4–10
GOSPEL	Jn 3:14–21

Reflection on the Readings

> For God so loved the world
> that he gave his only Son,
> so that everyone who believes in him…
> may have eternal life.

These words, found in today's Gospel, sum up the heart of the Gospel message. Through the words of the prophets, that same message was given in the Old Testament. Yet at times, the word was rejected. We hear, "But they mocked the messengers of God, despised his warnings, scoffed at this prophets." Down through the ages the choice of how we respond to God's love has always been ours.

This gift of God to us, the Christ, raises us up from sin to receive our "seat in the heavens." However, we may still choose to live in the darkness—a life of sin, desolation and hopelessness. Or we may accept the light of the life of Christ and live in that light.

We are not unlike the man born blind in the Gospel (Jn 9). Jesus is offering us sight too by inviting us to follow him and to view life with his light. Physical healing is given to the man born blind. Spiritual healing and awakening is offered to us, encouraging us to move from the darkness of sin to the light of Christ.

Suggestions for Prayer

1. Reflect on areas of your life that are still shrouded in darkness. What is left to let go of in order for you to accept the light that Christ offers? This week ask Jesus to continue to sustain you in your quest to grow in faith.
2. As we continue on our Lenten journey, we are encouraged to reflect on Christ's death for all people. We are invited to belong to his family. Ask forgiveness for those times we discriminated against members of that family because of race, religion, social status, sex, etc.
3. The themes of forgiveness and reconciliation continue throughout the Lenten season. Is there someone in your life from whom you are alienated? Take steps this week to mend the relationship, to reconcile, to forgive.

Suggestion for Journal Keeping

Read the Gospel of the man born blind (Jn 9). When the blind man is given the gift of sight, he first calls Jesus "a man." Next, he calls him "a prophet." Finally, he professes Jesus as "Lord." Who was Jesus to me when I began my journey as a catechumen? Who is he to me now? What has happened that I have received the gift of sight?

Mary Kay Meier

Fourth Sunday of Lent   [C]

READING I	Jos 5:9a, 10–12
Responsorial Psalm	Ps 34:2–3, 4–5, 6–7
READING II	2 Cor 5:17–21
GOSPEL	Lk 15:1–3, 11–32

Reflection on the Readings

We are at the halfway mark in the Lenten season—a time of renewed energy, a time for recalling God's continuing care. In the first reading, we hear of God's providence for his people. While the Hebrews were on the journey, manna was provided for them. On the celebration of this Passover, they ate the food they themselves had grown in their new homeland of Canaan. God had indeed led them into the promised land, and now they are experiencing again God's blessings.

In the reading from Paul's Second Letter to the Corinthians, we are given the image of Jesus Christ as the new Passover who has reconciled us, who gives us the message of forgiveness and redemption.

It is that message of God's continuing care and forgiveness that are highlighted in the memorable and beautiful parable of the Gospel reading. It is the story of a loving and compassionate father, a clear image of God. Each son represents a segment of the people of God. One son is like those who are self-sufficient and proud, but who eventually realize their predicament and return to the father to be forgiven and welcomed. Then there are those of us who stay at home, loyal and perhaps self-righteous. The most wondrous love of this father, who has waited for, longed for, the return of his lost son, reaches out to his loyal son as well. The elder son was confused and hurt by his father's actions; the father is understanding and compassionate toward him as well.

This is a truly powerful story for meditation. Do we understand the measure of God's deep and constant love for each of us, no matter who we are or what we have done with our lives up to this point? Regardless of our past, whether we are catechumens, candidates, elect or baptized, we all need assurance of God's mercy, love and continued presence with us.

Suggestions for Prayer

1. Reread the Gospel parable and put yourself into the story—perhaps as the runaway son, returning, or as the loyal stay-at-home elder son, or as an observer. How do you feel about your life? About yourself? About what is going on around you? Spend time with the Father. What does he say to you?

2. In some parishes, the Sunday of the second scrutiny may use the Gospel story of Jesus healing the blind man (Jn 9:1–41). Either Gospel encourages us to look at our lives with the light of faith—to see beyond the immediate situation. We are called to be honest about ourselves. Who is it that heals us, forgives us, welcomes us? How open are we to the action of God in our own lives? Spend some time in quiet reflection, looking at your openness to God's presence and action in your life.

3. Imagine yourself as the son walking the road back home. What thoughts do you have? What do you want to say to your father? Your family? Put these thoughts into a prayer for strength, for mercy and for gladness at being forgiven and welcomed back.

Suggestion for Journal Keeping

Keep your journal ready as you spend time in prayer and reflection. Use it to keep some of the insights and thoughts that come to you. At another time in the week, reread what you wrote. Do new insights come to you? You may want to talk with your sponsor or members of the catechumenate team about your reflections and feelings at this time.

Clare M. Colella

Fifth Sunday of Lent [A]

READING I	*Ez 37:12–14*
Responsorial Psalm	*Ps 130:1–2, 3–4, 5–6, 7–8*
READING II	*Rom 8:8–11*
GOSPEL	*Jn 11:1–45 or 11:3–7, 17, 20–27, 33b–45*

Reflection on the Readings

Jesus is faced with the painful reality of death in today's Gospel. Jesus weeps over the death of his dear friend Lazarus. As a way of pointing out the abundance of God's love, Jesus raises Lazarus back to life. Along with the raising of Lazarus is a central proclamation from Jesus: I am the resurrection and the life. Through the gift of the Sprit, that which was corruptible and broken through death is now made incorruptible and restored to eternal life.

All of the readings today proclaim the God of the living. In the Ezekiel text, we hear God's desire to bring life through the Spirit. In the text from Romans, St. Paul reminds us that because we share in the very Spirit of God, then we will share in fullness of life as experienced in Jesus' resurrection. Lazarus' restoration to life is a witness to the working of God's Spirit. Wherever the Spirit dwells, there life is found in abundance.

Yet these readings also heighten our awareness to that which keeps us from this fullness of life: death, existence without the Spirit, being held bound. The same Spirit that breathes life does so by breaking open the graves that oppress us, by untying the wrappings that keep us enslaved to death.

I am the resurrection and the life—not only for eternal life, but for freedom from sin and oppression in the world now, today. The Spirit is given to restore life where there was apparent death and sin.

Suggestions for Prayer

1. Create and pray a litany celebrating the God of the living. Recite or chant the refrain: "Blessed be the God of the living!" Following the refrain, mention experiences of life from God, such as "For the beauty of creation," "For the gift of my family," etc.
2. Jesus proclaimed: Untie him and let him go. What areas of your life keep you bound? Pray for what you need to be made free.
3. Return to the Gospel. Prayerfully reflect on the passage when Jesus calls forth Lazarus from the tomb. Hear Jesus call you by your name from your own tomb. Pray for what you need to live a renewed life.

Suggestion for Journal Keeping

Describe areas of your life that have come back to life after being dead. What were the circumstances leading to this renewed life? How were you changed because of this renewed life? Describe your relationship with God because of these experiences.

Thomas H. Morris

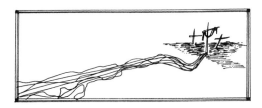

Fifth Sunday of Lent [B]

READING I	*Jer 31:31–34*
Responsorial Psalm	*Ps 51:3–4, 12–13, 14–15*
READING II	*Heb 5:7–9*
GOSPEL	*Jn 12:20–33*

Reflection on the Readings

New life is the symbol of today's narrative. The Gospel reads, "Unless a grain of wheat falls to the ground and dies, it remains just a grain of wheat. But if it dies, it produces much fruit." Jesus himself follows nature's cycle through his death and burial. New life is resurrected. He had spent his public life telling his followers about the Father's love. Now the hour has almost come. The sign of the love he has shared is about to be given for a final time. John's Gospel reminds us that we are called to follow Christ's example. If we are to share in his glory, we must also die to self.

Jeremiah reminded the people of God's new covenant, "The days are coming. . . when I will make a new covenant with the house of Israel. . . . I will be their God, and they shall be my people." This covenant is extended to us this day as we gather to hear the good news of Christ. It is no longer through observance of the law of the Old Testament, carved in the tablets of stone, that we glorify God. Today we are called to hear the words of Christ and to follow his example. Let us respond to both, and carry them in our hearts.

Suggestions for Prayer
1. As we acknowledge our need for God, we also need to acknowledge areas of our life that need to be strengthened. Read and reflect on the responsorial psalm for this week.
2. Take time this week for quiet. Be at peace with your God.

Suggestion for Journal Keeping

Read the Gospel account of the death of Lazarus. Imagine yourself at the tomb. Listen to the words Jesus says: " I am the resurrection and the life; whoever believes in me, even if he dies, will live, and everyone who lives and believes in me will never die. Do you believe this?" How do you respond?

Mary Kay Meier

Fifth Sunday of Lent [C]

READING I	*Is 43:16–21*
Responsorial Psalm	*Ps 126:1–2, 2–3, 4–5, 6*
READING II	*Phil 3:8–14*
GOSPEL	*Jn 8:1–11*

Reflection on the Readings

One of the joys of reflecting on the word of God in the Scriptures is that we today are continually learning from words written so long ago. The words of Scripture are ever new. This is expressed through Isaiah: "See! I am doing something new!" Let us take time to look and see what is new. What is the Lord doing? We have been on this Lenten journey for quite a while now—and on our conversion journey for an even longer time. We are getting to know ourselves better—and getting to know Jesus as well.

Today's readings assure us of God's continued presence and especially his forgiveness. What is made new may well be *us*—we put our past behind us and move on to what is ahead. Though we have done wrong, made mistakes, been weak, we find that God has "remembered not." The first two readings and the responsorial psalm go on to assure us that God has formed us, blessed us, called us to himself. We are forgiven and beloved. Through the Gospel episode, we are enlightened—Jesus speaks not only to the people of his time but to us also. With very few words and a simple action, he teaches us about honesty, forgiveness, conversion, as he challenges the complacent/self-righteous while he accepts and forgives the accused sinner.

This Sunday is the third scrutiny in parishes that are celebrating the catechumenate process. If your parish chooses the Gospel of the raising of Lazarus, read the reflection under Cycle A.

Suggestions for Prayer

1. Reread the Gospel episode of the woman caught in adultery. Picture yourself in this story. Is your life somewhat like the person accused—acknowledging the reality of your life, knowing you are forgiven and that you can begin a new life of discipleship? Or is it more like the accusers who, having found another's weakness, are reluctant to acknowledge their own sinfulness and walk away from the Lord unconverted? Spend some time in prayer with Jesus as he writes in the sand, then stands up. He knows what is in your heart. What does he say to you? How do you respond?

2. Paul's Letter to the Philippians reveals the deep faith and conviction he has about what is most important in his life. Having found Jesus Christ, nothing else really matters.

With the eyes of faith we see things differently—even our sufferings bring us closer to Jesus. Imagine Jesus looking at your life and love and forgiveness. Hear his invitation to you to look at your life through his eyes, with faith and a desire to be a disciple of his.

3. "The Lord has done great things for us; we are filled with joy!" The responsorial psalm proclaims specifically what the other readings and prayers seem only to hint at: that God has done wonderful things in our lives. Picture yourself in a comfortable setting with your friend, the Lord. Take time to get a graphic image of your friend. Feel familiar and comfortable with him. Then let your memory recall some of the good things that have happened in your life.

Suggestion for Journal Keeping

Since your journal is a personal record of your faith journey and your thoughts and prayers along the way, use some quiet time to write about your reflections on the liturgy and readings today. Use your journal to help concretize your prayer—you may want to write your prayer images and work with them again at a later time.

Clare M. Colella

Holy Week
Palm Sunday of the
Lord's Passion
At the Procession with Palms

GOSPEL A	Mt 21:1–11
GOSPEL B	Mk 11:1–10 or Jn 12:12–16
GOSPEL C	Lk 19:28–40

Reflection on the Readings

Hymns of praise resound! Hosanna! Blessed is he who comes in the name of the Lord! Today's proclamation is a reminder of the great excitement and wonder that welcomed Jesus into the city of Jerusalem. Jesus was such a powerful presence to people—in word and action—that the whole city was "shaken." There were songs of welcome and greetings, great cheers and a great procession.

There was something very simple and sacred about the triumphant entry into Jerusalem. People had been genuinely touched by Jesus. He lived a blessed and holy life that helped them come to know God's gracious love and forgiveness. Because of Jesus, people's lives were changed. And with the same enthusiasm that we would welcome a hero or heroine to our neighborhood, they gather to greet this special man who comes to them on a borrowed colt, surrounded by his companions.

The initial instinct of the people is to celebrate the gracious presence of God in Jesus. There is gratitude, rejoicing, praise in the air. Soon these same people will turn and run because of their own fear. But for now they welcome the one who has brought the freshness of God into their lives—Jesus.

Suggestions for Prayer

1. Reflect on the text from Matthew. At the end of the text, answer the question posed: Who is this?
2. Lead yourself through a guided imagery of the text from Mark. As you experience Jesus coming into the city, reflect on what you are grateful for that brings you to proclaim: Hosanna!
3. Pray the text from Luke. Recall in your own life the "mighty deeds" from God for which you wish to give praise.

Suggestion for Journal Keeping

The entry into Jerusalem is also an entry into the passion and death of Jesus. Yet Jesus could be obedient because of his profound trust in God. Reflect on your life experience: How have I met God in the very ordinary events of life? For what do I give praise and thanks? How do I describe God's love in my life? Can I trust God? If not, what do I need to trust God? After writing these reflections, recall Jesus' entry into Jerusalem. Continue to journal: Can I go with him? What does this mean for me?

Thomas H. Morris

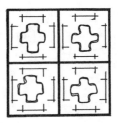

Palm Sunday Mass [A B C]

READING I *Is 50:4–7*

Responsorial Psalm *Ps 22:8–9, 17–18, 19–20, 23–24*

READING II *Phil 2:6–11*

(The Gospels and their related material follow these reflections.)

Reflection on the Readings

The readings preceding the Gospel narrative share a common vision: trust in God. The text from Isaiah, known as the Third Servant Song, speaks of one who has been faithful to proclaiming the message of God despite persecution and rejection. In Psalm 22, the psalmist moves from a cry of abandonment that is a response to the persecution resulting from trusting in God to the recognition of God's loving presence. And the text from Philippians recounts Jesus' trust in the will of the Father, thus being empowered to empty himself of everything but this loving relationship. Because of his fidelity to this truth, Jesus' life is affirmed and confirmed: God exalts Jesus so we can truly proclaim Jesus as Lord.

Trust in God—in God's providential love that will not bring disgrace but help, that will not leave us abandoned but singing praises, that will not leave us emptied and dead but raised up. It is only that kind of trust that can serve as the backdrop for Jesus' decision to accept his sentence of death on the cross.

Suggestions for Prayer

1. Reread the text from Isaiah. After sitting in silence, offer prayers of petition for the men and women in the world who stand up for truth and justice, even at the cost of their own lives.

2. Recall a painful time in your life when you felt abandoned by God. Slowly retell your experience in your prayer, pausing to ask: My God, why have you abandoned me? Ask God for the healing to be able to see how God was truly present with you in this pain.

3. Mantra prayer is a gentle repetition and recollection of a short phrase, usually accompanied to your breathing. Based on the readings and reflection, choose a short phrase that reflects your need, such as "God, teach me to trust." Slowly and prayerfully, repeat the phrase in rhythm to your breathing. Continue to pray the mantra until you feel the need to move to either silence or petition.

Suggestion for Journal Keeping

Recall events in your life (or in the life of family and friends) when you remained firm in your convictions, despite the comments or threats of others. What helped you to remain strong? Looking back on these events, how was God present? How is your experience similar to the experience of trust proclaimed in the readings today?

Thomas H. Morris

GOSPEL A *Mt 26:14–27:66 or 27:11–54*

Reflection on the Gospel

Today's passion narrative from Matthew's Gospel drains us. It is filled with emotions and experience that run very deep—betrayal, love, trust, denial, condemnation, death. For apparently senseless reasons, Jesus is killed. His life was centered on God's love and justice. His ministry helped bring about the liberation and reconciliation of people from all that oppresses and binds. Jesus' words and actions continued to reflect God's abundance, God's graciousness, God's desire to be on our side.

Yet Jesus' obedience to such an authentic life—a life that truly reflected God in the world—not only brought healing and peace, but also stirred up and challenged any way of life that was centered in selfishness and sin. Accepting Jesus' claim that God was truly on our side demanded a changed way of life that also reflected this love of God. This made some people uncomfortable, threatening them, unmasking their blindness. Their response was to kill Jesus.

Jesus could have fought back, but then he would have compromised the values he had lived by—the values of the reign of God. Instead, Jesus holds firm to his belief that God's way is truly the way of life, even if it costs death.

The stirrings from the narrative run deep because we hear the same challenge today: Can we live the values of the reign of God, even at the cost of our lives? Is this not what it means to embrace and carry the cross?

Suggestions for Prayer

1. Return to the passion narrative from Matthew. Choose one section that particularly struck you when you heard it proclaimed. Pray that passage slowly. What is God asking of you at this time of your life?
2. Religious art is a special way of entering into prayer. Gaze at either a crucifix or a painting of the crucifixion. What does it mean that Jesus died for us?
3. Pray the Jesus prayer. Slowly repeat the mantra, "Jesus, Son of the living God, have pity on me, a sinner." Continue to pray the mantra, focusing on Jesus' gift of love for you.

Suggestion for Journal Keeping

"Not as I will, but as you will." Write about the following: How do I know what God's will is for me? Who can help me understand God's will for me? How do I respond to God's will? What do I need to be able to fully accept God's will?

Thomas H. Morris

GOSPEL B

Mk 14:1—15:47 or 15:1—39

Reflection on the Gospel

The passion narrative from Mark's Gospel is painful: Jesus, who had lived a life of obedience to the will of the Father, is killed because of that very obedience. We are reminded of the various parts of the story that grip us: the sharing of a final meal with his friends, the betrayal from one of his companions, Jesus' own struggle in prayer, the denial of one so close to him, the condemnation to death, the rejection from the crowd that only days earlier welcomed him, the beatings and mockery Jesus endured, and his death on the cross. Painful memories, memories of apparent destruction and violence.

Yet we remember this central story of our faith today precisely because it is in and through the trust Jesus places in the Father that we learn the way of life that brings freedom from all oppression. Jesus died because he was faithful to witnessing to God's love in the world—a love that frees, reconciles, heals, restores order. That witness threatened some, frightened others, and angered enough people to bring Jesus to the cross. Yet Jesus continues to trust that God will be victorious—that the final word will be God's word of justice and love. Even Jesus' followers run in fear, not having developed the level of trust in relationship with the Father.

We are invited to stand at the cross today, to remember the cries of welcome as Jesus enters Jerusalem and the cries of condemnation as he leaves carrying his cross. We come to learn trust with Jesus in the ways of God.

Suggestions for Prayer

1. Prayerfully recall the men and women of our time who have died because of their commitment to the values of justice, mercy, peace and love—in Central and South America, South Africa, Northern Ireland, the Middle East, throughout the world. Pray for the grace to remain strong in your own convictions.

2. Using imaginative prayer, recall the basic story of the passion, walking with Jesus from the gathering to celebrate the passover to his death. As each scene changes, stop and ask God to help you know more deeply the meaning of Jesus' death for the world.

3. The Our Father is the prayer of those who place their trust in God, the prayer of those who embrace the cross of Jesus. Slowly pray the Our Father, pausing after each line. What does that line mean for you now?

Suggestion for Journal Keeping

What keeps you from trusting God fully? Draw images or list words that capture your feelings as you reflect on your relationship with God, your ability or inability to trust God. What do you need from God to help you trust God more completely?

Thomas H. Morris

GOSPEL C   *Lk 22:14—23:56 or 23:1–49*

Reflection on the Gospel

The passion narrative in Luke's Gospel holds in contrast Jesus' obedience to the will of the Father and the injustice that condemns him to death. Luke is rich in his imagery and stories surrounding the events of these last days of Jesus' life: the sharing of the Passover meal, the dispute over greatness, the agony in the garden and arrest, Jesus' turn to look at Peter after his denial, Jesus' condemnation and crucifixion, the dialogue with the criminals hanging with Jesus, Jesus' death and burial. Over and over again, Jesus is presented with the opportunity to strike back, or to run away. Instead, he remains faithful, refusing to compromise God's values that had directed and empowered him throughout his life and ministry. He remains the innocent victim.

Again and again we see in Luke's account Jesus' choice for self-sacrificing love. Self-sacrificing love means that the values of the reign of God as experienced through Jesus—freedom from oppression, compassion for all, liberation and acceptance, reconciliation and right relationships with God—were more important than Jesus' very own life. When faced with the choice of the reign of God or self-preservation, Jesus chose the reign of God. This does not mean self-annihilation. Rather, it means that Jesus lived from his deepest center—God-within—and responded to all of life in this way, whatever the cost. And now we are invited to lives of self-sacrificing love, of choosing God's values whatever the cost. We now can choose such love because Jesus—our Liberator and Redeemer—bestows the Spirit of God upon us.

Suggestions for Prayer
1. Reflect on incidents of oppression in your neighborhood—racism, sexism, ageism—and pray for the courage to bring God's word of liberation to those situations. Ask God to give you what you need to stand up for the values of the reign of God.
2. Jesus' death frees us from all sin and oppression. Recall areas of your life that are still not free, that are still enslaved. Pray: Come, Lord Jesus, and set me free from. . . .
3. Go to your parish church and pray the stations of the cross. Between each station, meditate on the meaning of the station in your life today.

Suggestion for Journal Keeping
The cross is a symbol of Jesus' self-sacrificing love. Recall times in your life when you experienced this self-sacrificing love from another person. Write about: How can I describe this love? How was I changed because of this love? How is God present in this love? What does this love tell me about God's love? What do I need from God to be able to love more freely, to be able to offer self-sacrificing love for others?

Thomas H. Morris

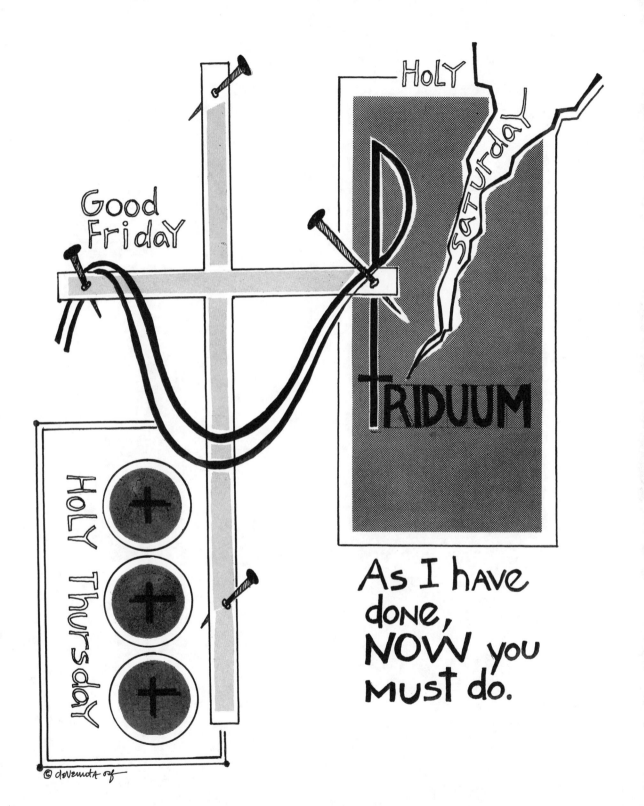

Holy Thursday Mass of the Lord's Supper [A B C]

READING I	Ex 12:1–8, 11–14
Responsorial Psalm	Ps 116:12–13, 15–16bc, 17–18
READING II	1 Cor 11:23–26
GOSPEL	Jn 13:1–15

Reflection on the Readings

Together with that of Palm Sunday, this Holy Week liturgy continues to offer an abundance of symbolic celebration, use of sacramentals, and exposure to the rich ritual heritage of our Church. Unless you take part in the liturgy itself, the simple reading of the prayers and Scripture seem comparatively barren. It is in the context of the praying community that the liturgy comes to full life.

The evening Mass of the Lord's Supper connects the first Passover with Jesus' Last Supper. God's care for his people—through the exodus event and on through Jesus' washing the feet of his disciples—is part of a covenant. The other part of that covenant is our response to God's presence and care, as shown through our service to others, our prayer, our love and care for others. This liturgy also focuses on the institution of the Eucharist, the Last Supper itself, in which Jesus gives himself through the bread and wine. The Eucharist, celebrated with the community, signifies our oneness with God and one another. If a seder meal is celebrated in your parish, the roots of our sacred meal as a family become more clear. The seder meal recalls the exodus event that becomes the Passover meal of Jewish heritage, the setting in which Jesus gave us the new Passover—his own self before his passion and death.

The centrality of the holy meal in the life of the community becomes clear when, as catechumens, elect or baptized members, we regularly gather to worship God and celebrate our life as a community of believers.

Suggestions for Prayer

1. As catechumens, you do not yet celebrate the Eucharist. The fullness of participation comes only after baptism and acceptance into the Church. As you pray with the community, listen to the readings and celebrate

to the fullness of your capacity at this time; pray for all those who are members, and particularly those who are preparing for full membership. Let yourself feel a hungering for the Lord in the Eucharist.

2. Washing the feet of the members of the community is a sign of the service to others, which a leader is called to give. Modeled after Jesus' actions with his disciples, it is a witness to our care for one another. Spend time praying for God's special blessing on the leaders of your parish.

3. The closing words of the Gospel are Jesus' command to his disciples, "As I have done for you, you should also do." The example of Jesus is one of service to others. What service, gifts, caring, do you offer to others as a disciple of Jesus? You may want to spend some time thinking and praying about your gifts within the community. How can you be of service to others? You may want to talk with your sponsor or a member of the catechumenate team about your thoughts and questions.

Suggestion for Journal Keeping

The first reading from Exodus describes the Passover meal. These three days are our Passover in Christ, as we journey with him from death to life. Now that Lent has ended, reflect on what you are celebrating. What is your Passover? From what form of death and toward what new life are you moving?

Clare M. Colella

Good Friday
The Passion of the Lord
[A B C]

READING I	*Is 52:13—53:12*
Responsorial Psalm	*Ps 31:2, 6, 12–13, 15–16, 17, 25*
READING II	*Heb 4:14–16; 5:7–9*
GOSPEL	*Jn 18:1—19:42*

Reflection on the Readings

The liturgy of the Church today is unlike that of any other day. It comprises three segments: the liturgy of the word, the veneration of the cross, and a Communion service. The setting and appearance of the church itself is stark and bare today. The quiet, solemn spirit is most appropriate.

A long reading from the prophet Isaiah unfolds a theology of suffering—that pain and suffering are redemptive, through our perseverance and fidelity we grow spiritually. Here we apply the "Suffering Servant" theme to Jesus who, personally innocent, accepted his suffering for all of us. It is he who redeems us through his death and resurrection.

In the passion narrative, we hear again, this time from the Gospel according to John, the story of our redemption. This event is not unconnected with you and me. Jesus is there because of his love for us. The emphasis on suffering should not be understood as an indication that suffering is the only way to grow spiritually. We can grow and gain insight through any occasion or event in our lives. It is fitting, however, at this time, to look at the reality of pain and suffering, and see in it a path to God.

The general intercessions offer both a prayer for many persons within the people of God and a reminder to us of many for whom we often neglect to pray. As a redeemed people of faith, we reaffirm our solidarity with the universal Church and beyond to all those who seek holiness in their respective faith journeys.

The second movement in the service is the veneration of the cross—a time for us to become very aware of the events of Good Friday as we honor the symbol of Jesus' crucifixion and death. Most of the time, the crucifix is an environmental fixture on the wall, a picture, an icon or a hanging. We tend to take it for granted. We are also more conscious of the triumphant resurrection of Jesus; so many times our crucifixes have the image of a resurrected, majestic, triumphant Jesus. But today we focus on the first part of the paschal mystery: Jesus suffered and died on a cross because of his love for us. The prayers and reproaches of this service emphasize God's continuing care for his people throughout time despite their inconsistent fidelity to him.

The final part of this service, for the baptized community, is the Communion service. Even without the usual celebration of Mass, participants desire to receive Jesus into their lives and hearts through the Eucharist. The prayers and reception of Communion serve as a bridge from Holy Thursday to Easter.

Suggestions for Prayer

1. Time to pray is a priority today. In the midst of a hectic pre-Easter schedule of family activities, we especially need an atmosphere of prayer and reflection. If possible, join in the parish services. But take personal quiet time to think about the events of the passion and death of Jesus—the great love that moved him to do what he has done for us. Do you really believe you are forgiven, loved, and redeemed by Jesus? What does this mean to you?

2. In a special way, we reflect today on the value of suffering for our purification, spiritual growth, self-knowledge, relationship with God. All of these are affected by our attitude toward pain and suffering. Take time to think about a time of suffering in your life—physical, emotional or spiritual. How have you grown through that experience? What are your feelings about suffering in your life? In the lives of loved ones? What are we to learn through suffering in our lives?

3. The reason for Good Friday is the power of love that bursts through death into new life. It is God's overwhelming love for his people, for us, that brought his Son to earth. It is Jesus' love for his Father and for us that brought him to his public life, death and on through to his resurrection. What is the measure of our love in response? To what extent are we willing to suffer because of our love, our discipleship?

Suggestion for Journal Keeping

What has been your experience of death and loss—the loss of a loved one, a painful change in your life, having to let go of someone or something you love? What do you remember about that experience? Have you sensed new growth, new life or wisdom springing from it? Have you learned about yourself? About your relationship with God? Others? God's care for you? As you take time to reflect, use your journal to keep track of your insights and prayer.

Clare M. Colella

Easter
The Resurrection of the Lord
Easter Vigil [A B C]

READING I   *Gn 1:1—2:2 or 1:1, 26–31a*

Responsorial Psalm   *Ps 104:1–2, 5–6, 10, 12, 13–14, 24, 35 or Ps 33:4–5, 6–7, 12–13, 20–22*

Reflection on the Readings

In this reading from the Book of Genesis, we hear the story of the creation of the world. From darkness came light, from the wasteland came life.

During the season of Lent and continuing into celebration of Easter, God continues creating through us. There was the darkness of sin and despair; now there is the light of Christ, our hope. There was death and destruction; now there is renewed life through Christ.

In the creation story we hear about the passages of time in which God created new life, the first day, the second day, etc. What is a day in God's time? No doubt it is unlike our perception. But like the creation of life in the world, the creation of our renewed life will take time. And God will see how good it is and be pleased!

Suggestions for Prayer

1. Make a determined effort each day during this Easter season to become more aware of the gifts of creation. Say a prayer of thanksgiving for them.

2. Spend time experiencing new life through relationships, work and recreation.

Mary Kay Meier

READING II   *Gn 22:1–18 or 22:1–2, 9a, 10–13, 15–18*

Responsorial Psalm   *Ps 16:5, 8, 9–10, 11*

Reflection on the Readings

Abraham and his wife Sarah had been waiting for a child for all of their wedded life. Finally, a miracle happened! Sarah gave birth to a son, even though she was well beyond childbearing years. Therefore, can you imagine the heartache and pain Abraham must have suffered as he prepared to make a sacrifice of this child? He loved the Lord without question. Without striking bargains or complaining, he accepted the will of God for him. He had passed the test. God's messenger now knows how devoted Abraham was to God. Abraham was blessed abundantly through countless descendants.

We sometimes think that because we love God, life should be easy. How disappointed and angry we can become when we realize daily life can become difficult and messy when we follow Christ. We cannot bargain with Christ, but, like Abraham, we can continue the struggle of putting complete trust in him.

Suggestions for Prayer

1. Reflect on a time when you were going through a difficult time in your life. How did you respond? Did you call upon God at the time? What was the result?

2. Repeat part of the responsorial psalm (Psalm 16) daily: "With God at my right hand, I shall not be disturbed."

Mary Kay Meier

READING III

Ex 14:15—15:1

Responsorial Psalm   Ex 15:1–2, 3–4, 5–6, 17–18

Reflection on the Readings

In the prayer for the blessing of the baptismal water, we hear these words:

> *Through the waters of the Red Sea*
> *you led Israel out of slavery*
> *to be an image of God's holy people*
> *set free from sin by baptism.*

As we listen to this reading during the Easter Vigil, we are reminded that the waters of the Red Sea prefigure the water of baptism. As Moses led his people from slavery to freedom through the sea, Jesus leads us from death to life through baptism. Through baptism you will share in Jesus' death and resurrection. You too will go into the water of death and liberation. Like Jesus you will die, leaving sin behind. Like Jesus you will rise, filled with his power and life. Jesus is our Moses, leading us to enter new life in our promised land—the Christian community.

Suggestion for Prayer

From what slavery do you need to be liberated? What part of you must die if you are to rise with Christ?

Robert M. Hamma

READING IV

Is 54:5–14

Responsorial Psalm   Ps 30:2, 4, 5–6, 11–12, 13

Reflection on the Readings

This reading is filled with very evocative words. On the one hand there is great sadness—forsaken, abandoned, afflicted, storm-battered, unconsoled. On the other hand there is great joy—tenderness, enduring love, pity. The prophet Isaiah compares our relationship to the love between a husband and wife. Our Creator has raised us high and made us his spouse. Yet we have been unfaithful and so become "a wife forsaken and grieved in spirit." But now the Lord takes us back with great tenderness and enduring love. He promises to be faithful to us even if we are unfaithful:

> *Though the mountains leave their place*
> *and the hills be shaken,*
> *My love shall never leave you.*

God's love is lavished upon us. We are adorned with precious stones.

This is the covenant of fidelity that the Lord makes with you. It is sealed in your baptism.

Suggestion for Prayer

Christian mystics such as John of the Cross have often compared our relationship with the Lord to a marriage. Reflect on God's love for you in this way. Do you find this a helpful image? Why?

Robert M. Hamma

READING V   *Is 55:1–11*

Responsorial Psalm   *Is 12:2–3, 4, 5–6*

Reflection on the Readings

An invitation is given to us. Come to the water. Come and eat. Come and be refreshed. Come and listen. Come and have new life. Come and renew the covenant with me.

Conversion is asked of us. Seek the Lord. Turn to the Lord for mercy. Forsake wicked ways. Listening to God's word will refresh us. This was the reason for our creation, to rejoice, celebrate and be made whole through him.

Suggestion for Prayer

Prayerfully read the responsorial psalm from Isaiah 12:2–6. Reflect on phrases such as, "I am confidant and unafraid," "Give thanks to the LORD," "Sing praise to the LORD for his glorious achievements" and others you choose that are meaningful to you.

Mary Kay Meier

READING VI   *Bar 3:9–15, 32—4:4*

Responsorial Psalm   *Ps 19:8, 9, 10, 11*

Reflection on the Readings

From the prophet Baruch, we are instructed to walk in the way of God and live in peace forever. It was when Israel turned away from God that her enemies destroyed her.

God calls us to the light, not the darkness. He has created all for our joy, not our demise. We are invited into oneness with God, rather than separation. All ways of giving glory to God have been revealed to us. It is in following his ways that we receive enduring peace. The responsorial psalm of this reading reminds us, "Lord, you have the words of everlasting life."

Suggestion for Prayer

In today's culture the advertising world tells us we can find peace and happiness in what we eat, drive, wear, or where we live, etc. This reading tells us we find peace and happiness in the Lord. Where are you in your search for peace? What modern-day pressures prevent you from responding to God's invitation to you?

Mary Kay Meier

READING VII   *Ez 36:16–17a, 18–28*

Responsorial Psalm   *Ps 42:3, 5; 43:3, 4*

Reflection on the Readings

Despite the disobedience and deeds of the people of Israel, God again proclaims his covenant with them, "You shall be my people and I will be your God." At the time the Israelites turned away from the Lord, they were overcome by enemies and scattered to foreign lands. But now the Lord, once more, welcomes them back to him by washing them clean of their impurities. It is to us he speaks: "I will give you a new heart and place a new spirit within you, taking from your bodies your stony hearts and giving you natural hearts." These words are fulfilled during the baptismal rite of this night's celebration. We are welcomed by the Lord despite our past. We are washed clean in the living waters. We are given new hearts. We are given new spirits.

Suggestions for Prayer

1. In your imagination, place yourself at a place of cool water. Imagine yourself touching it, gently. Scooping it into your hands, allow it to run down your face, your arms, your entire self. Reflect on those feelings your imagination has developed.
2. Use Psalm 51, the responsorial psalm of this reading, as your night prayer for this week.

Mary Kay Meier

EPISTLE *Rom 6:3–11*

Responsorial Psalm *Ps 118:1–2, 16–17, 22–23*

Reflection on the Readings

Through baptism we die with Christ. Our old self is washed clean. We are no longer slaves to sin but free people living in and with Christ. Christ will never die again. Death has power over him no longer. We are also freed from death, the death we experience from sin. Sin and darkness need control us no longer. Through the death of Christ we are alive in God. It is a time to celebrate! It is a time to praise God's power and might!

Suggestion for Prayer

As a catechumen still journeying toward the waters of baptism, reflect on this reading often during this week. Converse with God. Share with him your struggles in turning away from darkness to the light, from death of the old self to a new life.

Mary Kay Meier

GOSPEL A *Mt 28:1–10*

GOSPEL B *Mk 16:1–7*

GOSPEL C *Lk 24:1–12*

Reflection on the Readings

"He has been raised." "He is not here." "Go and tell his disciples." These are the words of good news that greet the women when they arrive at the tomb of Jesus. However, they probably weren't words of good news when they first heard them! The scene at the tomb was one of mystery, fear, doubt, confusion.

The women were still grieving their loss. They came to the tomb to attend to the ritual of anointing the body as prescribed by the law. Their concerns were getting past the Roman guards stationed at the tomb and rolling the stone away from the tomb. We need only to

place ourselves in the scene to begin to imagine their feelings, when, upon their arrival, they are greeted by a man wearing a dazzling white robe telling them their Lord was not there.

Jesus had tried to prepare his followers for the events leading to his death, but even those closest to him did not understand. They tried to protect him in the garden when the soldiers came, but fearing for their own lives, they fled. They were still in hiding on this morning of resurrection. Would you have believed three trembling women when they told you, "He is risen"? The women were the first to receive the news of the resurrection. They were the first to see him in his glory. They were the first messengers of the good news of his resurrection. Amazed, fearful and confused as they were, they were called to witness what the Lord had accomplished.

Suggestions for Prayer

1. It is the night of nights for Christianity! Celebrate his resurrection with praise and song.
2. Whether you be man or woman, reflect on the happenings of that resurrection morning. Remember a time you doubted Christ's presence or were confused by his words or perhaps frightened by his call. Thank him for "appearing" to you as he did.

Suggestion for Journal Keeping

According to Matthew's account of the resurrection, without warning Jesus stood before the women and said "Peace." Imagine yourself in that scene. How do you respond to him? What do you say? What do you do?

Mary Kay Meier

EASTER

A NEW BIRTH

...A SHARE IN THE RESURRECTION

Easter Sunday [A B C]

READING I	*Acts 10:34a, 37–43*
Responsorial Psalm	*Ps 118:1–2, 16–17, 22–23*
READING II	*Col 3:1–4*
OR	
READING II	*1 Cor 5:6b–8*
GOSPEL	*Jn 20:1–9*

Reflection on the Readings

In today's first reading Peter proclaims: "God was with Jesus." God worked in and through Jesus. His very name, Jesus, means "God is our salvation." Thus we might ask ourselves: When we pray or act in the name of Jesus, what are we saying? Are we not saying that we believe in a God who works in us and in the Church too?

Christian prayer is always in the name of Jesus. Praying in the name of Jesus does not necessarily mean that we understand all of what God is doing. Rather, it is an acclamation of faith and trust. It is an act of placing ourselves in God's hands rather than relying on ourselves alone. It is a statement of our intention and desire to enter into fuller union with the will of God.

As individuals, and as a people, we move toward belief. It is always ahead of us. The Gospel makes it clear that the disciples did not understand the consequences of the resurrection of Jesus from the dead, yet they believed. Our task is to ponder the consequences of ourselves, today.

Where are we looking for the Lord? Do we look in the empty tomb, or among the living where healing and reconciliation are happening?

Suggestions for Prayer

1. The word, the name "Jesus" is a prayer. Repeat it often. You can develop your own rhythm. You can add petitions such as "Be with me" or "Give me life."
2. The psalm announces: "This is the day that the Lord has made." Begin your day with these words on your lips. Add your own reasons for giving thanks to God for the day.
3. Pray that God's will shall become more evident. Reflect upon the encounters of your day and ask for God's guidance and wisdom, care and compassion.

Suggestion for Journal Keeping

The Church is sometimes called "the Easter people." Record the names of some of the people who have shared their faith with you, and who have accompanied you in the movement toward belief. How are they like Mary Magdalene, Peter or the other disciples? How are you a disciple?

Elizabeth S. Lilly

Second Sunday of Easter   [A]

READING I	*Acts 2:42–47*
Responsorial Psalm	*Ps 118:2–4, 13–15, 22–24*
READING II	*1 Pt 1:3–9*
GOSPEL	*Jn 20:19–31*

Reflection on the Readings

With the Psalm 118, the Church proclaims, "This is the day the Lord has made!" This is the day of Easter, not just twenty-four hours, but the fifty days of Easter, known in the early church as "the Great Sunday."

On this Second Sunday of Easter, as the newly baptized gather with the faithful to celebrate the Eucharist, the Gospel provides a mirror to remind us of the mystery of our assembly. At the disciples' gathering on the first day of the week, the risen Christ appears, breathing the Spirit on them and sending them forth. This is what happens each Sunday. Christ, risen from the dead, is among us and says to us, "Blessed are you who have not seen and have believed."

Although we do not see Jesus as did the apostles, we do see Christ in the ongoing sign of his presence, his body the Church. This community of Christians is called to remain faithful to the teaching of the apostles who are witnesses to the resurrection, to the common life, evidenced by sharing of goods and made possible by the breaking of the bread, and to perseverance in prayer.

Recalling how in Acts the Lord day by day added new members to this community, on the Second Sunday of Easter we rejoice with all the newly baptized whom the Lord has added this year. St. Peter reminds us, however, that baptism is not only initiation into a new community, but a new birth, a share in the resurrection of Jesus Christ. From the womb of the baptismal font come the newborn who already possess an inheritance to be revealed in the last days. Because of this great hope, the baptized see their trials in a new light and look forward to that day anticipated now by the joy and communion of the Great Sunday.

Suggestions for Prayer

1. The members of the early Jerusalem Church shared all their goods as a sign of their community life. To what concrete expression of common life do you think the Spirit is guiding you?

2. Peter encourages us to be steadfast during our times of trial. What current situations or experiences in your own life does this bring to mind? What is your response?

3. In your imagination, listen to Jesus speak these words to you. How are you responding? What kind of dialogue ensues?

> *Peace be with you.*
> *As the Father has sent me, so I send you.*
> *Blessed are those who have not seen and have believed.*

Suggestion for Journal Keeping

Thomas doubted, yet his doubt led to the strongest affirmation of faith in the New Testament. Do you find yourself ever afraid to doubt in the area of religion? Other areas? Reflect on experiences you may have had where doubt led to greater faith.

Emily J. Besl

Second Sunday of Easter   [B]

READING I	*Acts 4:32–35*
Responsorial Psalm	*Ps 118:2–4, 13–15, 22–24*
READING II	*1 Jn 5:1–6*
GOSPEL	*Jn 20:19–31*

Reflection on the Readings

Thomas, like the other disciples, had put all his hope in Jesus of Nazareth. He had dedicated his life to following this great teacher who he believed was the Son of God. When Jesus died, all his hope died too. This was not the way things were supposed to end. In frustration and despair he refused to believe the others when they told him, "We have seen the Lord!" Only when Thomas touched the wounds of Jesus did he finally believe.

When things don't go the way we think they should or when tragedy strikes our life as it did with Thomas in the death of Jesus, we can easily lose faith and fall into despair. Jesus asks us to believe though we do not see. Jesus asks us to have faith even when we do not understand.

It is faith in the risen Lord that transforms a frightened, discouraged group of disciples locked away in a hiding place as described in the Gospel into the strong self-confident community of faith that is described in the reading from Acts. The risen Christ offers them peace and gives them the gift of forgiveness of sins. Christ empowers them and sends them out to preach the good news of the resurrection.

Those who now believe can no longer be defeated. As the First Letter of John proclaims, "Whoever is begotten by God conquers the world. And the victory that conquers the world is our faith."

Suggestions for Prayer
1. Reflect on the following questions:
   (a) Was there a time in your life in which you felt alone and afraid like the disciples in the beginning of the Gospel?
   (b) Were you able to find peace? How?
2. Thomas believed because he touched the wounds of Jesus. We can strengthen our faith by touching the wounded in our world. Think of an individual you know personally or a group in our society that is wounded. Ask for God's healing power for them. Ask God how you can help be an instrument of healing.
3. In the Gospel, the disciples proclaim, "We have seen the Lord!" Think of the events and people in your life that help you to say, "I have seen the Lord!"

Suggestion for Journal Keeping

The risen Lord sends us on a mission with the words, "As the Father has sent me, so I send you." Think of these words and ask yourself, "What is God asking of me?" Write in your journal three concrete ways in which you can carry out this mission in your life today.

Kathryn A. Schneider

Second Sunday of Easter [C]

READING I	*Acts 5:12–16*
Responsorial Psalm	*Ps 118:2–4, 13–15, 22–24*
READING II	*Rv 1:9–11a, 12–13, 17–19*
GOSPEL	*Jn 20:19–31*

Reflection on the Readings

Belief is a gift from God. We do not earn it, but we must choose to receive it. We must be open to faith to discern God's action within us. The Gospel begins with the account of the locked doors. Yet, despite locked doors, God is present.

How often do we place ourselves behind locked doors? We act out of fear and in the search for security. Locked doors are our defenses, barriers between nations and individuals.

The Gospel is about freedom, salvation and healing. One sign of the attitude of openness to these is the hands that are open and touching. We are called to be open to the peace of God, the gift of God's presence, in an attitude and posture without fear, an attitude that is forgiving.

Suggestions for Prayer

1. Pray for the gift of belief. Like Thomas, we pray that our eyes will be opened to see God. In the name of Jesus, we pray to see God in each other.
2. Pray for a release from fear and for the freedom of the Spirit. You may construct a list or litany of things that bind you and pray with this model: "From (name something such as fear or envy or bitterness) release me, Lord. Fill me with your Spirit of peace."
3. Pray not only with your mind and heart, but with your body also. Find a time and place to rest, a time of quiet, when and where you can sit peacefully. Find a comfortable position. Open your hands and unbind your arms and legs. Feel the presence of God in your midst and sense any tension or tightness. Relax.

Combine this body prayer with the second suggestion. Each time you name that which binds, close your hands into a fist. When you pray for peace, open your hands.

Suggestion for Journal Keeping

Reflect on all the pressure you feel to preserve your personal security. Reflect on the fears that are raised, such as social rejection or national danger. Note all the instant cures, from beauty aids to massive weapons. Where do you find it easy to move beyond quick answers, and where do you find it difficult to examine more closely your symbol of security. What do you discover about your need for God?

Elizabeth S. Lilly

Third Sunday of Easter [A]

READING I	*Acts 2:14, 22–33*
Responsorial Psalm	*Ps 16:1–2, 5, 7–8, 9–10, 11*
READING II	*1 Pt 1:17–21*
GOSPEL	*Lk 24:13–35*

Reflection on the Readings

To the eucharistic assembly of recently and formerly baptized, as well as catechumens still on the journey, the readings announce in yet another way the mystery of Easter realized anew in the sacraments of initiation.

Today's Gospel recounts how the two disciples on the road to Emmaus had come to know Christ in the breaking of the bread. When he sat down with them to eat, the stranger took bread, blessed it, broke it, and gave it to the disciples. These familiar actions unmistakably brought to mind the Eucharist. Upon recognition Jesus vanished, emphasizing that no longer would he be visible in this glorified body, but in the sacraments. Christ is encountered not only through sacramental symbols, through the meal, but also in the Scriptures. Thus the age-old pattern in Christian worship of word and sacrament is illustrated here as the means by which the risen Christ is made known to us.

God's raising Jesus from the tomb climaxes Peter's summary of the good news in the first reading, foreshadowed in Psalm 16. The redeeming love exemplified in God's rescue of the psalmist is decisively at work in the resurrection of Jesus, and in turn now opens up for us the path of life in baptism.

Eternal life, however, was purchased for us by the ransom of the blood of the Lamb. Here the early Church perceived a reference to the anointing in confirmation. Just as once the blood of the Passover lamb anointed the doors of the Israelites, putting the angel of death to flight, so now with the seal of chrism Christ stands guard at our door, shutting out for the initiated the power of death.

Suggestions for Prayer

1. In the responsorial psalm today, we chant the words first applied to Jesus, but now extended to us who are regenerated in the womb of the font. Sing this psalm in prayer this week in thanksgiving for the call to baptism.

2. Christ appears in the Emmaus story as a preacher who explains the Scriptures. Who have been important preachers in your life? What aspects of their message were significant to you at the time?

3. The image of a path appears in the first reading and the psalm, while the two disciples encounter Jesus on the road. The RCIA is often compared to a journey, with its sequential steps and stages. For what particular moments on the journey do you especially thank God? Which companions on the road have especially been instruments of God for you?

Suggestion for Journal Keeping

At first, Jesus is a stranger to the two disciples; they don't recognize him. Their awareness of who he is comes later. In what ways have you grown to gradually recognize the presence of Christ in people or events in your life?

Emily J. Besl

Third Sunday of Easter   [B]

READING I	*Acts 3:13–15, 17–19*
Responsorial Psalm	*Ps 4:2, 4, 7–8, 9*
READING II	*1 Jn 2:1–5a*
GOSPEL	*Lk 24:35–48*

Reflection on the Readings

Because of Jesus' resurrection, there is no unforgivable sin. As Peter reminds the people in this passage from Acts, even though they had handed Christ over to death, God raised him up from the dead. "Repent, therefore, and be converted, that your sins may be wiped away."

Peter spoke from experience. Having encountered the risen Jesus whom he had three times betrayed, he knew of Jesus' forgiveness firsthand. The other disciples also shared this awareness. Jesus' greeting of peace in the Gospel was likewise a word of forgiveness to them who had betrayed him. He communicated that peace through touch, through sharing a meal.

Jesus' forgiveness is offered to all. But in the second reading St. John reminds us that true knowledge of Jesus means putting our sins behind us and living according to his commandments. If we do not do this, our claim to be disciples is a lie. But if we do, God's love is perfected in us.

Suggestions for Prayer

1. Reflect on one or more of the following questions:

   - Do you truly believe that there is no unforgivable sin?
   - Is there any sin in your past that blocks you from approaching Jesus?
   - Is there any element of fear in you as you approach him? Why?

2. In your imagination, place yourself in the room with the disciples. Listen to Jesus' words:

   Peace be with you.
   Look at my hands and my feet, that it is I myself.
   Touch me and see.

3. Psalm 4, the responsorial psalm, is one of the traditional psalms for night prayer. Read it prayerfully each night before sleep.

Suggestion for Journal Keeping

Describe an experience of betrayal and forgiveness. What were the emotions involved? What light does this shed for you on today's readings?

Robert M. Hamma

Third Sunday of Easter [C]

READING I	Acts 5:27–32, 40b–41
Responsorial Psalm	Ps 30:2, 4, 5–6, 11–12, 13
READING II	Rv 5:11–14
GOSPEL	Jn 21:1–19 or 21:1–14

Reflection on the Readings

Forgiveness is a constant theme in Scripture during this Easter season. We know that Peter had denied Jesus, and Thomas had not believed the accounts of the meetings with the risen Jesus. Yet they are named in particular in today's Gospel. They are in the company of the Lord.

What they come to understand, as we hear in the Acts of the Apostles, is that Jesus' love is a forgiving love. Again and again, we, like the apostles, are invited to return to his company even when we have refused or ignored the invitation before.

Not only is each of us forgiven, we are commissioned to share the love of God. To accept forgiveness is to begin to live a forgiving life. The signs of this in today's Gospel are the commands to give nourishment and care to others.

Suggestions for Prayer

1. Mealtime is a good time to pause and pray. It is a time to give glory to God and to thank God. It is a good time to ask God's blessing on our lives. The traditional prayer before meals gives us a model.

   Bless us, O Lord, and these your gifts
   which we are about to receive
   from your bounty
   through Christ, our Lord. Amen

2. Place yourself in the presence of God. Remember people who are difficult for you to forgive. Let go of the reasons why forgiveness is difficult. Leave your mind open for the grace of God to be known. Repeat as often as necessary. Spend time with this prayer.

3. Reread the Gospel and hear the words of Jesus spoken personally to you—cast your net, come and eat, tend my lambs, follow me. Imagine you are responding. Which word speaks most urgently to you? Recognize that the Spirit of God is acting in you in your response. Give thanks for the freedom to respond.

Suggestion for Journal Keeping

Mealtime is a time of nourishment, but it is also a time of healing, of reconciling, of building community. Reflect on the meals of your life, past and present. Think of those present, their relationships, the time spent together, the care in the presentation, and any other factors. Do they contribute to community?

Elizabeth S. Lilly

Fourth Sunday of Easter   [A]

READING I	*Acts 2:14a, 36–41*
Responsorial Psalm	*Ps 23:1–3a, 3b–4, 5, 6*
READING II	*1 Pt 2:20b–25*
GOSPEL	*Jn 10:1–10*

Reflection on the Readings

In the early centuries of Christianity, baptism was imagined as a brand with which Christ marked the sheep belonging to his flock. This ancient tradition is called to mind today by the readings.

Christ is the gate of the sheepfold; it is through him that we have entry into the community of believers, the Church. The life he offers is not mere existence among like-minded friends, but sharing in the fullness of the life of God.

Those whom Christ has marked with the seal of baptism, and who recognize his voice calling each by name, follow their Shepherd as he walks in front of them. The second reading emphasizes a practical aspect of following this Shepherd: the way he walks leads to suffering. But for Christ's flock, accepting suffering is possible because of the promise of resurrection.

Shaken by Peter's preaching on the first Pentecost, his hearers respond to the message about Jesus with conversion and baptism. That journey of initiation is unfolded in the early Church's interpretation of Psalm 23. The green pastures represent catechesis in preparation for baptism where we are nourished on the word of God. Buried with Christ, we pass fearlessly through the dark valley and the shadow of death to the restful waters of baptism. Guided in right paths by the Advocate, the Holy Spirit, our heads are anointed with oil in confirmation, while Jesus spreads the table of the Eucharist before us. The overflowing cup of Christ's saving blood inebriates us with joy as the psalm gives us a foretaste of the peaceful, refreshing garden in which we shall lack nothing good when we at last with our Shepherd are at rest.

Suggestions for Prayer

1. "The sheep hear his voice, as the shepherd calls his own sheep by name and leads them out." Pray with this passage from the Gospel and allow various images to come to mind. What is it like to hear Jesus call you by name? What name do you hear? Where does he seem to be leading you?

2. In the second reading, Peter urges us to put up with suffering for doing what is right. What experiences does this call to mind? Pray for those who have hurt you and ask for the grace of forgiveness.

3. During the coming week, pray Psalm 23 reflecting on your own journey toward initiation.

Suggestion for Journal Keeping

In the first reading, Peter urges his listeners to reform or repent, while the second reading uses a similar word, "return." These different words are all used to convey the Greek word *metanoia*, which literally means a change of heart or change of mind. In what ways has the Good Shepherd prompted you to change your heart? How have you responded? What obstacles existed? How will this change continue?

Emily J. Besl

Fourth Sunday of Easter [B]

READING I	*Acts 4:8–12*
Responsorial Psalm	*Ps 118:1, 8–9, 21–23, 26, 28, 29*
READING II	*1 Jn 3:1–2*
GOSPEL	*Jn 10:11–18*

Reflection on the Readings

The Jewish people at the time of Jesus expected a powerful Messiah. This Savior, who had been prophesied for generations, was expected to be a great king of Israel who would defeat its enemies and place Israel above all nations. So when the Messiah came in the form of the humble teacher, Jesus of Nazareth, most were unable to recognize him. He taught, healed, preached and called himself not king, but shepherd.

In the Gospel, Jesus describes himself as the Good Shepherd who lays down his life freely for his sheep. He leads his flock with self-sacrificing love. Those outside his flock do not recognize his voice. But those with faith recognize his voice and follow. This image of the Good Shepherd with its emphasis on gentleness and love is in direct contrast to society's values of power and competition. Those tied to the values of the world fail to recognize Jesus and reject him. Yet those who hear Jesus' voice in faith become children of God.

Children of God run the risk of being rejected as Jesus was. In Acts, Peter and John are arrested for preaching about Jesus' resurrection and for healing a crippled man in Jesus' name. John explains, "The reason the world does not know us is that it did not know him." Just as

Jesus was the stone rejected by the builders, which has become the cornerstone, so too will the followers of Jesus risk being rejected by the world, but find a privileged place in the kingdom of God.

Suggestions for Prayer

1. Reflect on the following questions: Are there obstacles in your life that keep you from hearing the voice of Christ, the Good Shepherd? How can you remove those obstacles?
2. We hear the call, the voice of the Good Shepherd, in many ways. Is there a person in your life who helps you to hear the voice of Christ? Bring that person to your mind in your prayer and ask God to help that person to continue to be an instrument of God's call.
3. Prayerfully read Psalm 23.
   - Imagine that the waters in the psalm are the waters of baptism.
   - Imagine that the table in the psalm is the table of the Eucharist.
   - Imagine that the oil in the psalm is the oil of confirmation.
   - Now prayerfully reread Psalm 23.

Suggestion for Journal Keeping

In your journal, write descriptive words that name the attributes of the Good Shepherd. Do you think these words could also describe values held by our society? How are they the same? How are they different?

Kathryn A. Schneider

Fourth Sunday of Easter [C]

READING I	*Acts 13:14, 43–52*
Responsorial Psalm	*Ps 100:1–2, 3, 5*
READING II	*Rv 7:9, 14b–17*
GOSPEL	*Jn 10:27–30*

Reflection on the Readings

"My sheep hear my voice. I give them eternal life. . . . " The word of God is the gift of everlasting life. The word of God is the love that calls forth life, that seeks out life.

The Church is charged with the mission of speaking the word of God in every time and place. Everywhere we turn, we should hear the word of salvation, of love, compassion and life. And we should speak this word; we should echo it in our lives.

What we know of this word of love and life we know because we have first been loved and called to life. Our response to this understanding is to give praise to God. In the Church's constant prayer of praise, we hear the proclamation of love. The more we join the Church in praise, the greater is our experience of God's love and life.

In Christ we already share in the eternal life of God. Our experience of this union and life grows as we experience the love of Jesus and we praise him for his compassion, forgiveness and mercy.

Suggestions for Prayer

1. Prayer is growing in intimacy with God. Identify a place that helps you relax so the intimacy becomes possible. Imagine the lamb held by the shepherd. Then place your needs in the hands of God.

2. Repeat the psalm as a morning prayer. It offers both comfort and an example of prayer. We are the Lord's people and we give thanks and praise.

3. Translate the image of the Good Shepherd with his flock into a contemporary image of compassion, of life-giving presence and action. Pray for the grace and courage to bring that life to the relationships and situations that you meet.

Suggestion for Journal Keeping

Select one situation in which you could offer a word or action of comfort. Brainstorm ideas for possible action. Decide to act. Keep a record of your action. Integrate your prayer and your action. Change your course if need be.

Elizabeth S. Lilly

Fifth Sunday of Easter [A]

READING I	*Acts 6:1–7*
Responsional Psalm	*Ps 33:1–2, 4–5, 18–19*
READING II	*1 Pt 2:4–9*
GOSPEL	*Jn 14:1–12*

Reflection on the Readings

As the Easter season continues, the readings carry on their mystagogical task of unraveling various facets of Christian initiation and the Church.

Because of the unity between God and himself, Jesus stresses that he is the means of encounter of God: to see Jesus is to see God. Now, however, his role is carried on by the Church, which also becomes the sacrament of God in the world and the way, the truth, the life. The exalted, risen Jesus continues his words and works in his body, the Church. In the second reading, Peter urges us to "come to the Lord," to join ourselves to Christ by joining fully in the Church. Already the promise of Jesus in the Gospel to return is fulfilled by his abiding presence in the Church through the gift of the Spirit.

The "house" of God mentioned in the Gospel refers not only to heaven, but to wherever God is. Thus, the "many dwelling places" in God's house are the members of the Church, living stones built into a spiritual temple on Christ the cornerstone, bonded by the Spirit. Addressing Christians of different races and nationalities in the second reading, Peter boldly emphasizes the unity of baptism which transcends all such barriers and distinctions. Living out this unity is not always easy, however, as is evident in the first reading where the Jerusalem community is threatened by a split between its Greek- and Hebrew-speaking members.

In assuring that believers will do the works he does and greater ones, Jesus is not necessarily referring to miracles, but to works of service and the sacraments. Just as Jesus did not seek his own glory but God's, so Christians as a "holy priesthood" are dedicated through baptism to the worship and service of God. Their very lives are to be an act of worship.

Suggestions for Prayer

1. In the second reading, Peter says that we are to offer "spiritual sacrifices" to God and to "proclaim the glorious works of the One who called you." This is what we do in our daily lives, and what is expressed each Sunday in the eucharistic prayer. Prayerfully read Eucharistic Prayer III, reflecting on the works of God that

you now proclaim and the sacrifices in your life that you dedicate to God.

2. As demonstrated in the first reading, the Christian community must always organize itself for service of the needy. Who are the needy whom you serve? Do you recognize the face of Christ there?

3. Jesus says, "Whoever has seen me has seen the Father." Who in your life is a sign of God for you? What qualities or events come to mind? For whom are you an expression of the love of God?

Suggestion for Journal Keeping

Jesus is the way to God. The path to God lies in patterning our lives after Christ. Describe some instances in which you experienced yourself able to imitate the self-giving love of Christ.

Emily J. Besl

Fifth Sunday of Easter [B]

READING I	Acts 9:26–31
Responsorial Psalm	Ps 22:26–27, 28, 30, 31–32
READING II	1 Jn 3:18–24
GOSPEL	Jn 15:1–8

Reflection on the Readings

Saul was a great persecutor of the early Christians until one day, on the road to Damascus, he encountered the risen Lord. Saul, who would eventually be called Paul, experienced a great conversion. The great persecutor became the great preacher in the name of Jesus the Lord. His great love for the Lord drove him to seek entrance into the Christian community. Many feared him because they thought he was a spy. Yet Barnabas believed in Saul, for he saw him risk death to preach the good news. Saul found new life in Jesus Christ and with the community that proclaimed Jesus as Lord.

In order to have new life, we like Saul must live on in Jesus Christ. Christ is the vine, we are the branches. Cut off from Christ, we wither and die. Yet, if we live on, connected with Christ, we receive the nourishment we need to grow and bear fruit. One way we are able to remain in Christ is through the Church. We receive our nourishment in the form of God's word as proclaimed in Scripture, the celebration of the sacraments and the witness and support of members of the Church community.

As we receive this nourishment, we must bear good fruit. John's letter reminds us that this fruit is love that is expressed in word and deed. Others will know we are committed to the truth not through our words alone. Rather, they will know by how we live our lives and how we love one another.

Suggestions for Prayer

1. Barnabas was Saul's sponsor into the Christian community. Bring your sponsor to mind. Think of how he or she has helped you to feel more welcome in the Christian community. Pray that God may continue to help him or her in witnessing to you.

2. The psalm proclaims, "I will praise you, Lord, in the assembly of your people." Take these words of praise from the eucharistic acclamation in the Mass and meditate on their meaning:

> *Christ has died.*
> *Christ has risen.*
> *Christ will come again.*

3. Reflect on the following questions:
   - Have you ever felt cut off from Christ?
   - How did that feel?
   - How is that different from times when you feel connected with Christ?

Suggestion for Journal Keeping

In your journal, list some ways in which you feel you receive nourishment for your life in Jesus Christ. List two or three ways in which you have borne good fruit through your love as expressed in your words and deeds.

Kathryn A. Schneider

Fifth Sunday of Easter [C]

READING I	Acts 14:21–27
Responsorial Psalm	Ps 145:8–9, 10–11, 12–13
READING II	Rv 21:1–5a
GOSPEL	Jn 13:31–33a, 34–35

Reflection on the Readings

"Behold, I make all things new!" Change and movement are part of life and they are part of faith. Christians are people coming to faith in God through Jesus the Christ. A life in faith is a life of changing to new life characterized as a life of moving from sorrow to joy.

"I give you a new commandment: love one another." The model for coming to faith is relationship. Jesus always sees himself in relation to the Father and to others, in a bond of love.

Before each of us is the command to love one another. This is not only an individual requirement, but the hallmark of the community of believers.

God opens the door of faith through love. The Church sustains, encourages and challenges us to grow in faith. The Church is a community, always in conversion, where encouragement and support come in the form of instruction, worship and discipline.

Suggestions for Prayer

1. Pray for faith. To pray is already an evidence of faith, but we always need to pray for openness to God's life. The Church gives us a model with the Act of Faith.
2. To become something new means that one must die to something old. In prayer, name the things that are dying, or that need to die in yourself, and ask for the discipline of love to grow in your life. Close your prayer in the name of Jesus.
3. Read the life of someone committed to change in the area of social justice. Reflect upon the place of faith in that person's life and examine the place of faith in your own. In prayer, seek the strength and direction to bring about changes in any unjust situation.

Suggestion for Journal Keeping

Your sponsor is a member of the Church, appointed to walk with you on the journey of conversion. Record any questions you want to discuss and reflect your experience of being with your sponsor. What can you do to make the most of your time together?

Sixth Sunday of Easter   [A]

READING I	*Acts 8:5–8, 14–17*
Responsorial Psalm	*Ps 66:1–3, 4–5, 6–7, 16, 20*
READING II	*1 Pt 3:15–18*
GOSPEL	*Jn 14:15–21*

Reflection on the Readings

Anticipating Pentecost, today's readings focus on the gift of the Spirit, outcome of the resurrection, bestowed upon the initiated.

Obedience marks the beginning and end of today's Gospel. Obeying Christ is proof of love and condition of receiving the Spirit, since the words and deeds of the Church reveal the Spirit's presence just as the words and deed of Jesus showed he was from God. A legal term, *paraclete* means an advocate, mediator or helper. The Spirit is called "another" mediator because Jesus is the first, and through the Spirit Jesus will come back as promised and remain. His departure thus results not in absence, although the world thinks Jesus has disappeared, but rather in continued presence through the Spirit.

Our pledge of triumph, the Spirit among us, gives us basis for hope. Although he was put to death, Christ lives in the Spirit, says the second reading. So we to whom the Spirit gave rebirth in baptism hope to be glorified like Christ. Difficulties and persecution, then, pose no threat since this is the way we share in Christ's victory.

Before his ascension, Jesus announced to the apostles that they would receive the Holy Spirit and be his witness to Jerusalem, Judea and Samaria, and even to the ends of the earth—that is, first to the Jews, then to the Gentiles. The first reading presents the spread of the Gospel to Samaria, outcasts of Israel, who joyfully accept the word of God and are baptized. An unusual occurrence, the reception of the Spirit apart from baptism is meant to stress the relationship of the Spirit and the Church. Each new Christian community must be associated with the apostles. It is the Spirit in the Church who brings unity with the apostolic witnesses, with the risen Christ, and through Christ with God.

Suggestions for Prayer

1. Meditate in prayer on those words of Jesus.

   I will come to you.
   I am in my Father and you are in me
   and I in you.
   Another Advocate will be with you always.

2. Peter advises you to be ever ready to reply should anyone ask you the reason for your hope. In what words or images would you express your hope? What would your reply to such a question be?
3. Pray Psalm 66, giving thanks that the Gospel has been preached to "all the earth," and consequently to you. "Listen now while I declare what he has done for me." What thoughts are prompted by this line?

Suggestion for Journal Keeping

"The one who obeys my commandments is the one who loves me." Reflect on an experience in which you obeyed because you loved. What was involved? What light does this shed on your relationship with Christ?

Emily J. Besl

Sixth Sunday of Easter   [B]

READING I	Acts 10:25–26, 34–35, 44–48
Responsial Psalm	Ps 98:1, 2–3, 3–4
READING II	1 Jn 4:7–10
GOSPEL	Jn 15:9–17

Reflection on the Readings

God is love. So essential is this love that those who love become children of God and those who do not love know nothing of God. Love becomes the measure. God's love is gracious and open to all. It is hard for us to understand the love of God. As humans, we love some people and do not love others. It is hard to believe that God offers love to all.

Peter came to understand this better when he witnessed the gift of the Holy Spirit given to Cornelius and his friends and relatives. This gift was significant because Cornelius was a Gentile and not a Jew. In the early Church, many argued that because Jesus and his first followers were Jews, one must become a Jew before one could be baptized a Christian. Thus, uncircumcised males would have to be circumcised before they could be baptized. Peter came to understand that these were artificial barriers to baptism, that God shows no partiality and that those who respond to God's gracious gift of love with love are worthy to be called children of God. They are worthy to be baptized in the name of Jesus Christ.

In the Gospel of John, Jesus teaches us that God loves us first. Through this love we become friends with God. When we get in touch with this great love in our lives, we respond in love.

All Jesus asks of us is this, "Love one another as I love you."

Suggestions for Prayer

1. Think of a time when you felt loved by God. What was it like?
2. Is there someone in your life who loves you in a way that reveals God's love to you? Bring that person to your prayer and thank God for him or her.
3. Read today's psalm slowly and prayerfully. Reflect upon how God has revealed himself to all the nations or, in other words, to diverse groups in society.

Suggestion for Journal Keeping

How is God's love different from the way we, as humans, usually love?

How is God calling you to love? Whom is God calling you to love?

Kathryn A. Schneider

Sixth Sunday of Easter   [C]

READING I	Acts 15:1–2, 22–29
Responsorial Psalm	Ps 67:2–3, 5, 6, 8
READING II	Rv 21:10–14, 22–23
GOSPEL	Jn 14:23–29

Reflection on the Readings

Peace is the gift of God dwelling within us. Peace is the gift of Jesus to the disciples. Peace is our desire, and yet peace seems so often to be absent.

In the first reading, we hear that even in some of the early Christian communities, peace was not always evident. We also hear of the model for discerning that peace, that gift of God. The apostles sought to restore peace in the community by uniting their will with the Holy Spirit.

Turning to God, opening ourselves to the work of the Spirit within us, and hearing the word of God in the community of disciples are all important aspects of prayer. Our prayer always follows the model of Jesus. We praise God, and we petition for our needs and the needs of others.

Suggestions for Prayer

1. The sign of the cross is a prayer expressing our faith in the fullness of the gift of God's presence with us. Say this blessing slowly, allowing images, memories and stories to come to mind with each name—the Father, the Son, and the Holy Spirit. For example, reflect upon God the Creator, the Shepherd, God the Savior, the Anointed One, God who loves us and makes us holy.

2. St. Francis prayed that he would become a channel of God's peace. God's gift to us is not for us alone, but for the good of the world. Pray the Prayer of St. Francis.

3. Acknowledge that you have received the gift of God's peace. Picture the unpeaceful situations of your life as layers that you can peel away. In your imagination, fold back each layer you encounter until you come to rest in God's peace in your heart.

Thank God for peace. Ask for strength to be a peacemaker. Pray in the name of Jesus.

Suggestion for Journal Keeping

Take one couplet from the Prayer of St. Francis, for example, "Where there is hatred, let me sow your love," and reflect on specific situations in your life where you can pray for God's grace of peace.

Elizabeth S. Lilly

Ascension [A B C]

READING I	*Acts 1:1–11*
Responsorial Psalm	*Ps 47:2–3, 6–7, 8–9*
READING II	*Eph 1:17–23*
GOSPEL A	*Mt 28:16–20*
GOSPEL B	*Mk 16:15–20*
GOSPEL C	*Lk 24:46–53*

Reflection on the Readings

Not simply recalling an historical event, the feast of the Ascension celebrates what we are and will be as the Church. Rather than focusing on the departure of Christ, this feast reminds us of his presence manifest in our midst in the Church. As St. Leo preached on this occasion centuries ago, what was previously visible in the Redeemer is now present in the rites. No longer limited by space or time, Christ has gone away only to be available through the Spirit in the sacraments. And because he lives among us, St. Leo says, "Where the Head has gone, the Body hopes to follow." That the ascension of Christ is a promise of what lies ahead for believers is reflected in the prayers of today's liturgy. In the first preface, we remember that Christ left our sight "not to abandon us, but to be our hope," and in the opening prayer we ask, "May we follow him into the new creation, for his ascension is our glory and our hope."

The first two readings are repeated each year. In the first, we have the beginning of Luke's second volume, the Acts of the Apostles, where Jesus' ascension inaugurates the Church's mission of witnessing for Christ, even to the Gentiles. Although the disciples hope for the immediate second coming, Jesus corrects their preoccupation by turning their attention to the Spirit among them: this is the return of Christ for now.

In the second reading, the past event of the ascension is discussed in the context of the present reality of the Church. When St. Paul prays for the Ephesians for knowledge, he does not mean conceptual knowledge, but rather the experience of the power of God among believers. Christ is the sign of such strength, whom God raised and seated at his right hand, making him the head of the Church, his "fullness." Thus the glory of Christ is our hope; we see our inheritance in him.

In Year A, the Gospel is from Matthew. Here Jesus transmits to the apostles the authority he has from God. In sending them out to make disciples by baptizing and teaching, Jesus charges the apostles to continue his ministry. Experiencing Christ's promise fulfilled through the Spirit and the sacraments, the Church witnesses to the resurrection by showing in its life and activity that Jesus lives.

In the Gospel of Mark read in Cycle B, Jesus also commissions the apostles to go forth, preaching the good news leading to baptism. In this way, Christ continues to work after the ascension—through the disciples. The various signs performed by the believers are indications that the kingdom of God is being established through the work of the Church.

In contrast to his scene in Acts where it marks the beginning of the Church's ministry, Luke's account of the ascension in his Gospel concludes Jesus' ministry on earth on Easter Day. With this farewell scene, Luke describes a definite close to the earthly ministry of Jesus, declaring that no longer can Jesus be known as he was on earth. From now on, Christ will be discovered in the Church.

Suggestions for Prayer

1. *Apostle* comes from a word meaning to be sent. In prayer this week, consider to whom Christ has sent you. In what ways are you "preaching the good news" or "making disciples" through your daily words or actions?

2. Listen to the Letter to the Ephesians as if it were written to you. You may want to dwell especially on these lines.

   "the great hope to which he has called you"
   "the wealth of his glorious heritage to be distributed among the members of his Church"
   "the surpassing greatness of his power for us who believe"

3. In the reading from Acts, the angels ask the apostles, "Why are you standing there looking up at the sky?" What would be your response as you consider the same question?

Suggestion for Journal Keeping

Scripture scholars tell us that the Gospel accounts for the ascension are not literal descriptions of an historical event, but are stories that emphasize the religious truths described above. Reflect this week in your journal on whether or not these conclusions affect your faith, and, if so, in what ways.

Emily J. Besl

Seventh Sunday of Easter   [A]

READING I	*Acts 1:12–14*
Responsorial Psalm	*Ps 27:1, 4, 7–8*
READING II	*1 Pt 4:13–16*
GOSPEL	*Jn 17:1–11a*

Reflection on the Readings

Between the feasts of Ascension and Pentecost, we listened to the account that links the two events in the Book of Acts. Listed here are the names of the apostles to whom we are united through the Spirit as suggested by last week's reading. Utterly dependent on God to act, all the community can do is wait and pray. Perhaps we should find here an image of us as the Church persevering in prayer, petitioning God for the gift of the Spirit whose presence we ought never take for granted.

Prayer occurs in the Gospel also, as Jesus prays on behalf of his disciples who must remain in the world. The Spirit will enable them and all Christians to be, as Jesus was, in the world and for the world, yet not of it. In his disciples, Jesus has been glorified, through their fidelity as well as their future works of preaching and service. Called to union with one another, the disciples find the model and source of their unity in the communion and mutual love of Father and Son.

The second reading continues from Peter's letter, repeating the theme of suffering for being a Christian. Baptismal life leads to glory, eternal life, unity and joy, found paradoxically in the way of suffering. Undergoing persecution for Christ is a cause of joy because the Spirit of God rests on a suffering Church as the pledge of future glory. Nothing, then, can take our joy away because the Holy Spirit is on us.

Suggestions for Prayer

1. Jesus prays for his disciples who must remain in the world but not of the world. Do you ever experience a conflict between Christian values and those of the world? What do you do to resolve this conflict?
2. Reread the letter from Peter. What experiences come to mind? Have you had to suffer in any way for being a Christian? "Pray for those who persecute you," as Jesus admonishes, and for forgiveness.
3. This week in prayer join those gathered in the upstairs room persevering in prayer and petitioning God for the gift of the Holy Spirit.

Suggestion for Journal Keeping

Empowering the Church, the Spirit prepares each member of the community for ministry. As the season of Easter draws to a close, consider the gifts you have been given and in what way you might use your gifts for the building up of the body of Christ.

Emily J. Besl

Seventh Sunday of Easter   [B]

READING I	*Acts 1:15–17, 20a, 20c–26*
Responsorial Psalm	*Ps 103:1–2, 11–12, 19–20*
READING II	*1 Jn 4:11–16*
GOSPEL	*Jn 17:11b–19*

Reflection on the Readings

Jesus is the word of God. When Jesus speaks, God speaks. God's words are truthful and transformative. When we accept God's word as truth and allow this word to touch our lives, our lives are changed. As Jesus states in his prayer, we are no longer of this world. The values of Jesus' kingdom stand in stark contrast to the values of society. Those who allow Jesus' truth to touch them adopt the values of the kingdom and often feel out of step with society. Society can often reject and be cruel to those who do not conform. For this reason, Jesus prays for protection for those who hear God's words and allow their lives to be transformed by them.

The central value of God's kingdom and the message of God's truth is love. God's love is selfless and without limit. It is a love that is showered upon friend and enemy alike. It is a love that stands in stark contrast to society's values of power, self-promotion and materialism. God calls on us to allow our selves to be touched by this love and to share this love with one another. If we do so, we may risk society's scorn. Yet at the same time, we allow ourselves to share completely in the joy promised by Jesus.

Suggestions for Prayer

1. In the Gospel, Jesus prays to God for his friends. Do you have friends who are in need of your prayers right now? If you do, bring them to your mind in prayer.
2. Psalm 103, the responsorial psalm, is a psalm of praise. Read this psalm prayerfully. At the end, add your own prayer of praise for the good things God has accomplished in your life.
3. Meditate on these words:

> *God is love.*
> *God dwells in me.*
> *I dwell in God.*

Suggestion for Journal Keeping

Write a short prayer based on Jesus' prayer in the Gospel. Include in this prayer how you hope God's word will touch and transform your life.

Kathryn A. Schneider

Seventh Sunday of Easter [C]

READING I	*Acts 7:55–60*
Responsorial Psalm	*Ps 97:1–2, 6–7, 9*
READING II	*Rv 22:12–14, 16–17, 20*
GOSPEL	*Jn 17:20–26*

Reflection on the Readings

Jesus prays for unity, for the oneness of the relationship between the Father and the Son to be the source of union for the believers. The prayer in the Gospel is a petition. It also contains a description and reflection of Jesus' life and a promise of a continuation of the work of unity. The center of the union is the activity of praising God.

Union between loved ones is a normal desire. Family members, friends, lovers, desire to be in each other's company. That union or reunion is life-giving. The desire for union with God is described as thirst. The union with God is described as the very essence of life, as life-giving water.

God's love is inclusive, from beginning to end. God's love is a gift. This is not at all simple to grasp in our lives that are surrounded by competition, and by exclusive company and associations. We also experience fragmentation due to the many roles we play or the many hats we wear. Jesus' prayer for unity calls us to wholeness and to an integration of God's will and our lives. The readings express the immediacy of God's love. Union with God is now. And this union includes us.

Suggestions for Prayer

1. Become familiar with a prayer or hymn of praise that is prayed by your community. The Gloria, for example, a prayer of the universal Church, gives praise to God. On a local scale, there are many hymns that are familiar in this country or even a song of your own church. Keep a copy of the words of the prayer and say them daily. Know that when you are doing that you are in union with the Church.

2. Place a basin or bowl of water before you. Touch the water, letting drops splash and circles widen. Pray that this element of creation will become a source of hope and life. Recall rivers that divide, and water that has been diverted, polluted or run dry. Pray that these waters may again flow clear and clean.

   Pray to be fully immersed in God's life-giving water.

Suggestion for Journal Keeping

Recall the roles you played, the relationships in which you were involved in one day or one week. Where do these converge? How do they bring you to an integrated wholeness?

Elizabeth S. Lilly

Pentecost Sunday [A B C]

READING I	*Acts 2:1–11*
Responsorial Psalm	*Ps 104:1, 24, 29–30, 31, 34*
READING II	*1 Cor 12:3b–7, 12–13*
GOSPEL	*Jn 20:19–23*

Reflection on the Readings

The psalm proclaims:

> *The earth is full of your creatures.*
> *If you take away their breath,*
> *they perish and return to their dust.*
> *When you send forth your spirit,*
> *they are created,*
> *and you renew the face of the earth.*

The Holy Spirit is our breath. God breathes new life into us by sending us the Holy Spirit. We are created anew and together with God we work to renew the face of the earth.

In the Gospel, the disciples are like creatures whose breath had been taken away from them. Jesus, the one in whom all their hope lay, had been taken away and killed. Hidden in a room with doors locked, they are without hope, purpose or identity. It is as if they had perished and returned to dust. Then the risen Lord enters and breaths new life into them. Christ greets them with words of peace and sends them on a mission to continue God's work. Christ gives them the breath of new life by giving them the gift of the Holy Spirit.

This gift manifests itself on the day of Pentecost. In Acts, the Holy Spirit transforms a frightened group of disciples into brave and powerful preachers who make bold proclamations about the marvels that God has accomplished.

In his Letter to the Corinthians, Paul reminds us that it is this same Holy Spirit that we receive in Baptism. We are made into new creations, united with other Christians in our proclamation, "Jesus is Lord." This same Spirit that unites us provides us with gifts to be used for the common good. Fired with hope, purpose and new identity, the Holy Spirit sends us on our mission to work with God to renew the face of the earth.

Suggestions for Prayer

1. Reflect on the following questions: Have you ever felt afraid, without hope or identity? What was that like? How is that different from the times you felt the presence of God in your life?
2. In the reading from Acts, the fact that each spoke a different language proved to be a barrier to hearing the word of God. But then each hears Peter preaching in his or her own tongue. Are there any barriers in your life that keep you from hearing the word of God? Ask God to help you hear and be touched by the word of God.
3. Meditate on this proclamation: *Jesus is Lord!*

Suggestion for Journal Keeping

God asks us to use our gifts to renew the face of the earth. Write in your journal some concrete ways in which you can reach out to others to help renew the face of the earth.

Kathryn A. Schneider

Trinity Sunday [A]

READING I	Ex 34:4b–6, 8–9
Responsorial Psalm	Dn 3:52, 53, 54, 55
READING II	2 Cor 13:11–13
GOSPEL	Jn 3:16–18

Reflection on the Readings

"Blessed be God the Father and his only-begotten Son and the Holy Spirit: for he has shown that he loves us." The entrance antiphon for Trinity Sunday announces what this feast celebrates: God has shown his love for us. Not concerned with pondering abstract metaphysical categories of person and nature, today's readings focus on our *experience* of the triune God as acting *for us* in the work of saving and recreating the world.

Israel's idolatry had provoked Moses to break the tablets of the covenant. But because of Moses' pleas God restored the tablets and turned toward Israel in love and compassion. He is a "merciful and gracious God, slow to anger, rich in kindness and fidelity." Given confidence by this encounter, Moses responds by inviting the Lord to remain and to receive Israel as his own, dwelling among them.

The love which God bestowed on Israel is revealed in Jesus, the decisive sign of God's self-giving, of his commitment not to condemn but to save an alienated world. Allusions to Abraham's willingness to sacrifice his son Isaac are suggested by describing God giving his "only" Son: such is the extent of God's love for us.

The love of God is manifested in Jesus as self-sacrifice, so the disciples of Jesus must express this same kind of love in their lives. Belief in the Trinity, then, requires not mere meditating on an abstraction, but a life lived concretely in harmony and peace expressed in the holy kiss. Often used in the opening rites of the Mass, Paul's greeting here sums up Christian faith in the Trinity: Jesus, by ransoming us, has won the grace of our redemption; in Jesus' life and death we encounter the love of God made flesh; this leads us to incorporation in the Church where the Spirit transforms us day by day into the house of God and the image of Christ.

Suggestions for Prayer

1. Meditate on the passage from Exodus describing the mercy and kindness of God. Is your response similar to that of Moses who invited the Lord to "come along"?
2. The responsorial psalm is taken form the well-known Canticle of the Three Young Men in the Book of Daniel, a traditional part of morning prayer. Pray this canticle each morning this week to dedicate your day to God.
3. If we live in harmony and peace, the God of love and peace will be with us, St. Paul says. Consider in prayer how you might be better able to foster harmony in your surroundings

Suggestion for Journal Keeping

Think of an experience you have had of being loved unconditionally.

Recount the events in light of today's readings, highlighting your response.

Emily J. Besl

Trinity Sunday [B]

READING I	*Dt 4:32–34, 39–40*
Responsorial Psalm	*Ps 33:4–5, 6, 9, 18–19, 20, 22*
READING II	*Rom 8:14–17*
GOSPEL	*Mt 28:16–20*

Reflection on the Readings

To be a Christian is to live in unity with the Trinity. The words of today's Gospel focus on the mystery into which we are baptized. The Trinity is a mystery that we can never fully grasp. But the reality of the Trinity reveals to us that God is a community of love. The Father, Son and Holy Spirit exist eternally in a relationship of mutual equality. To be baptized in the name of the Father, the Son and the Holy Spirit is to be immersed into relationship with the Trinity.

In today's second reading, Paul points out how our prayer manifests this immersion into the Trinity. In union with our brother Jesus we cry out, "Abba!" This is the name by which Jesus himself called God when he prayed. It is a Hebrew word used by children meaning "Daddy." Both our prayer itself and the very inclination to pray are the works of the Spirit, calling us into relationship with God. Paul says, "Those who are led by the Spirit are sons of God." The Holy Spirit unites us with Jesus and we are immersed into his loving union with the Father. We are co-heirs with Christ, sons and daughters of God.

This is the movement of all Christian prayer. In union with Jesus, by the power of the Holy Spirit, we give glory and praise to the Father. This is the mystery into which you will be baptized.

Suggestions for Prayer

1. Sit in a straight-backed chair, feet flat on the floor, hands folded on your lap. Breathe deeply. Each time you exhale pray the word *Abba!* Center all your thoughts and energy on this word. Pray this way for about ten minutes.

2. One of the most popular traditional prayers is the Glory Be. In it we praise the triune God:

   Glory be to the Father, and to the Son, and to the Holy Spirit.
   As it was in the beginning, is now, and ever shall be, world without end. Amen.

To grow in your appreciation of this prayer, reflect on Paul's prayer in Ephesians 3:14–21.

Suggestion for Journal Keeping

In today's first reading, Moses calls on the Israelites to remember the key events that made them a people. Through God's self-revelation in the burning bush, through signs and wonders worked amidst the Egyptians, and by means of the passage through the Red Sea, God made Israel his own people.

Describe in your journal some key events in your spiritual journey. What is your burning bush? What signs and wonders has God worked for you? What is your Red Sea?

Robert M. Hamma

Trinity Sunday [C]

READING I	*Prv 8:22–31*
Responsorial Psalm	*Ps 8:4–5, 6–7, 8–9*
READING II	*Rom 5:1–5*
GOSPEL	*Jn 16:12–15*

Reflection on the Readings

Jesus promises the disciples that the Spirit of truth will come who will guide them to all truth. Our temptation might be to want it all now or to assume that we already have all truth. We live in the promise, opening ourselves to the truth. We will come to truth in God. We do not possess truth, but rather will come to be possessed by truth.

The truth of God is a relational truth. Our experience of God is the loving relationship of the Father, with the Son, in the Spirit. The relationship expressed in the Trinity is one of harmony and peace. This interrelatedness can encompass us.

When we trust in this gift of peace, we can begin to live with greater and greater hope. One result of this Spirit-induced hope will be an increase in our awareness and appreciation and participation in the delights of creation.

Suggestions for Prayer

1. Pray for the Spirit of truth, the spirit of wisdom. Reread the first reading and imagine all the places that are described. Imagine yourself, too, created in God's image, an image of delight. After taking some time with these images, thank and praise the creative God.

2. Learn this traditional prayer of praise:

Glory be to the Father, and to the Son, and to the Holy Spirit.
As it was in the beginning, is now, and ever shall be, world without end. Amen.

Let these traditional words come to your mind in the morning and in the evening. Let them give direction and perspective to your thoughts and your actions.

3. God's hope will not leave us disappointed. Form a statement of faith or belief in God's gift of life and love. Then allow events that might seem hopeless to come to mind. Address each one with your confession of hope, your statement of faith. Ask God to guide you in living in hope. Pray in the name of Jesus.

Suggestion for Journal Keeping

Recollect a relationship that significantly helped you discover who you are. Describe the person, the place and the situation. Was this a single event or did it continue over time? Was your discovery immediate or did you come upon the self-knowledge in reflection?

Elizabeth S. Lilly

The Body and Blood of Christ (Corpus Christi) [A]

READING I	Dt 8:2–3, 14b–16a
Responsorial Psalm	Ps 147:12–13, 14–15, 19–20
READING II	1 Cor 10:16–17
GOSPEL	Jn 6:51–58

Reflection on the Readings

The feast of Corpus Christi, or Body of Christ, celebrates the two dimensions of that mystery: the Eucharist and the Church. The body of Christ that is the Eucharist strengthens and sustains the body of Christ that is the Church.

Prefigured by the manna in the desert, the Eucharist is the food God provides for the journey. Not cultivated or harvested by human efforts, the manna that comes down from heaven is, like the Eucharist, given by God's gracious word, the true source or life. Some early Christian writers saw another reference to the Eucharist in the water from the rock, signifying the blood of Christ as well as the font of baptism: the water and blood flowing from the side of Christ as he hung upon the cross.

A further image of the Eucharist is found in the New Testament in the multiplication of the loaves in which Jesus' discourse in the Gospel occurs. Jesus himself is the living bread from heaven, the "best of wheat" mentioned in Psalm 147. Just as bread exists not for its own sake, but to nourish and give life, so Jesus lives not for self but dies "for the life of the world." We who drink the blessed cup of his blood participate in his sacrificial death, embracing his way of life and trusting in the hope of sharing his resurrection. Communion with Christ now in the Eucharist is a pledge of complete communion with him in the great and promised feast at the end of time.

In contrast to the Corinthians who seem to have had a rather individualistic view of the Lord's supper, Paul stresses that the Eucharist binds us not only to Christ but also to one another. We who eat of the one loaf are really one body. It is through eating the body of Christ that we become the body of Christ, participating in the Eucharist, the sacrament of the Church.

Suggestions for Prayer
1. Spend time in prayer reflecting on the rich image of Christ identified as food. How does it help you to understand or appreciate the mystery of Christ's presence in the Eucharist?
2. Before or after meals, pause for prayer to give thanks to God for sustaining and nourishing you through the gift of food.
3. To share in the eucharistic body of Christ entails patterning one's life after Christ who gave himself for the life of the world. In what ways are you being called to lay down your life for others?

Suggestion for Journal Keeping
Recall an experience of a dinner or other meal in which you felt united with those around the table. What insight does this lend to your experience of the Eucharist?

Emily J. Besl

Corpus Christi [B]

READING I	*Ex 24:3–8*
Responsorial Psalm	*Ps 116:12–13, 15–16, 17–18*
READING II	*Heb 9:11–15*
GOSPEL	*Mk 14:12–16, 22–26*

Reflection on the Readings
Most of us are familiar with the slogan of the American Red Cross, "give the gift of life;

give blood." Blood is life, and to give blood is to give life.

In each of today's readings, blood plays a central role. In the first reading, it is used to seal the bond of unity, the covenant that God makes with the Israelites. Moses says, "This is the blood of the covenant that the Lord has made with you." And the people respond, "All that the Lord has said, we will heed and do."

In the Gospel, Jesus takes a cup of wine and says, "This is my blood of the covenant, which will be shed for many." Jesus recognizes that his obedience to the Father's call will lead to his death, but that this will be "for many." The gift of his blood forms a new covenant between God and humanity, one which, as Hebrews says, "cleanses our consciences." As the disciples drink of the cup, they say yes to the new covenant.

Today's feast of the Body and Blood of Christ celebrates the life of Christ in us. The Church is his body and he nourishes us through the gift of the Eucharist. Just as the Israelites and Jews responded with obedient fidelity to God, we are called to give our lives faithfully to the Lord. This is true worship of the living God, our ratification of the new covenant.

Suggestions for Prayer
1. Sit quietly. Listen to your heart as it pumps the lifeblood through your body. Reflect on the importance of your blood for your life. Offer your life again to God.
2. The Eucharist is the spiritual source of our Christian lives. As you prepare for initiation, pray for an increase in your hunger and thirst for the Eucharist.
3. Today's responsorial psalm is read by Christians in light of the Gospel. Join your prayer to that of Jesus as you pray this psalm.

Suggestion for Journal Keeping

Write about what the Eucharist means to you. Discuss this with your sponsor or spiritual guide.

Robert M. Hamma

Corpus Christi [C]

READING I	*Gn 14:18–20*
Responsorial Psalm	*Ps 110:1, 2, 3, 4*
READING II	*1 Cor 11:23–26*
GOSPEL	*Lk 9:11b–17*

Reflection on the Readings

One name for the Church is the body of Christ. Today's feast focuses on how the body of Christ is nourished and in turn gives life. From the Old Testament, from the early Christian community and from the Gospel we hear accounts of blessings associated with the giving of life. The dying and rising of Jesus, the freedom from enemies and the abundance of nourishment give and sustain life.

The Church becomes the body of Christ precisely when it acts in the way of Jesus, e.g., by being present to the hungry and the broken. Sometimes this is on such a grand scale that it becomes news. More often, and perhaps more importantly, are the times when bringing the presence of Jesus into our world is such an ordinary part of the fabric of our lives that we only recognize it when we stop and reflect. For example, sitting with a sick person, feeding a child, preparing a family dinner, and sharing a meal with a stranger are all life-giving acts. These are opportunities to thank God for the gift of life.

Suggestions for Prayer

1. Pray a blessing before each meal. The traditional prayer is given in the suggestion for the Third Sunday of Easter, Cycle C. Vary this with your own prayer, praising God, acknowledging him as the giver of all gifts, and asking for his blessing. Pray in the name of Jesus.

2. We often experience the body of Christ in the dying, the hungry or the broken. In remembering the saving acts of Jesus' rising, or his feeding the hungry, we enter into communion with God. This remembering is a part of daily Christian life. Pray in remembrance of God's saving action in your life.

3. Pray for wholeness in your body. In the midst of our own sufferings, aches, pains, illness, and brokenness we can turn to God. Pray through these aspects of your life. Pray in hope and trust in the life of God through Jesus.

Suggestion for Journal Keeping

How does the Church remember the life of Jesus in your community today? What are the signs of hope, of life and of healing? Who conveys this message to those searching for meaning, for wholeness? Who brought this good news to you? How are you sharing with others?

Elizabeth S. Lilly

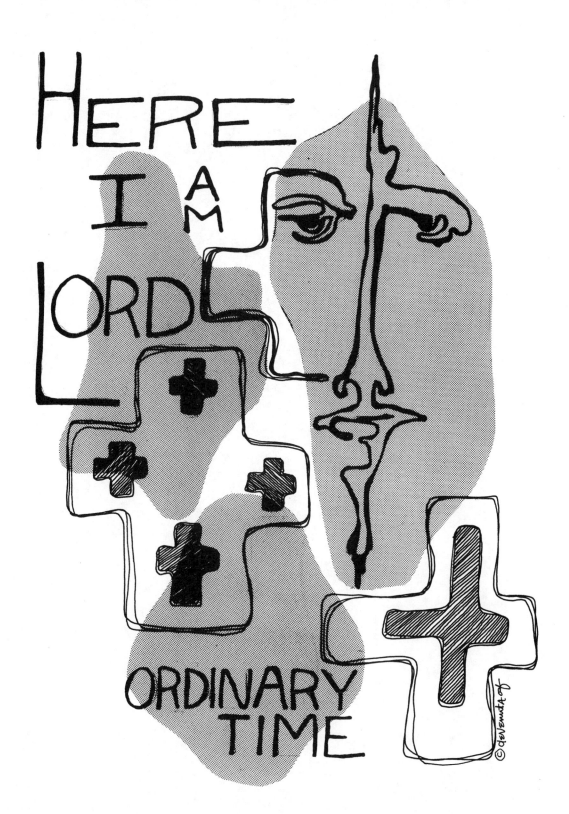

Second Sunday of the Year [A]

READING I	Is 49:3, 5–6
Responsorial Psalm	Ps 40:2, 4, 7–8, 8–9, 10
READING II	1 Cor 1:1–3
GOSPEL	Jn 1:29–34

Reflection on the Readings

Today's readings hearken back to last week's feast, the Baptism of the Lord. Jesus' baptism by John was the beginning of his public ministry. Many Scripture scholars believe that it was for Jesus an experience of hearing the Father calling him to his mission. In today's Gospel we hear John the Baptist relate that his baptizing Jesus is a religious experience for him as well. At first, John says, he did not recognize Jesus, even though he was the very reason for John's baptizing. But when he saw the Spirit descend upon him, he recognized Jesus as "the Son of God." For Jesus, his baptism was a call to ministry; for John, it was a confirmation of his ministry.

As you prepare for your own baptism, today's Scriptures can serve as a reminder of the calling you have received. The image of the servant, described by Isaiah in the first reading, can be applied not only to John the Baptist and Jesus, but to you as well. The Lord has also formed you as his servant from the womb. The Lord has given you a mission to be a light for others.

In the second reading, Paul reflects on his call to be an apostle. For Paul, the word *apostle* does not only apply to the twelve, but to anyone who is sent to preach the good news. All Christians are called to an apostolic life. Furthermore, all the baptized, "who have been sanctified in Christ Jesus," are "called to be holy."

Suggestions for Prayer

1. To what kind of mission or service do you sense the Lord is calling you? Reflect on your gifts and the needs you see around you. Respond by praying repeatedly the psalm refrain, "Here am I, Lord; I come to do your will."

2. Reflect on the word *servant.* How do the words of John the Baptist in the Gospel express the meaning of being a servant? What kind of a servant was Jesus? What about you?

3. John recognizes Jesus when the Spirit descends upon him and says that Jesus is the one who will baptize with the Holy Spirit. Pray for the gift of the Spirit so that you may fulfill your mission.

Suggestion for Journal Keeping

Reflect on a time—perhaps when you were ill or otherwise needy—when someone was a servant for you. Write down some of the qualities required of a servant. Which of these qualities do you need to grow in? Why?

Robert M. Hamma

Second Sunday of the Year [B]

READING I	*1 Sm 3:3b–10, 19*
Responsorial Psalm	*Ps 40:2, 4, 7–8, 8–9, 10*
READING II	*1 Cor 6:13c–15a, 17–20*
GOSPEL	*Jn 1:35–42*

Reflection on the Readings

Responding to a call is only the beginning. A single action or decision affects others as well as ourselves. A choice for God, for Jesus Christ, for an exploration of the faith, or getting to know a community of believers becomes a pivotal time in our lives. Our choices, like our lives, are not in isolation. Once we set a course for ourselves, we continue to make other choices affirming—or changing—that pivotal one.

In the first and third Scripture readings today, we hear stories of "call"—Samuel called by the Lord, the first disciples called by Jesus. Once these persons heard the call, and understood even a little who it was that called them, their response was total: "Here I am!" A second level or implication is indicated in the readings as well: we hear the call through others. There are other people in our lives who advise, guide, lead, listen, and encourage us.

Having heard a message and responded to it, we enter a new community—those who are there to welcome and be with us. During the catechumenate process, we are listening, asking, searching, growing. The important thing is that we continue to be honest with ourselves and others. We do not always know what the end of the journey will be. We don't even have a guarantee of the direction our lives will take on this journey. But we do know that, having said yes, we are learning about ourselves and about others who are also seeking.

In daily life, it is not so simple to hear the call of God or to work out what it means to respond to that call. Sometimes others are most valuable in helping us understand what a call to discipleship means in ordinary terms. As Eli aided Samuel, and Andrew told his brother Simon, others help us. As you are preparing for entrance into the Catholic community, it may be helpful and inspiring to hear other members of the parish who are willing to share their faith and what it means in their lives.

The second reading, from Paul's First Letter to the Corinthians, reminds us of our value as persons, that we are greatly loved by God. The people of Corinth are an example of a community of people who have heard the message and who struggle to remain faithful to it. Being faithful isn't always easy—which is also why getting to know others who are on a faith journey may be helpful at this time.

Suggestions for Prayer

1. Obtain and listen to the song "Here I Am, Lord" (Dan Schutte, S.J., NALR) or "Speak Lord, I'm Listening" (Gary Ault and Damean Music). Listen to the words of the song as if you are praying them as well. Then simply compose your own prayer conversation with the Lord.

2. Recall a time when you were aware of being asked to make a choice that would influence your life. To whom did you turn for help in clarifying the decision and its implications? As you recall the time, keep the persons involved in prayer and thank God for the choice and its aftermath—what you have learned from it.

3. Find a spot where you can see highways, roads or paths. Become aware of these as a way for people to go from one place to another. Watch people—or imagine them—making ordinary choices about directions to go in. Sometimes making decisions about traveling is easier than choices about life directions. Now become aware of Jesus walking with those on the way. Concentrate on Jesus accompanying you, in spirit and through other persons in your life. Talk with Jesus about your choices and decisions right now.

Suggestion for Journal Keeping

What is required of you at this time to respond faithfully, to the best of your abilities, to the call of Jesus: "Come, follow me"? How can you keep a joyous, peace-filled response alive in your life? Reflect, and write some of the thoughts you have.

Clare M. Colella

Second Sunday of the Year [C]

READING I	Is 62:1–5
Responsorial Psalm	Ps 96:1–2, 2–3, 7–8, 9–10
READING II	1 Cor 12:4–11
GOSPEL	Jn 2:1–11

Reflection on the Readings

The occasion of a wedding feast becomes the scene of Jesus' first sign of his glory. A miraculous transformation of water into wine opens his disciples into further belief. This transformation is effected quietly. Jesus' mother prompts him with a simple statement, "They have no wine." And Jesus himself commands, in a simple way, "Draw some out now and take it to the headwaiter." That this miraculous transformation occurs is not dramatic. But the result certainly is astounding. Water becomes wine.

In the first reading, Isaiah uses a simple image to convey to the people the effect of God's favor upon Israel. He speaks about a young man marrying his bride. What could be more ordinary? A man and woman stand before their family and friends and proclaim simple words as they vow themselves to one another. The effect, however, is beheld over an entire lifetime of faithfulness. Husband and wife become a "royal diadem" and "glorious crown." God takes to himself a people, Israel, and calls them "espoused" and "my delight."

The culmination of this relationship is to be found in Jesus and his new covenant. The fruit of this covenant is the gift of the Spirit as St. Paul reminds us in the second reading.

A simple wedding celebration. Jesus' quiet, commanding words effect a powerful transformation. The waters of our lives become the choice, rich wine of his Spirit. Rejoice!

Suggestions for Prayer

1. Spend some quiet time reflecting on one or more of the following: What are the gifts you have been given in your life by Jesus? How does the Spirit call you to best use your gifts in service to the needs of others?
2. Imagine Jesus standing before you and commanding, "Now take some and draw it out!" What part of you might he be talking about? Is there an area in your life that needs transforming? Offer that part of yourself to Jesus, and in your prayer use the words of Isaiah, "I shall be called a new name."

Suggestion for Journal Keeping

Describe someone you know who has gone through a personal transformation. What was the cause? What was the cost? In your own estimation, was that transformation positive or negative? Was it the "marvelous deed" proclaimed in the psalm for this Sunday?

Steven M. Lanza

Third Sunday of the Year [A]

READING I	*Is 8:23—9:3*
Responsorial Psalm	*Ps 27:1, 4, 13–14*
READING II	*1 Cor 1:10–13, 17*
GOSPEL	*Mt 4:12–23 or 4:12–17*

Reflection on the Readings

Today's Gospel marks the beginning of Jesus' ministry as recounted by Matthew. Throughout this year, the liturgy draws from Matthew. This passage emphasizes two of Matthew's favorite themes: Jesus the fulfillment of the hopes of Israel, and Jesus the teacher.

The first part of the Gospel is a quotation from the prophet Isaiah in today's first reading. Jesus comes from Galilee, a place that was until that time inhabited by Gentiles and held in low regard by the Jews. Matthew sees here a fulfillment of Isaiah's words in which this land, once degraded, is now exalted. Jesus' coming fulfills the hopes expressed by Isaiah and is described with rich imagery.

Jesus begins to teach with the proclamation: "Repent, for the kingdom of heaven is at hand." There is much to be said about what the coming of the kingdom means, and Matthew will lead us to understand this in the weeks ahead. Yet already in today's Gospel we see that it calls for a change. This change is dramatically portrayed in the lives of the first disciples who leave their fishing nets to follow Jesus as well as in the miraculous healing that accompanies Jesus' teaching. So, too, for us, the coming of the kingdom will mean a letting go of something, but also the discovery of something new.

Suggestions for Prayer

1. What do you hope for? How does Jesus fulfill your hopes? Reflect on these questions and conclude by praying the responsorial psalm.
2. What kind of a teacher is Jesus? What do you want to learn from him? What must you let go of in order to learn? Reflect on these questions and pray with Jesus' words to the disciples, "Come after me."

3. One of the changes that the kingdom brings is the end of factions and divisions. Reread the second reading and reflect on how you can be a reconciler.

Suggestion for Journal Keeping

In today's readings from Isaiah, Psalm 27 and Matthew, the theme of light and darkness is emphasized. In your journal make two columns with the headings *Light* and *Darkness*. Under each, list the words that the readings associate with each. In what sense can the words under darkness describe your life? How does Jesus lead you to light? What is required of you for this passage?

Robert M. Hamma

Third Sunday of the Year [B]

READING I   *Jon 3:1–5, 10*

Responsorial Psalm *Ps 25:4–5, 6–7, 8–9*

READING II   *1 Cor 7:29–31*

GOSPEL   *Mk 1:14–20*

Reflection on the Readings

Making a decision at one time in our lives doesn't always mean that the case is comfortably closed. Sometimes we have second thoughts about what we are doing. Sometimes we hesitate, waver. Sometimes we need to affirm a choice we have already made.

So it is with the call to holiness. It may be that we are eager for holiness but reluctant to pay the price of discipleship. For others, or at another time in our lives, we may just want to maintain the status quo, being unwilling or unable to invest the energy and time that changes require. We may go through times of wanting to let go of an already-made commitment. Our sense of what is important may change. We may simply get tired of trying. There *is* a cost in discipleship.

These ambiguities are part of human nature. Our Scripture readings today deal with this. Jonah, at first reluctant, finally does agree to do what God has asked—to preach conversion to the people of Nineveh. Jonah's efforts are rewarded by the belief and conversion of the people. Jonah was effective. Paul's letter to the people of Corinth is a sort of echo of Jonah—time is short; you are called to lead a holy life. It too is a call for conversion and discipleship.

The Gospel episode opens with Jesus continuing the proclamation of John the Baptist: "This is the time of fulfillment. This is the time for conversion." Mark's Gospel recounts this as the time when the disciples responded readily and wholeheartedly to Jesus' invitation to follow, to learn his ways.

The disciples, and we, have made a choice. It is central in our lives; our attitudes, values and priorities may have to change. They may have already changed. We have heard a call to discipleship. Typically, the call from God is indicated in the desires and hopes of our hearts. So we gather, ask, learn, pray, ponder, discern: How do we hear the call? What does it mean to respond to that call? What is being given, promised? What does it mean for me to reform my life and believe the good news? What is being asked of me?

Suggestions for Prayer

1. Reread the Gospel story. Take time to picture graphically in your mind the seashore setting, Jesus walking, seeing Simon and Andrew and calling to them, "Come after

me." Picture yourself in that setting. See Jesus approach you, hear his words to the fishermen, watch the others get up to follow him. Does he call to you? What do you feel? What do you do?

2. Think of someone you know who is making a real effort to live a life of goodness, of holiness. Reflect on the qualities and characteristics of one who follows Jesus. Pray the prayer of St. Francis: "Make me a channel of your peace. Where there is hatred, let me sow your love. Where there is injury, pardon; where there is doubt, faith; where there is despair, hope; where there is darkness, light; where there is sadness, joy. O Divine Master, grant that I may seek not so much to be consoled as to console; to be understood as to understand; to be loved as to love. For it is in giving that we receive; it is in pardoning that we are pardoned. It is in dying that we are born to eternal life."

Suggestion for Journal Keeping

Sit in a comfortable position, in a quiet area; let your hands rest, open palms upward, in your lap. Have your journal nearby and ready to write in. With your eyes closed, let your mind picture the important elements in your life right now— your family, loved ones, your home, work. Focus on those you feel are gifts, blessings to you. In the midst of this surrounding, you see Jesus approach you, look at you intently, then ask you to be his follower, his disciple. What do you feel? What is your first response to him? Do you hesitate? Why—or why not? Continue to image Jesus and yourself together in the setting of your life. What is changing? Open your eyes and write in your journal.

Clare M. Colella

Third Sunday of the Year [C]

READING I	Neb 8:2–4a, 5–6, 8–10
Responsorial Psalm	Ps 19:8, 9, 10, 15
READING II	1 Cor 12:12–30 or 12:12–14, 27
GOSPEL	Lk 1:1–4; 4:14–21

Reflection on the Readings

Ezra, the priest, reads the words of the law before the people. They react quite strongly: weeping, prostrate on the ground. The ancient scroll from which Ezra reads is the visible, concrete manifestation of God's love to his people; and as the psalm says, the words of the Lord are "spirit and life." The people react as they do because the word of God proclaimed in the law is powerful and life-giving.

And yet, as powerful and life-giving as the words of the old law are, we are gifted with a new law, the ultimate revelation of God's love to us because words written on a scroll are not enough. Just as words between lovers can never quite communicate the depth of their love for one another, God's eternal word to us in the law, or Scripture, is not the whole story. The story is enfleshed in Jesus.

Love must be embodied. It is not enough to say, "I love you." Those words must be acted upon. God has acted upon the words of his law. As Jesus says in the Gospel, "Today this Scripture passage is fulfilled in your hearing." Jesus is the fulfillment of the favor of the Lord God.

Because of that favor, we followers of Jesus are bound together in one body of love. We are many members, united by the living word that Jesus offers us through his real, bodily presence.

Suggestions for Prayer
1. Take some time to reflect on the following:
   - One or two powerful experiences in your life when someone who loved you showed you love-in-action.
   - A time when your family or friends acted together to some good end, where cooperation or unity produced something truly beneficial.
2. Consider when you have been or could have been, in the words of the Gospel:
   "glad tidings to the poor"
   "liberty to captives"
   "sight to the blind"
   "release to prisoners"
3. Think of the times you have attended liturgy with the "one body" of the faithful. Visualize in your prayer those different kinds of people who attend. As you do so, continue to say in your prayer: "Rejoicing in the Lord is our strength!"

Suggestion for Journal Keeping
Jesus stands before you and proclaims, "Today this Scripture passage is fulfilled in your hearing!" How do you feel? How do you react? What glad tidings would that fulfillment entail? What freedom, insight or release?

Steven M. Lanza

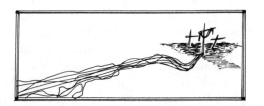

Fourth Sunday of the Year [A]

READING I	*Zep 2:3; 3:12–13*
Responsorial Psalm	*Ps 146:6–7, 8–9, 9–10*
READING II	*1 Cor 1:26–31*
GOSPEL	*Mt 5:1–12a*

Reflection on the Readings

In today's Gospel, Matthew again presents Jesus as the teacher. Just as Moses ascended Mount Sinai to receive the law, Jesus, the new Moses, now goes up on a mountainside and begins this great sermon. Throughout the Sermon on the Mount, Jesus proclaims that the kingdom of God is coming, bringing the law and the prophets to a new fulfillment and revising the ways of the world.

The sermon begins with the beatitudes. These eight sayings announce a new order in which God's love and justice triumph over evil. They proclaim where the kingdom of God is coming and point Jesus' followers in that direction. Understood in this way, we could rephrase the beatitudes as follows: "The reign of God is coming to those who are poor in spirit," or "God is showing mercy to those who are merciful." This perspective allows us to capture Jesus' emphasis on God's action and to go "where the action is." This is the perspective of the responsorial psalm as well. It is the Lord who is securing justice, feeding the hungry, setting captives free.

How? We might follow Paul's lead and go to the "lowly and despised" to find out. There we might discover what the Lord is doing and see what happens to us as well. We might find ourselves beginning to hunger and thirst for the kingdom of God.

Suggestions for Prayer
1. Reflect on the beatitudes in light of your present-day circumstances. Which of the beatitudes is the Spirit calling you to focus on? What must you do to live this beatitude?
2. Do you know anyone whom our society would consider lowly or despised? What can this person teach you? How could you learn from him or her?

Suggestion for Journal Keeping
Following the examples in the reflection, rewrite the beatitudes. Make God the subject of each one. What is God doing in each beatitude, and for whom? Then rewrite the beatitudes again, this time negatively, e.g., "How unhappy are the greedy?" "The kingdom of God does not belong to them." What does this exercise teach you?

Robert M. Hamma

Fourth Sunday of the Year [B]

READING I	*Dt 18:15–20*
Responsorial Psalm	*Ps 95:1–2, 6–7, 7–9*
READING II	*1 Cor 7:32–35*
GOSPEL	*Mk 1:21–28*

Reflection on the Readings
As we grow in love for someone, it seems there is always more to get to know about him or her—new insights, new "revelations." Sometimes *we* change, so we see and understand dif-

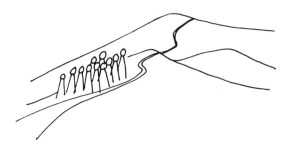

ferently than before. The time we spend reading and reflecting on the Scriptures helps us learn about persons of faith—and hopefully gain insights into ourselves. In particular, reflection on the Gospels gives us a deeper knowledge of Jesus Christ, his works and teachings. The readings evoke our personal reflection on our belief in Jesus Christ. We need to be more deeply aware of who it is we have faith in and follow, so that we can be strengthened to live out the Gospel and turn our hearts to God. We may gain insight as well into what barriers we may have to that faith and discipleship.

The readings from Deuteronomy and from Paul's Letter to the Corinthians point to a person who, dedicated to the Lord, serves as a spokesperson for God. Jesus, speaking and acting with authority in the Gospel event, is that person. He teaches and challenges the demons, the barriers that hinder discipleship. The external miracle of casting out demons points to the interior grace of obedience to God and the authority of one who speaks in God's name. It is faith and love that heal—on the part of the penitent (the disciple) as well as on the part of the person assuring forgiveness and healing.

Once we have chosen to begin or renew a life of discipleship we need to look carefully at our lives and into our hearts. What is there that may be a hindrance to our readiness to follow Jesus? What might need to be rooted out, changed radically, so that we might be more faithful to the Gospel teachings?

Brokenness and selfishness are a part of our lives. Part of the process of discipleship is examination of our habits and motivation with a view to changing our lives.

Suggestions for Prayer

1. Write in brief list form several feelings or values you have that may be barriers to discipleship, e.g., materialistic values, holding a grudge against someone, reluctance to help the poor, etc. Choose one to begin with. Meditate on its influence on your life. Concretely imagine how your life will change as that "demon" or problem value is diminished. Pray for strength and perseverance in exorcising that issue from your life. Picture the positive, compassionate values replacing it, influencing your personal spiritual growth. Plan concretely how your life can change.

2. Together with your sponsor or spiritual guide, focus on a value or quality you would like to develop that will help you be a better disciple. Prayerfully reflect on the costs of developing that quality. Picture yourself with Jesus talking over your efforts at growth in holiness. In your own words, pray for strength and joy, as you become a more faithful follower of Jesus.

Suggestion for Journal Keeping

Choose one quality or characteristic you hope to develop in your life. Write about it, how you will take concrete, realistic steps to affirm that quality. Create a prayer, in your own words, asking for Jesus' help in your process of growth.

Clare M. Colella

Fourth Sunday of the Year [C]

READING I   *Jer 1:4–5, 17–19*

Responsorial Psalm   *Ps 71:1–2, 3–4, 5–6, 15, 17*

READING II   *1 Cor 12:31—13:13 or 13:4–13*

GOSPEL   *Lk 4:21–30*

Reflection on the Readings

Jeremiah is just like any other human being. He looks and acts much like others around him, except for one major difference. He preaches the word of God. He challenges people to be faithful to God. In the words of the psalm, the prophet "sings of salvation."

But, like Jesus' experience in the Gospel, not everyone wants to hear what the singer sings. Jesus, like Jeremiah, looks like any other human being. He stands up in the synagogue to read from the scroll of the law and preach on it. His garments look like the garments that all the others are wearing. Those neighbors who listen to him have watched him grow up, like their own sons and daughters. He is one of them. And yet, he is more. The words that Jesus speaks are prophetic, challenging. And he sings of salvation. But because they thought they thoroughly knew him, they were unable to accept his song that day.

As St. Paul reminds us, it is necessary to go beyond the superficial, to become much more mature than we have been. We need to grow up, and to grow into a deeper faithfulness. This means seeing with more than our eyes and going beyond the appearance of things and people to the heart of the matter, to the realities of the kingdom: faith, hope and love.

As Jesus indicates in the Gospel, we must see with our hearts in order to accept his message. We need to be open to his challenge; otherwise, he will walk straight through us, away from our midst, until that time when we are ready.

Suggestions for Prayer

1. Consider the following:
   - What makes the message of Jesus hard for you to hear and accept?
   - Are there times when you have been angry at God? What caused your indignation?
2. Do you have a favorite song about love? If so, play it or recall it and afterward reflect on the following:
   - What makes that song special to you?
   - What feelings does the song create within you? Offer these feelings to God, our loving Redeemer.

Suggestion for Journal Keeping

Jesus has just opened his heart to you, one friend to another. But, for whatever reason, you were not receptive to his message and became upset at what Jesus had revealed to you. Sadly, he walks away. You have second thoughts and run to catch up with him. You tug on his sleeve, turning him around, and you say to him, "I'm sorry. I really do want your friendship. I need you because. . . ." Complete the statement.

Steven M. Lanza

Fifth Sunday of the Year [A]

READING I	Is 58:7–10
Responsorial Psalm	Ps 112:4–5, 6–7, 8–9
READING II	1 Cor 2:1–5
GOSPEL	Mt 5:13–16

Reflection on the Readings

Most of us would describe our lives as ordinary. There are ups and downs, successes and failures, disappointments and hopes. Sometimes this realization can make us feel unworthy of the Gospel. The Gospel, we think, is a call to heroic love, and we are not often heroic.

Today's readings can help to refute such thinking. The Gospel tells us we are to be salt and light. Of all the seasonings, salt is the most ordinary. Of all life's daily necessities, light is one of the most basic. Jesus affirms the ordinary. He calls us to be salt and light, to be common elements that give flavor to life, that help people find their way.

Writing to the people of Israel in a time of discouragement, Isaiah describes what it means to be a light. Share your bread with the hungry, give shelter to the homeless, remove malicious speech from your midst—then your light will shine. For us to be light, we most actively cast out the darkness both within and around us. Then the light of God will be seen.

The source of our power is the Spirit. As St. Paul says to the Corinthians, their faith does not rest on his wisdom or eloquence, but on the power of God. So for us, our ordinariness, even our weakness, is what the Lord wants to use to make us light and salt for the world.

Suggestions for Prayer

1. Look around you and ask where there is darkness in your world. Who do you know who is suffering, physically, emotionally, spiritually? How can you be a light to this person?

2. What is the "bushel basket" that keeps you from sharing your light? Is it fear, shyness or perhaps a past hurt? Present your weakness to the Lord and pray for strength. Reflect on the promise of healing in Isaiah to those who share their light.

3. Sit in a quiet and darkened place with a candle lit before you. Focus your attention on it as you pray to Jesus, "You are the light of the world."

Suggestion for Journal Keeping

Today's readings remind us that the best way to get out of our woundedness or discouragement is through love. Is there such an area in your life? If so, reflect on it in your journal. Why do you feel this way? What loving thing can you do to pierce the darkness with the light?

Robert M. Hamma

Fifth Sunday of the Year   [B]

READING I	*Jb 7:1–4, 6–7*
Responsorial Psalm	*Ps 147:1–2, 3–4, 5–6*
READING II	*1 Cor 9:16–19, 22–23*
GOSPEL	*Mk 1:29–39*

Reflection on the Readings

Today's readings focus on Jesus' great compassion for the poor, the brokenhearted, the sick. In the first reading from the Book of Job we read of one of his poor and downtrodden. Paul affirms that it is in his lowliness and service to others that he carries out the work of the Gospel.

As we seek to know and follow the will of God in our lives, we become more familiar with the varied aspects of Gospel values. Jesus, through his actions as well as by his words, teaches that care for one another, compassion for the needy, and service of others are hallmarks of the Christian disciple.

There is another aspect of today's readings that we may consider: the problem of pain and suffering. By his steadfastness in faith throughout his difficulties, Job exemplifies trust in God, deepened and strengthened through suffering. Through a thoughtful reading of today's Scriptures we are called upon to make a personal response to the suffering of others, according to the example of Jesus. Proclaiming the good news and healing were two aspects of the same event for Jesus. For us and for others, the healing we experience, or nourish in others, may be physical, spiritual or emotional. While suffering and pain are part of our lives it is also clear that healing the sick and caring for the brokenhearted are integral to the ministry of Jesus and his followers.

Our attitude toward and response to pain and suffering—our own and others'—reflects in some measure our faith and trust in God. Our ready compassion, or lack of it, may well be an indication of how thoroughly we are taking on the mind of Jesus Christ. Do we see the face of God in those who need compassion, mercy, service? Are we aware that our service to others is also a key step in our own growth in faith?

Suggestions for Prayer

1. All around us, daily, are stories and evidence of persons in pain and suffering. Take time to learn more about someone who is in pain. Reflect on a concrete way to make your prayer and faith tangible in the service of others. Then go out to be of service.

2. Recall a time of pain in your own life. Try to understand how you grew through that experience or are growing as you grapple with it now. In your own words, ask God to help you understand how wisdom and faith can be deepened through such painful experiences. Pray for compassion with others who are suffering.

3. With your sponsor, or on your own, choose and read at least two Gospel stories of Jesus' ministry to the poor, sick, brokenhearted. You may well find a simple pattern of compassion, forgiveness and healing in Jesus' actions. He also asks for conversion, for faith in God, as a response to healing. Take time to read more, to get to know Jesus as a man "who went about doing good."

Suggestion for Journal Keeping

As you take time to work with one of the above prayer suggestions, keep track of your thoughts, questions and efforts in your journal this week. Be honest in your evaluation of your own compassion and sense of service. Affirm that which is good and faith-filled. Specify what you are focusing on in order to grow in a healthy Christian life-style. You may find yourself wanting to talk with your sponsor or spiritual friend. Use opportunities to help others and yourself grow spiritually.

Clare M. Colella

Fifth Sunday of the Year   [C]

READING I	*Is 6:1–2a, 3–8*
Responsorial Psalm	*Ps 138:1–2, 2–3, 4–5, 7–8*
READING II	*1 Cor 15:1–11 or 15:3–8, 11*
GOSPEL	*Lk 5:1–11*

Reflection on the Readings

Isaiah is the recipient of a terrifying vision. He sees the Lord God. Yet he is a sinner, and knows himself to be a sinner. Terror turns to invitation when his sin is removed by the Lord and Isaiah offers to be sent out as God's own prophet.

While Simon Peter is not the recipient of a terrifying vision, he is nonetheless amazed at the miraculous catch of fish and the power of Jesus. Peter probably felt he was a highly competent fisherman, and yet it is Jesus, the carpenter-preacher, who shows him where the fish are that day. Amazement turns to realization on the part of Peter and the others. They know themselves to be imperfect. They discover the Master, Jesus, and he in turn invites them to become more than they are, "Do not be afraid. From now on you will be catching men."

St. Paul also encounters the Lord, his Master, and because of that experience becomes more. Indeed, he is transformed from one who persecutes the Church to one who is its biggest promoter among the Gentiles. He knows himself, his previous attitudes and actions, and describes the transformation as being "born out of the normal course."

In all three readings for this Sunday, there is self-knowledge, an encounter with divinity and

a transformation in Isaiah, Paul and Simon Peter for the greater glory of God's kingdom. The prophet and the disciples experienced what we pray in the psalm: "You built up strength within me."

Suggestions for Prayer

1. After you reread the Gospel passage for this Sunday, set it aside, close your eyes and imagine that scene with Jesus in every detail. Place yourself in Peter's sandals—or those of one of the other disciples.

    What happens and how do you feel about it?

    When Jesus says, "From now on you will be catching men," how do you react?

2. Transformation or conversion is not usually abrupt, as portrayed in these passages. Conversion to a new way of life usually takes a very long time. Can you reflect on the stages of your own growing and deepening faith in Jesus?

Suggestion for Journal Keeping

In his letter to the Corinthians, St. Paul says, "I handed on to you as of first importance what I also received" (that Christ died, was buried, rose from the dead and was seen by certain witnesses). If you personally were to "hand on" the core of the good news of Jesus, how would you do so? What would you proclaim?

Steven M. Lanza

Sixth Sunday of the Year [A]

READING I	*Sir 15:15–20*
Responsorial Psalm	*Ps 119:1–2, 4–5, 17–18, 33–34*
READING II	*1 Cor 2:6–10*
GOSPEL	*Mt 5:17–37 or 5:20–22a, 27–28, 33–34a, 37*

Reflection on the Readings

Today's Scriptures again present us with Jesus, our teacher. We have heard his proclamation, "Repent! The kingdom of heaven is at hand." Now we hear him tell us what that means. It is not simply a matter of not murdering or not committing adultery. What Jesus requires is the rooting out of anger and of lust in our lives, actively making peace with those who have harmed us, removing the cause of temptation in our lives.

Jesus calls us to holiness. It is a holiness that must surpass that of the scribes and Pharisees. Our holiness should not focus only on external fulfillment of the law, but must be the result of an internal transformation of our hearts. This holiness is first of all a decision. Your entrance into the catechumenate was your first public commitment to this way of life. At baptism, you will finalize your decision to be a disciple, to be holy. Now, as Lent draws near, it is the time to renew your commitment to the process of change and growth.

Holiness is not beyond us. As Sirach says, "If you choose you can keep the commandments." God does not "give strength for lies," but God does give strength for holiness. Nor is the choice a question of something extra. As Sirach tell us, fire and water, life and death are set before us. We receive whatever we choose. But for those who choose life, "eye has not seen what God has prepared for those who love him."

Suggestions for Prayer

1. Is there someone in your life with whom you need to be reconciled? Bring that person before the Lord in your prayer. Ask for the wisdom to understand that person, to see him or her as Jesus does. Pray for the strength to forgive and seek forgiveness.
2. Reflect on the impact that our society has on your approach to sexuality. How have you been influenced by it? To what extent do you see women or men as sex objects? How does that affect your marriage or other relationships?
3. What is Jesus' attitude toward divorce? What is your attitude? Discuss this difficult Scripture passage with your sponsor or another member of the parish catechumenate team.

Suggestion for Journal Keeping

Write out the Ten Commandments. For each one, write what more Jesus calls you to in fulfilling the law.

Robert M. Hamma

Sixth Sunday of the Year [B]

READING I	*Lv 13:1–2, 44–46*
Responsorial Psalm	*Ps 32:1–2, 5, 11*
READING II	*1 Cor 10:31—11:1*
GOSPEL	*Mk 1:40–45*

Reflection on the Readings

On the surface, two of today's readings deal with physical bodily illness: leprosy and uncleanness. Just below that surface, we are looking at spiritual illness—sin. The balancing of sinfulness and forgiveness gives us hope as we approach the season of Lent. In our search for faith, and through our efforts to know the Catholic community and its beliefs, we both acknowledge our need for help in spiritual growth and affirm the presence of a strong, active faith in the community. For all members of the community, the effort to grow in faith is an ongoing experience. We continue to seek to know more about Jesus, to know him better. It is an easy thing to become complacent about our faith, about our relationship with Jesus and our participation in the Church. That is why each year the Church, through its season of Lent, offers us a time of penitence and spiritual re-energizing.

The leper in the Gospel story approached Jesus with the belief that he could be healed. Whether he believed in Jesus' proclamation of the good news or in Jesus' power to forgive, the faith he had was sufficient. Jesus perceived his desire for healing from leprosy, but he knew on a deeper level the man's need for spiritual strength.

We grow in faith through our experiences, reflection, insight, through being loved and accepted, by being "touched" by the lives of others. When we acknowledge our need for help we can more readily receive the support and care of others; we can grow and learn more fruitfully.

We may even find ourselves, because of that deeper experience, going out to proclaim to others our growing faith. As catechumens, we are on the way, engaged in learning, searching. The touch of Jesus may come in a variety of ways, through a variety of persons. But the outreach and compassion are there to the best of the ability of the members of the community. Jesus is present among us.

Suggestions for Prayer

1. As in weeks before, you are encouraged to read more of the Scriptures. Your sponsor may help you this week choose additional stories of Jesus' healing. Particularly focus on stories that deepen awareness of persons who approached Jesus with faith in his ability to heal. Note how often physical healing is accompanied by forgiveness and a call to conversion. Pray Psalm 32, which is the responsorial psalm in the liturgy today.

2. If you or someone you know has had an experience of physical or spiritual healing, take time to renew your awareness of that experience. Pray in your own words for a deeper understanding of your relationship with God and the faith that is the outgrowth of that relationship.

3. Often in our society, people are made to feel like outcasts when they do not measure up to certain arbitrary standards. The mercy and compassionate healing of Jesus were extended to the outcasts in his society. Who are our outcasts today? How can you become more aware of them? What can you do to help heal the brokenness in a self-righteous or insensitive society that keeps them outcasts? Take time to look around you, and ask God for wisdom, compassion and energy to help the healing in those situations.

Suggestion for Journal Keeping

In what area of your life have you experienced healing, forgiveness or reconciliation? What wisdom or insight comes to you as a reflection on that experience? Healings may be simple reconciliation between friends who were harsh or angry; they may be as unique as a physical healing. Though we may put other words on the experiences, almost all of us have had a time of healing. As you recall an experience, it may be helpful to write it down, then reflect on what came about because of it. You may also want to talk it over with your sponsor or spiritual guide.

Clare M. Colella

Sixth Sunday of the Year [C]

READING I   *Jer 17:5–8*

Responsorial Psalm   *Ps 1:1–2, 3, 4 and 6*

READING II   *1 Cor 15:12, 16–20*

GOSPEL   *Lk 6:17, 20–26*

Reflection on the Readings

Jesus is clear and decisive. On one side is offered blessedness. On the other side is offered woefulness. Those who are blessed are poor, hungry, weeping and the followers of Jesus. Those who will be woeful are those who are rich, filled, well spoken of, and happy. What is going on here? Choosing Jesus does not necessarily mean comfort and fulfillment here and now. In fact, it may mean derision, scorn and hardship.

But St. Paul also knows we are a resurrection people, given a great hope and promise in the new life Jesus holds out to us—even beyond death. In his letter to the Corinthians, he makes clear that our hope is not limited to this life. To limit the pay-off to this life alone makes our faith worthless. Again, clear and decisive language.

The prophet Jeremiah is just as firm in his message. Trust in God and in God alone. We may be experiencing a "year of drought," our life may be parched, or we may find ourselves in a seemingly hopeless situation, and yet "happy are those who hope in the Lord."

Suggestions for Prayer

1. Reflect on one of the following;
   * Are there dry, waterless, parched areas of your life (situations, events, relationships) that you wish to raise up in trust to the Lord?
   * What seemingly hopeless or dead-end situations are reported in today's newspaper or news? Perhaps a particular situation resonates with you. Spend a day abstaining from meat as a form of hopeful prayer regarding this situation.
2. Reread the Gospel passage and then close your eyes, placing yourself in the large crowd of disciples.
   * Are you rich or poor?
   * How do you feel about the words of Jesus?
   * How are the others reacting around you?
   * What will you do about your feelings?

Suggestion for Journal Keeping

Make a list of the affluent aspects of your lifestyle that you would be able to give up in order to embrace Jesus. Make a corresponding list of those aspects you would be unable to give up. Do the words of Jesus in the Gospel hold any challenge to the items placed on either list?

Steven M. Lanza

Seventh Sunday of the Year [A]

READING I	*Lv 19:1–2, 17–18*
Responsorial Psalm	*Ps 103:1–2, 3–4, 8, 10, 12–13*
READING II	*1 Cor 3:16–23*
GOSPEL	*Mt 5:38–48*

Reflection on the Readings

The first sentence of the reading from Leviticus and the last sentence from the Gospel offer a striking parallel: Be holy, as God is holy; be perfect, as your Father is perfect. This is the context in which we should hear Jesus' words in the Gospel. By human standards, what he asks is indeed foolish. But his call is to abandon our human perspective and to take on the perspective of God. We are called to love as God loves— "for his sun rises on the bad and the good."

Not only may this call seem foolish to us, but it may also seem impossible. Who can love like this? We might remember Jesus' words to his disciples when they were shocked by another one of his teachings: "Nothing is impossible for God." We are called not only to love as God loves, but to love *with* God's love. Paul reminds us that we are holy because the Spirit of God already dwells within us. It is the Spirit, the love of God dwelling within us that enables us to follow the call of Jesus. And when Paul says, "The Spirit of God dwells in you," the *you* is plural. It is in the community of the Church that we find our strength. No one can live Christianity all alone. Nor is it an "all at once" power. It is a gradual process through which the Spirit of God "perfects" us, as God is perfect.

Suggestions for Prayer

1. Reflect on the following questions:

   Is there anyone for whom you bear hatred in your heart?

   In what ways do you live by the rule "An eye for an eye"?

   How do you respond when people place demands on you?

2. Who is your persecutor? Pray for that person as well as for those who are considered the enemies of our nation.

3. Spend some time in silence reflecting on the presence of the Holy Spirit dwelling in you. Pray for the love and strength of the Spirit to flow through you. You may find the words of this traditional song helpful:

   Spirit of the living God, fall afresh on me. Melt me, mold me, fill me, use me.

Suggestion for Journal Keeping

Jesus' words in this Gospel are often cited as the foundation for a Christian stance of non-violence. Reflect on this in your journal. How can we as Christians be non-violent in a violent world?

Robert M. Hamma

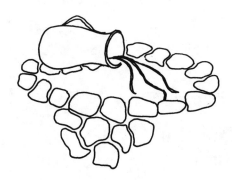

Seventh Sunday of the Year [B]

READING I	*Is 43:18–19, 21–22, 24b–25*
Responsorial Psalm	*Ps 41:2–3, 4–5, 13–14*
READING II	*2 Cor 1:18–22*
GOSPEL	*Mk 2:1–12*

Reflection on the Readings

This week's readings focus on repentance, forgiveness, healing and conversion. The reading from the Book of Isaiah and the responsorial psalm assure us that our sin and the past are forgiven. When we turn our hearts and lives to Jesus, we can leave the past behind us. It is the Lord who "wipes out" our offenses, who because of his love and forgiveness, remembers our sins no more. We are healed of our sinfulness when we choose to be faithful to the Lord.

The Gospel episode uses a physical healing to point to the power of interior spiritual healing—"Your sins are forgiven." The question of one of the scribes may be somewhat like our hesitancy. We ask, "Am I really forgiven? Does God really forgive me?" Perhaps we do not forgive ourselves, we do not fully seek reconciliation. Perhaps we doubt our own goodness and our ability, with the help of God and the support of others, to become more faithful to the Lord. God has promised his mercy. Paul's letter to the people of Corinth reminds them of God's fidelity, his presence through the Spirit. The companions of the paralytic, in today's Gospel, must have had a good measure of faith to bring him to Jesus. The miracle of healing is a faith event—an occasion for people to believe in Jesus, his teaching and power. A miracle of this sort is a clearly visible sign of the deeper reality, the inner spiritual healing and forgiveness. It shows God's power active through Jesus' ministry.

Through our reflections on today's Scriptures, we find ourselves challenged as well as comforted. Do we truly believe in God's forgiveness, in his healing power in our lives? What barriers or burdens might we have that we have not yet let go of? What keeps us from spiritual growth? How strong is our faith, our desire for faith?

Suggestions for Prayer

1. Take a few moments to reflect on your sense of faith in God's forgiving power as it applies to you. Then read the Gospel story inserting yourself into it: Are you a bystander in the crowd, a skeptical scribe, one of the companions on the rooftop, the paralytic? Think about your presence and your response to Jesus' words and actions. How do you feel? What insight might you gain as a participant in the imaginative story? Picture yourself alone with Jesus after the event. Talk with him about your feelings and your faith.

2. Are there persons or circumstances in your life that need forgiveness, reconciliation? Are you spontaneous and generous with forgiveness of others? Is there something within you that needs forgiveness? Is that easy or difficult? Picture yourself in a comfortable quiet place with Jesus, a trusted friend. You may want to reread the section from Isaiah, the responsorial psalm or the Gospel. Talk things over with Jesus. Let your thoughts and prayer come spontaneously. You may want to talk with your sponsor or spiritual companion about forgiveness and reconciliation in your life.

3. Position yourself comfortably, with open hands, palms upward in your lap. In quiet surroundings, let your mind and heart choose an aspect of your life that needs reconciliation and healing. Place that aspect, as if it were a cool, dark stone, in thought, in your open palms. With closed eyes, meditate on your stone, letting go of pain, painful memories, self-doubt or fear connected with it. Put behind you the pain of the past. Begin to sense the warming light of love and forgiveness changing the stone—yourself. The love of Jesus, present within you and given vitality through the love of others, can change that stone into a warm, light-filled ball. Imagine yourself as that warm light source of love. Know that you are loved. Know that you are called to love others. Let your thoughts become a prayer.

Suggestion for Journal Keeping

Write your reflections from the prayer experience. Let your thoughts and prayer continue the healing process in your life.

Clare M. Colella

Seventh Sunday of the Year [C]

READING I	*1 Sm 26:2, 7–9, 12–13, 22–23*
Responsorial Psalm	*Ps 103:1–2, 3–4, 8, 10, 12–13*
READING II	*1 Cor 15:45–49*
GOSPEL	*Lk 6:27–38*

As kingdom people, God requires from us radical mercy. Our efforts to cooperate with the goodness of God's kingdom focus on others rather than on ourselves—even those who hate and mistreat us. Jesus tells us in the Gospel that the measure of our judgment will be the measure by which we have shown radical mercy toward others.

This radical mercy is not a new reality. Its roots go back to Old Testament times. The prophet Samuel draws a vivid picture for us of the young David, who had within his power Saul's life—a life that he spares out of love of the Lord God.

St. Paul writes of the natural person and the spiritual person. These are not opposing realities. The spiritual builds upon the natural. God's graces build upon what is natural to us. For us to reach for a God-centered radical mercy is not a violation of ourselves, but a progressive movement for those who would be as the Lord is. We will bear the heavenly likeness. As the psalm says, "the Lord is kind and merciful."

Suggestions for Prayer

1. Examine yourself on one of the following: David was merciful to Saul. Where have you recently modeled this behavior? Where have you had power over another and yet used that power to show mercy? The spiritual builds on the natural. Imagine yourself, what you look like. Imagine your spiritual self. *Now* what do you look like?

2. In the Gospel, Jesus says to be merciful, as our heavenly Father is merciful. Where have you felt the mercy of God in your life?

Suggestion for Journal Keeping

Reread the Gospel. Set it aside and consider it in silence for a few moments. Imagine yourself as the Pope, speaking before the United Nations. You, the Pope, will use this Gospel as a starting point for your address. What will you say to the representatives of the nations?

Steven M. Lanza

Eighth Sunday of the Year [A]

READING I	*Is 49:14–15*
Responsorial Psalm	*Ps 62:2–3, 6–7, 8–9*
READING II	*1 Cor 4:1–5*
GOSPEL	*Mt 6:24–34*

Reflection on the Readings

Chances are, you could find a course on stress management at your local college. This is not surprising, given the complexity and fast-paced nature of our society. There is always more to do than there are hours in the day. Often we wish we could just get away from it all. But except for an occasional vacation or day off, that's not a viable solution.

Today's Gospel provides us with Jesus' approach to stress management: stop worrying about what you are to eat, or wear, or any of the countless concerns that plague you. Instead, seek first the kingdom of God. In other words, trust that God, who knows what you really need, will provide that for you. How often are we so preoccupied that we forget to look at the birds in the sky or the flowers in the field? How often are we so busy acquiring things that we forget to give thanks to the one who provides?

The choice Jesus offers between serving God or money is really a choice between the true God and a false god. Money cannot buy what is most precious, or restore it if it is lost. Jesus offers us freedom from slavery to money and the worry that accompanies it. He offers us freedom to love, to be grateful, to build up the values that are truly lasting—those of his kingdom.

Suggestions for Prayer

1. Look around your home and reflect on the plants or pets that you keep there. In what ways can they teach you about trust and reliance on God?
2. How can the complementary images of God as Mother (Isaiah) and Father (Matthew) deepen your own appreciation of God's love for you?
3. Paul calls himself a "steward" and says that the first quality of a steward must be trustworthiness. How do you balance your responsibilities with Jesus' call to rely on God?

Suggestion for Journal Keeping

Reflect in your journal on what it means to you to "seek first the kingdom of God and his righteousness" in your personal life, family life, social life.

Robert M. Hamma

Eighth Sunday of the Year [B]

READING I	*Hos 2:16b, 17b, 21–22*
Responsorial Psalm	*Ps 103:1–2, 3–4, 8, 10, 12–13*
READING II	*2 Cor 3:1b–6*
GOSPEL	*Mk 2:18–22*

Reflection on the Readings

A covenant of love—that's what today's readings focus on. But the term "covenant" may be unfamiliar. How is the covenant described? A love relationship? A relationship of fidelity? Compassionate care between persons? Hosea speaks of God's willingness to take back his unfaithful people, an image particularly powerful because of Hosea's own readiness to accept back his unfaithful wife.

The theme of overwhelming love, forgiveness, acceptance is carried through into Paul's imagery of the covenant being written in our hearts, for it is our faith, our spirit that binds us to God as ministers of that new life-giving covenant. The responsorial psalm phrases it as being kind and merciful. The Gospel uses the covenant imagery of marriage but goes on to use the image of wisdom, matching the new with the new, a relationship of appropriateness. If we are the new people of God, we live in the new covenant of love as taught and modeled by Jesus.

When Jesus, the bridegroom, is present among us, it is most appropriate to celebrate. Do we stand ready to affirm our covenant of love? Are we faithful to him? Has our journey of faith challenged us to make a choice for Jesus, for the Gospel teaching, in our lives? As we grow in faith and love, we may well find the thought of a covenant reassuring and strengthening—a reminder that God is faithful to his promises and to his people. These are the months when, as catechumens and faith community, we take time to read and reflect on the Scriptures, becoming familiar with the themes and teachings of the Word. We look more thoughtfully at the lives and actions of other Catholics, to learn better what it means to live out our faith. We reflect more deeply on our own lives, working out the will of God for us, establishing and deepening our relationship with God. These are the times of forming our covenant with God—uniquely personal yet lived out in the fellowship of other believers.

Suggestions for Prayer

1. The Hebrew people kept alive the stories of covenants between God and their ancestors—from Adam, Noah, Abraham, Jacob, Joseph and Moses on through their prophetic leaders and kings. The sense of being cared for and protected by God was very much a part of their religious heritage. We often do not keep active memories of those times when we sense God's care for us. In deepening your sense of covenant, take time to recall times in your life and the lives of others you know when God's presence, care, love have been evident. Let your thoughts formulate themselves as prayer to God who loves you and cares for you very much.

2. "We are called, we are chosen. . . . " "Anthem" by Tom Conry (N.A.L.R.) is one of many songs that focus on the caring relationship between God and each one of his people. Find and listen to the words of a song reflecting on God's care for you. Let the song become a prayer for you.

3. The new way of living—the covenant of love—calls for compassion, forgiveness, concern, acceptance, fidelity, service. Look at your practice of those qualities in your life. They are Gospel values. How will you take steps to grow in these qualities?

Suggestion for Journal Keeping

Write a brief story of at least one event in your life in which you felt especially protected or cared for by God. After some quiet reflection, formulate a prayer expressing your thoughts.

Clare M. Colella

Eighth Sunday of the Year [C]

READING I	*Sir 27:4–7*
Responsorial Psalm	Ps 92:2–3, 13–14, 15–16
READING II	*1 Cor 15:54–58*
GOSPEL	*Lk 6:39–45*

Reflection on the Readings

Both the first reading, from the Book of Sirach, and the Gospel, from Luke, center on speech. In Sirach, the prophet warns not to judge another until he or she has spoken. Speech for the prophet is revelatory. It opens a horizon toward the other's inner self.

Luke shares with us some powerful images used by Jesus in speaking to his disciples: a blind guide, a beam in the eye of one who wishes to remove another's splinter, a good tree producing rotten fruit. These are powerful images because they are contradictory.

Jesus himself is a powerful Word "spoken" by his heavenly Father. He is described in the beginning of the Gospel of John as the eternal Word with and from God. By his words and deeds, Jesus reveals to us the love of god—a love so great that God shares our human dilemma, our death.

Does this seem contradictory: an all-powerful God who shares with us our powerlessness, a God who dies? But from death springs life, a life that never ends. Defeat becomes victory. A more powerful statement could not be made. The Word who is Jesus is the Word of life.

Suggestions for Prayer

1. Take the time to speak these phrases aloud. Reflect quietly on each of them.

One's speech reflects one's mind.
Your toil is not in vain when done in the Lord.
O death, where is your sting?

2. The psalm says, "It is good to give thanks to the LORD." Imagine a Thanksgiving table, loaded down not with food but with everything for which you are thankful to the Lord. What's on the table? What's most important to you on (or around) that table?

Suggestion for Journal Keeping

Jesus uses many powerful images in his speech besides those he uses in this Gospel. Record a handful of these powerful images/words/phrases that Jesus uses—from memory. Why are these words so powerful to you that you recall them?

Steven M. Lanza

Ninth Sunday of the Year [A]

READING I	Dt 11:18, 26–28, 32
Responsorial Psalm	Ps 31:2–3, 3–4, 17, 25
READING II	Rom 3:21–25, 28
GOSPEL	Mt 7:21–27

Reflection on the Readings

With today's Gospel, we come to the conclusion of the Sermon on the Mount. Jesus sums up his preaching with two parallel sayings about words and actions. It is not enough to say, "Lord, Lord." No matter what one's religious credentials are, it is putting Jesus' words into practice that really counts. We must hear his words and do what he says. To do this is to build

one's house on rock rather than sand. In both sayings, Jesus has as the ultimate horizon the final judgment, pictured as a storm. Here, as we will see in Matthew 25, those who have put his teaching into action are welcomed into his kingdom, while the others are sent out of his sight.

Just as Moses presented the Israelites with two ways, a blessing or a curse, so Jesus, the new Moses, offers us the same choice: a blessing for obeying his commands, a curse if we choose idolatry. As any parent knows, obedience involves listening and doing. Idolatry, on the other hand, is not listening. Idolaters listen only to themselves, making their desires into gods and worshiping them. Idolaters bring the curse upon themselves.

Jesus offers us life. Following his commands strengthens us when the storms of life befall us.

Suggestions for Prayer

1. Moses' words at the beginning of the first reading led to the Jewish custom of wearing a reminder of the covenant on the wrist and around the neck. Christians sometimes wear medals or crosses. Do you consider this helpful to you?

2. Pray with today's responsorial psalm. Do you find the image of God as a rock helpful? Why?

3. Reflect on some of the storms you have experienced in your life. How would your awareness of God today have helped you then? Recall one of these storms in detail, picturing Jesus with you during that time. What does he say or do?

Suggestion for Journal Keeping

The catechumenate is a time of growth in prayer and action. How have you been growing in prayer? How are you putting Jesus' teaching into action?

Robert M. Hamma

Ninth Sunday of the Year   [B]

READING I	Dt 5:12–15
Responsorial Psalm	Ps 81:3–4, 5–6, 6–8, 10–11
READING II	2 Cor 4:6–11
GOSPEL	Mk 2:23—3:6

Reflection on the Readings

The clear theme of today's readings is the keeping of the sabbath, the importance of taking time for rest and worship. What a wonderful message to we who so often are caught up in a hectic daily pace! Keeping the sabbath is for the Hebrew people and for us a time free from routine work in order to remember and renew our relationship with God. Whether on Saturday—for Jews and some other religious groups—or on Sunday, like the Christian practice, we are called to make holy our time and actions. We celebrate Sunday as the day of the resurrection. The responsorial psalm today depicts a joyful celebration—our worship.

The myriad of detailed rules about what could or could not be done on the sabbath and the overwhelming legalism of the Jewish leaders in the time of Jesus led him to rebuke the Pharisees: "The sabbath was made for man, not man for the sabbath." It is to be a time of re-creation and renewal. Therefore we are encouraged to take personal and family time on this one day, to pray, to celebrate in worship, to read Scripture, to enjoy fellowship with our parish community, to attend to the spirit.

We need rhythms and changes to keep our sense of balance, perspective and growth. The weekly rhythm of a special day of prayer serves as a reminder and an energizer. It helps us to realize that we are a community of faith. Our busy schedules seldom allow us to take quiet time; we forget to set aside time for the Lord. On Sunday, the catechumenate community gathers to break the word of Scripture. You are spending extra time together on Sunday and perhaps also during the week. This is holy time. How do you feel about this time you share with the parish community? Do you also find a few extra moments to pause, in solitude, to pray, to listen to the Lord in your own life?

Most often we have to plan —we have to *make* time and arrange our activities so that regular quiet time is possible. Even our time driving a car can be made into quiet time by turning off the radio and by putting ourselves in the presence of God.

Suggestions for Prayer

1. In the Book of Exodus 31:12–17 we read of the Lord giving to Moses the rule of keeping the sabbath holy, "a token between you and me throughout the generations to show that it is I, the LORD, who make you holy." Set aside some quiet time in church simply to be in the presence of the Lord, remembering that it is he who made you, gave you life, gifts, all that you have. Enjoy his presence and listen for the inspiration within you on keeping your relationship with him alive.

2. Really listen to the words of the Mass as the celebrant prays on behalf of the whole community. Notice how the prayers of the community are a balance to our personal prayers —conscious of the whole Church, of our communal worship, of needs and persons we individually do not keep in mind. Use a missal to reread the prayers of the Mass, taking time to reflect on them.

3. Set aside quiet time at least three days during the week to create a "sabbath-atmosphere": let go of other tasks, tensions, worries. Hand them to the Lord for a few minutes while you take time to reflect and pray. Be faithful to the prayer time you choose each week, each day.

Suggestion for Journal Keeping

If you are accustomed to making Sunday a special, different kind of day, what will you do to strengthen the spiritual element? If keeping Sunday as a day of prayer and community building is not familiar to you, reflect on how you might begin to develop the sabbath sense. You may want to talk with your family, sponsor and catechumenate team about the changes that may be ahead of you.

Clare M. Colella

Ninth Sunday of the Year [C]

READING I	*1 Kgs 8:41–43*
Responsorial Psalm	*Ps 117:1, 2*
READING II	*Gal 1:1–2, 6–10*
GOSPEL	*Lk 7:1–10*

Reflection on the Readings

A centurion approaches Jesus through Jewish elders and asks the Lord to heal a valued servant of his. This soldier is a symbol of the occupation force dominating Israel at the time. He is perceived as an enemy. This particular centurion, however, is sensitive to the people. He has built a synagogue for them, and he does not ask Jesus to visit his house. To actually visit would make Jesus ritually impure since this is the home of a non-believer.

Is this centurion truly a non-believer? Not in the eyes of Jesus. The Gospel reports that he is "amazed." This is usually the word used by the evangelists to describe the crowd's reaction to Jesus' teaching (Mt 7:28; Mk 7:37). Instead, Jesus is moved to heal the centurion's servant because of the soldier's great faith in him. This is not the only time in the Gospel story that a centurion exhibits great faith in the Lord. At Jesus' death, in each of the Synoptic Gospels (Mt 27:54, Mk 15:39, Lk 23:47), a centurion reacts with a certain amount of faith.

A seeming non-believer comes to belief in Jesus. Solomon predicts this universal faith in the Most High. Perhaps the temple to which he refers in the first reading can be interpreted, from our point of view, as Jesus himself.

Fidelity to the person of Christ is the message of Paul in the second reading. We must forge intimate bonds of union with the Lord Jesus and in the words of the psalm "go out to all the world and tell the good news." Having met the Lord, perceiving his power and favor, how can we do anything less than tell his wonders?

Suggestions for Prayer

1. What does it mean in your life to go out and spread the good news of Jesus (at home, at work, with family and friends)? How would you do this?
2. In the first reading, Solomon speaks of the "fear" of the Lord by believers. What do you think he means by "fear"? Do you fear God?
3. Prayerfully consider the Gospel. Who are you and what do you feel?

   The centurion who wants Jesus to heal a valued servant/friend?

   The elders who petition for him?

The people who witness this petition and Jesus' amazement?

The servant in need of healing?

Suggestion for Journal Keeping

We are commanded by Jesus to spread his good news, to help bring all to belief in the Lord. Spend some time in reflection on the wonderful, transforming and amazing good news of Jesus. Imagine yourself as one of the Gospel evangelists. Spend some time in your journal completing the following:

"I have good news. Jesus has the power to heal and this is what I have experienced. . . ."

Steven M. Lanza

Tenth Sunday of the Year [A]

READING I	Hos 6:3–6
Responsorial Psalm	Ps 50:1, 8, 12–13, 14–15
READING II	Rom 4:18–25
GOSPEL	Mt 9:9–13

Reflection on the Readings

In the time of Jesus, the tax collectors were among the most despised people in all of Israel. They were seen as traitors, for though they were Jews themselves, they collected taxes for the Roman oppressors. They often overcharged people in order to make a better living for themselves. To befriend and eat with a tax collector was considered not only socially unpopular, but also religiously impure. The fact that Jesus befriended and ate with tax collectors and sinners scandalized the religious leaders. Jesus rebuked them for their rigidity. They had become experts at following the letter of the law and at offering sacrifices at the temple. Yet, they had lost the understanding of the spirit of the law, and their sacrifices had become empty and meaningless. Jesus challenges them to reach out to others with love and mercy. He teaches that the meaning of the law is love and that this love is meant for all, especially those who are lost, especially the sinners.

Just as it was easier for the Pharisees in the time of Jesus to offer sacrifice in the temple rather than reach out in mercy to sinners, so too was it easier for the Israelites in the time of Hosea to offer sacrifice rather than form a faith relationship with God. The Israelites to whom Hosea preached had adopted a practice of offering sacrifices to God whenever they were in need, but turned away from God whenever things were going well. Hosea teaches that it is love and knowledge of God that God seeks, not empty sacrifices. It is not through bargaining with God, but through forming a real faith relationship with him that we will, as the psalmist prays, see the saving power of God.

Suggestions for Prayer

1. Reflect with your sponsor on the following questions:

   Do I bargain with God?

   Do I get angry with God when things don't go my way? Why?

2. Who is the "tax collector," "sinner," "social outcast" in your life? Bring that person to your prayer and ask God to help you reach out to that person.

3. Jesus says to Matthew, "Follow me." Repeat these words to yourself prayerfully and silently, and meditate on how Jesus is asking you to follow him.

Suggestion for Journal Keeping

Write three things that you can do to help build your faith relationship with God.

Kathryn A. Schneider

Tenth Sunday of the Year [B]

READING I	*Gn 3:9–15*
Responsorial Psalm	*Ps 130:1–2, 3–4, 5–6, 7–8*
READING II	*2 Cor 4:13—5:1*
GOSPEL	*Mk 3:20–35*

Reflection on the Readings

The seasons of our lives are times that let us know all is not perfect or complete. We are on a journey in life—a journey of faith and self-knowledge. With today's readings, we recognize the polarizations within ourselves as the same ambiguities all persons share to some extent: weakness and hope, human sinfulness and redemption. Some ambiguities and confusion we learn to live with. Others are more radical and cause us to make a choice: the basic choice of doing good or not—choosing God or choosing evil. The two are not compatible in our lives. As long as we are alive, we continue to make choices. A fundamental choice to seek God as the center of our lives does not clear away all other burdens or difficulties ahead of us. Redemption has been promised, and we can be strong because, as Paul writes, we do not lose heart; we are renewed each day in Jesus through abundant grace.

In the midst of "ordinary time," we see again how our lives are ordinary: common ele-ments of search, question, weakness, failure, blessing, growth are shared by everyone. Yet how individual our life is, how unique in the way we work out our relationship with Jesus! What binds us together as a community of believers (or a community of searchers) is the effort to seek out and do the will of God. That is the assurance Jesus gives us today, that because we seek to follow God's way we are his people. Not because we are perfect; we aren't. But we are called to grow in love: recognizing, acknowledging and overcoming the very human barriers we have to giving and accepting love.

Suggestions for Prayer

1. Reflect on the words of today's opening prayer at Mass: "God of wisdom and love, source of all good, send your Spirit to teach us your truth and guide our actions in your way of peace." What is the truth we seek to learn? How can our actions more and more show the truths we live by?

2. Think of a time in your life when your words or actions have hurt another, and how that hurt you as well. Have you grown beyond that weakness? Are there any "loose ends" that may need to be dealt with or healed? Talk it over with the Lord; listen to his inspi-ration for your life.

3. As you continue your exploration of the faith and life of the Catholic community, you are becoming yourself a member of this "family of God." As a family we are growing together. Take the time to reflect on your family of faith. How do you feel? What do you think about this family and your faith? Let your thoughts be phrased as prayer. You may choose to talk to your sponsor or the catechumenate team about what you feel and think.

Suggestion for Journal Keeping

What have been the areas of greatest growth for you in recent months—spiritual insights, a specific facet of conversation, relationship to God, to others? Who or what has motivated that growth? Take some time to reflect on these questions. Use your journal to help "track" your growth and developing faith, even your questions and doubts. They are the opening edge of new growth.

Clare M. Colella

Tenth Sunday of the Year [C]

READING I	*1 Kgs 17:17–24*
Responsorial Psalm	*Ps 30:2, 4, 5–6, 11, 12, 13*
READING II	*Gal 1:11–19*
GOSPEL	*Lk 7:11–17*

Reflection on the Readings

In church, when we gather for the liturgy of the word, we hear after each of the readings, "The word of the Lord." All respond, "Thanks be to God."

Thanks be to God, indeed! The word of the Lord is active. It is not just a collection of syllables—subject, verb, object. To those who truly listen, it goes beyond spoken language and effects a change in those who hear the proclamation.

In the first reading for this Sunday, the woman responds to the prophet Elijah and the miracle he works by saying, "The word of the Lord comes truly from your mouth." This word is powerful and is able to restore the breath of life to her son. The word, as given by the prophet through his action, is a word of life.

The only son of the widow of Naim also experienced this powerful word of the Lord and its life-giving potency. Is it any wonder that when the young man is given back his life by the word of God, he too "sat up and began to speak"? The word engenders further words.

St. Paul, in the second reading, conveys this word of life and graphically applies it to his own background. He tells of his own persecution of the Church and how, after the Gospel was revealed to him by Jesus, his whole life was turned around.

The word of God converts us all from darkness to light, from our former ways to those of the Lord. In the words of the Gospel passage, "God visits his people." And those whom he visits are made new.

Suggestions for Prayer

1. The Gospel reading and the first reading are about Elijah and Jesus giving back life to those who are dead. The second reading is about St. Paul who has been given new life by the revelation of Jesus.
   - What areas inside of you need the healing presence of the word of the Lord? What keeps you from giving yourself totally to his message?
   - Is there anything you see in the Church itself that keeps you from giving yourself to the message of Jesus? What might this be?
2. React to the following phrases from the readings:
   - "Have you come to call attention to my guilt?" (First Reading)
   - "I was born and called through his grace." (Second Reading)
   - "The Lord said, 'Do not weep.'" (Gospel Reading)

Suggestion for Journal Keeping

Reread the Gospel passage. Imagine all the sights and sounds. Imagine further that you are the widow of Naim and it has been some months after the miraculous raising of your son by Jesus. At first, you were speechless. Now you are able to say something. Having been given back your son from the dead, write a letter expressing what you feel to Jesus. In what way does this miracle make you a new person?

Steven M. Lanza

Eleventh Sunday of the Year [A]

READING I	*Ex 19:2–6a*
Responsorial Psalm	*Ps 100:1–2, 3, 5*
READING II	*Rom 5:6–11*
GOSPEL	*Mt 9:36—10:8*

Reflection on the Readings

"I will be your God and you will be my people." This is the essence of the covenant God made with Abraham. God chose the Israelites to be a sign of God's care for and presence in the world. They were to be a nation set apart by virtue of their relationship with and their worship of the one true God. To this covenant, God remained ever faithful, though the people of Israel time after time turned away from God. God demonstrated faithfulness when he freed the Israelites from slavery, when he sent Jesus to teach us to love one another, and when he raised Jesus from the dead.

As Christians, we are the spiritual heirs to this covenant. To remain faithful, God calls us to follow Jesus Christ and to continue his mission on earth. Jesus came to announce the kingdom of God. He wanted all to know that the kingdom of God was not a kingdom on earth with a powerful leader and a strong defense. Rather, the kingdom of God is the reign of God. The kingdom exists wherever God's will is fulfilled. We glimpse the kingdom every time we see a person reach out to another in genuine love. It is to this harvest that Jesus calls the apostles and each one of us. Just as Jesus called the twelve apostles to announce the reign of God by curing the sick, raising the dead, healing the leprous and expelling demons, so too must we announce the reign of God. Perhaps we think we do not have the powers that were given to the apostles. Yet, we can announce God's reign, God's presence, by the way we love. We can care for those who are sick, mourn with those who have lost a loved one, accept and love those with stigmatized diseases and expel the fears of the frightened. Every time we reach out to another in love, we announce through our action that the reign of God is at hand.

Suggestions for Prayer

1. The mission of the apostles and our mission to announce the kingdom of God is the mission of the church. Speak with your sponsor and ask him/her how the Church attempts to fulfill its mission. In other words, how does the universal Church as well as your local parish work at announcing the kingdom of God?

2. Meditate on these words of the psalmist:
   The LORD is good:
   his kindness endures forever;
   and his faithfulness to all generations.
   Remember these words especially if you ever feel unworthy of God's love.

3. The Gospel ends: "Without cost you have received; without cost you are to give." What

gift have you received from God that you can share with others?

Suggestion for Journal Keeping

Write one way you can announce the reign of God through your words or actions.

Kathryn A. Schneider

Eleventh Sunday of the Year [B]

READING I	*Ez 17:22–24*
Responsorial Psalm	*Ps 92:2–3, 13–14, 15–16*
READING II	*2 Cor 5:6–10*
GOSPEL	*Mk 4:26–34*

Reflection on the Readings

Hope emerges as a theme from the readings today. But our hope is about lasting things. For Christians, it is about the coming of the reign of God. That is our ultimate hope. The images used are those of planting and harvesting. The hope we have is perhaps like that of a planter of seeds who does his best to assure the fruitful harvest. The mystery of growth, the mystery or gift of faith, is the link between seed and harvest.

The first reading from the prophet Ezekiel uses the image of God as the planter and caretaker—a wonderful parallel to the Gospel parables. Paul's letter to the Corinthians here reminds us of God's care: we have every reason to be confident in our hope. We are one with the Lord, his kingdom is within us, we are part of that kingdom.

Are our lives lived as though we are confident in the Lord's care of us? As catechumens

and faith community our faith is always developing, growing, unfolding, as a seed/plant does. Around us much challenges our growth in faith. Forces in society and sometimes even elements within us challenge our hope. As followers of Christ, we have heard the word—the mustard seed of faith. We have our assurance that throughout the growing season and its difficulties, we are cared for by God, the planter, the gardener. We are not left on our own. The good that has been begun in us God will continue to nurture. He will not abandon us. The tension between being planted in faith and not yet fully ready as a harvest is the tension of being "on the way." We have a deep inner-rooted hope, yet we are aware of our fragility. Prayers and readings such as we have today give us the encouragement, the inspiration, to continue in our growth.

Suggestions for Prayer

1. The experience of planting a seed, or transplanting a seedling, is a co-creative experience. We work in partnership to nurture a plant through its fullness. Take heart—plant some seeds, care for them, watch them grow. Let yourself feel the wonder of the first shoots and leaves as they emerge. Let your care be a reminder of God's care.

2. Reread the Scriptures and the prayers of today's liturgy. Imagine yourself as a disciple of Jesus, in the outdoor setting, hearing the parables of the Gospel. Looking around you see the plants growing—the images Jesus chose are natural to your life. Formulate your own prayer for nourishment in your faith journey.

3. Several traditional prayers of the Catholic Church speak of hope. One of them is the "Act of Hope." With your sponsor, find a copy of that prayer. Reflect on it, coming to

understand its meaning. You may want to write your own "Act of Hope."

Suggestion for Journal Keeping

What is your basic outlook on life? Is it an attitude of hope, confidence? Is it harmonious with belief in a loving, nurturing God? Spend some time reflecting on this; then write about it. You may want to talk it over with your sponsor as well.

Clare M. Colella

Eleventh Sunday of the Year [C]

READING I	*2 Sm 12:7–10, 13*
Responsorial Psalm	*Ps 32:1–2, 5, 7, 11*
READING II	*Gal 2:16, 19–21*
GOSPEL	*Lk 7:36—8:3 or 7:36–50*

Reflection on the Readings

One of the primary tasks for us Christians is to forgive. When they ask him how they should pray, Jesus himself bids his disciples to petition heaven to "forgive us our sins, as we ourselves forgive everyone who is indebted to us" (Lk 11:4). This does not mean that we do not acknowledge sin or that we cannot challenge one another to holiness as we strive to turn away from sinning. It does mean, however, that while acknowledging sin and challenging one another to holiness, we exercise mercy and forgiveness.

The Lord God certainly treats David in this fashion. In the first reading, God, through the prophet Nathan, accuses David, his anointed king, confronting him with his sins. But even though David has sinned, God does not abandon him or cast him aside. David is the leader of God's people and God does not go back on his covenant, his holy word. That covenanted relationship stands forever, and it is a relationship built on love, a love that funds forgiveness.

Jesus himself is the fulfillment of that Old Testament covenant, offering all men and women a new ultimate covenant based upon his own sacrifice. What greater sign could we be given of God's tremendous love for us? The woman who washes the feet of Jesus with her tears recognizes this great sign of love in Jesus. She does not deny her sins. In coming to Jesus, she acknowledges who she is and what she has done—just as did David before the prophet.

St. Paul tells us that "Christ lives in us." Because of his Spirit, we acknowledge who and what we are, confident that mercy and forgiveness will be given us. In turn, he invites us to act the same way to all those we meet.

Suggestions for Prayer

1. Spend some time reflecting on one of the following: Do you believe that Jesus died that our sins might be forgiven? What is the deepest part of yourself that needs Jesus' healing forgiveness? Can you offer that to him in prayer?

2. Spend some quiet time putting yourself into the Gospel scene. Imagine the supper. Imagine the host, Simon, and the honored guest, Jesus. Imagine the others present and the woman who enters. Who are you? Simon? One of the other guests? The woman? What are you feeling? Why?

3. If the prophet Nathan confronted you with a list of transgressions, what would he say? How would you react?

Suggestion for Journal Keeping

Would you assess yourself as a merciful and forgiving person? Why or why not? Is there any relationship of yours at present that needs healing forgiveness? How might this be achieved?

Steven M. Lanza

Twelfth Sunday of the Year [A]

READING I	*Jer 20:10–13*
Responsorial Psalm	*Ps 69:8–10, 14, 17, 33–35*
READING II	*Rom 5:12–15*
GOSPEL	*Mt 10:26–33*

Reflection on the Readings

Jesus knew that the life of his disciples would not be easy. After all, in order to preach his message, they would have to tell people to love their enemies, to offer the other cheek to those who strike them, and to give their riches to those who have nothing. These were not popular notions, then or now. For this reason, Jesus tries to reassure his followers by teaching them that God is watching over them. He tells them not to fear those who can kill the body, for it is the soul that gains eternal life. He promises that those who follow him and acknowledge him before others, he will acknowledge before God in heaven.

Just as the life of the disciples was not easy, neither was the life of the prophet Jeremiah. People denounced him and his friends abandoned him. Yet he persevered in his work to call the Israelites back to true faith in God.

Like the prophets, the disciples and the psalmist who bears insult and becomes an outcast for serving the Lord, at times we may feel alone and abandoned by God. Yet we must remember that God is ever faithful. As Jeremiah proclaims, "The LORD is with me, like a mighty champion." True discipleship carries risk. In living by and witnessing to the message of Jesus Christ, we risk ridicule, rejection and isolation by those who cannot accept Jesus' message of love. Yet, by risking these things, by remaining faithful, we win what is truly important: a privileged place in God's kingdom.

Suggestions for Prayer

1. In the Gospel, Jesus tells the disciples not to be afraid. Repeat these words silently and prayerfully and allow God to dispel your fears:

     Do not be afraid.
     I am with you.
     I love you.

2. Many people throughout history have risked much to serve the Lord. Some are famous; most are not. Bring to mind a person who has risked much to remain faithful to God. Perhaps this person is a saint like St. Paul, or a person from recent times like Mother Teresa or Dorothy Day, or perhaps this person is your sponsor or someone in your

community. Thank God for this person and ask God to help you nurture one quality of this person in yourself.

Suggestion for Journal Keeping

Are there things that frighten you about being a disciple? List them. Discuss this list with your sponsor or with a close friend.

Kathryn A. Schneider

Twelfth Sunday of the Year [B]

READING I	*Jb 38:1, 8–11*
Responsorial Psalm	*Ps 107:23–24, 25–26, 28–29, 30–31*
READING II	*2 Cor 5:14–17*
GOSPEL	*Mk 4:35–41*

Reflection on the Readings

This week's readings have a different sense of hope—there is an urgency, an impact, quite different from the seed/plant image of last week. Today we are in the midst of storms. We hope for safety and rescue.

The parallel in today's readings from Job and from Mark are linked by the responsorial psalm: in the midst of the storm, we cry out in fear, in faith, in hope. The psalm verse is remarkable in its imagery of storm: Give thanks to the Lord, his love is everlasting. It is as if we are to remember, in the midst of our own life's storms, that the Lord is very present and very much our protector, if we but turn to him.

Our lives, individually and as a community, come upon some difficult times. Our faith may be challenged by almost unanswerable questions. Relationships and harmony may be devastated by anger, pain, guilt, unforgiveness, selfishness. We all deal with storms. One of the most amazing experiences about storms in nature is that they come to an end. Much fear is engendered; real damage can be done. But storms do end. There is strength that comes from having survived a storm, a sort of natural wisdom. But we do not survive only on our own strength. Prayer in the midst of our storm gives us strength because it helps us remember who we are, beloved people of God, and where our strength truly is, with God. The voice of God addressing Job and the voice of Jesus calming the storm both assure us of God's presence and power in our lives.

Suggestions for Prayer

1. Remember a time of difficulty in your life, a storm on your journey. How did the storm arise? How did you come through it? What have you learned? Write your own prayer from the experience of that storm.

2. Think about what you have been learning in your faith growth. You are stronger than you were before, but you still have a way to go yet. With that in mind, formulate a prayer beginning, "Lord, I know that I can survive a storm in my life when . . ." and continue in your own words.

3. Part of the real value in Christian fellowship is that we are not alone—others are there to be our strength and support, inspiration and guide. Who might be the persons in your community who are *there* for you when you need someone? Think of them, and ask God to give them the strength and grace they need in their lives. You may want to let them know you are praying for them too.

Suggestion for Journal Keeping

Write a letter to God, talking over a storm that is recent in your life. Let God know, in your own words, your fears, doubts, hopes about that storm. Then spend quiet time, open for inspiration and wisdom. Write down your thoughts.

Clare M. Colella

Twelfth Sunday of the Year [C]

READING I	*Zec 12:10–11; 13:1*
Responsorial Psalm	*Ps 63:2, 3–4, 5–6, 8–9*
READING II	*Gal 3:26–29*
GOSPEL	*Lk 9:18–24*

Reflection on the Readings

St. Paul says that we are all made sons and daughters of God by our faith in Jesus Christ. At your baptism, you will put on a white robe, symbolizing that you have put on the Lord by faith. Because we belong to the Lord, we inherit all that is promised. And what is promised?

In the first reading, the Lord God promises to pour out upon the inhabitants of Jerusalem "a spirit of grace and petition." This spirit is promised to us. We are inhabitants of the new Jerusalem through baptism. But it is clear from the remainder of the reading that this spirit does not necessarily mean that everything in our life will be easy or be wonderful. The grace of God can be a difficult thing. Remember, Jacob wrestled with an angel (Gn 32: 24). We, at times, must also wrestle with the demands of God's grace.

Like Peter, because we believe, we recognize and proclaim Jesus as the Messiah, the Anointed One of God. We share in this anointing at baptism. But the Anointed One must suffer and die. And we must follow. To live the life of Jesus, we are invited to deny ourselves and take up his cross daily. Living for others, rather than solely for ourselves, is surely a denial of self and perhaps a cross.

John Paul II said that the Gospel and we Christians are a "sign of contradiction." To live for others, rather than ourselves, to embrace the difficult grace of God, the cross, is a sign of contradiction to an increasingly self-absorbed and egotistical world. Like the psalmist, though, our desires go beyond self-fulfillment. Our soul thirsts for God and what he alone can offer.

Suggestions for Prayer

1. Spend some time in front of a cross or crucifix meditating on Christ's sacrifice.
   - What was that death like?
   - Are you able, as a follower of Jesus, to accept some measure of that same denial of self, to die to self and live for others?
2. At the beginning of Mass, we sign ourselves with the sign of the cross. During the Rite of Becoming a Catechumen your senses were signed with the sign of the cross.
   - What does it mean to you personally when you make this mark upon your own body?
   - Is this gesture so automatic that its significance is lost?
3. In what ways have you suffered and how has this suffering helped others or yourself? Do you offer your suffering to the Lord?

Suggestion for Journal Keeping

In your journal, react to the following statement taken from the Eucharistic Prayer for Reconciliation II:

God our Father, we had wandered far from
*   you,*
but through your Son you have brought us
*   back.*
You gave him up to death
so that we might turn again to you
and find our way to one another.

Steven M. Lanza

Thirteenth Sunday of the Year
[A]

READING I	*2 Kgs 4:8–11, 14–16a*
Responsorial Psalm	*Ps 89:2–3, 16–17, 18–19*
READING II	*Rom 6:3–4, 8–11*
GOSPEL	*Mt 10:37–42*

Reflection on the Readings

Welcoming a stranger is difficult. Sometimes even welcoming friends is a challenge. The woman in today's first reading went beyond mere hospitality. She added a room to her house for the prophet Elisha!

In the Gospel, Jesus tells us that we will be rewarded for the welcome we offer to prophets, holy men and disciples. Jesus knew about hospitality and he knew about being sent away unwelcome. He ate in many homes, and he was driven away from more than one place.

We are reminded in today's readings to make room for Jesus and for holy people. We have a choice: to welcome or to drive away, to open our hearts or to close them. Welcoming strangers is

difficult. Jesus reminds us that "whoever receives you receives me," and that if we open our hearts we "will not lose our reward."

Suggestions for Prayer

1. What is the cross in your life? Are you willing to pick it up and follow Jesus?
2. Have you ever felt welcomed into someone's home? What was it like? What happened? Have you ever felt that way when praying?
3. Spend some time making yourself ready to welcome the Lord. Find a quiet place and ask the Lord to come and visit you. Sit quietly and wait; make time for the Lord!

Suggestion for Journal Keeping

Read over the second reading. Ask yourself what it means to be baptized into Christ's death. What does baptism mean to you at this time?

Michael P. Enright

Thirteenth Sunday of the Year
[B]

READING I	*Wis 1:13–15; 2:23–24*
Responsorial Psalm	*Ps 30:2, 4, 5–6, 11, 12, 13*
READING II	*2 Cor 8:7, 9, 13–15*
GOSPEL	*Mk 5:21–43 or 5:21–24, 35b–43*

Reflection on the Readings

Touch is one of our basic human senses. We touch others and others touch us in many different ways. We touch others physically by putting our arms around their shoulders, hugging them or kissing them. Others touch us by the look in their eyes, by the words that they speak, by the acts of charity that they do for us. Touching is a beautiful means of communication. By our touch, we can communicate comfort and support. We can communicate love and affection. We can communicate a sense of unity. Unfortunately, through touch, we can also communicate sinful desires such as lust or violence.

In the Gospel today, *touch* or its equivalent is used at least six times. Jairus says, "My daughter is at the point of death. Please, come lay your hands on her." The woman suffering from a hemorrhage for twelve years believed that by touching Jesus' cloak, she would be made well again. When the woman touched Jesus' cloak, she was healed, but Jesus felt power going out of him. It was through touch that the life of Jesus was communicated to the woman and healed her. Jesus also took the dead child by the hand, that is, he touched her and she was restored to life.

Today God continues to communicate himself to us through the humanity of Jesus. When Jesus touches us and we touch Jesus, we are healed of our sin and ailments and are made one with the Father through him. This happens especially in the sacraments of reconciliation, anointing of the sick, and the Eucharist, and, during the catechumenate, through the laying on of hands and anointing.

Suggestions for Prayer
1. Reflect on one or more of the following questions:
   - Do you believe that Jesus communicates his life, love and healing through human touch?
   - Can you forgive the times you may have been touched unwholesomely?
   - Do you believe in the healing power of the sacrament of anointing of the sick? Why?
2. In your imagination, you are lying on your sickbed. Jesus is standing beside you, holding your hand. He says: "Do not be afraid; only have faith." "Go in peace and be free from your complaint."
3. Pray the responsorial psalm as your evening prayer this week.

Suggestion for Journal Keeping
Describe an experience of a life-giving touch that strengthened you and gave you a sense of unity and belonging. What emotions were involved?

Michael J. Koch

Thirteenth Sunday of the Year [C]

READING I	*1 Kgs 19:16b, 19–21*
Responsorial Psalm	*Ps 16:1–2, 5, 7–8, 9–10, 11*
READING II	*Gal 5:1, 13–18*
GOSPEL	*Lk 9:51–62*

Reflection on the Readings
Anyone who owned twelve oxen in ancient Israel was most likely a very wealthy man. To sacrifice those oxen and burn one's tools for cultivating the soil, one's life work and survival, would have been a radical act. This is precisely what we are told Elisha did in the first reading, as he responded to the call of the Lord given through Elijah, a prophet of God. His response

emphasized his understanding of the radical commitment required of one who desires to follow the Lord. For Elisha to follow the Lord meant a total renunciation of all his possessions. He then leaves his land and follows Elijah, becoming a prophet of the Lord.

Jesus' journey to Jerusalem became a witness of his radical commitment to the kingdom of God, and nothing could deter him from being faithful to this commitment. If anyone desired to be Jesus' disciple, that same radical commitment was required from them. But what does that actually mean for the disciple of Jesus? Responding to three potential disciples, Jesus makes it clear that to follow him will require a new single-mindedness that will challenge their current life. No longer will they enjoy a roof over their heads, for they will need to be detached from all things that give security and protection. What they previously understood as their responsibilities under the law or enjoyed as familial relationships will no longer have the same priority as following Jesus.

But perhaps the most important element of being Jesus' disciple is to know that one must also walk the road with Jesus to Jerusalem, the place where all security, all former responsibilities and relationships were surrendered. Jerusalem is the place of the total renunciation and radical sacrifice for all times in the passion and death of Jesus Christ.

Suggestions for Prayer

1. Reflecting on your life in your family, workplace, parish or neighborhood, how do you hear yourself called by God to live a more committed Christian life? What keeps you from living it? After reflecting on this, invite God to enter your life, asking for what you need to help you in your commitment as a Christian.

2. As you reflect on your life today, what is one area or one problem from which you would like to become detached or freed? In silence turn this area of your life over to God.

3. In silent prayer image Jesus standing before you, inviting you to share with him your feelings, fears, concerns, etc., about being his disciple. Listen to Jesus respond to you.

Suggestion for Journal Keeping

In your journal write a dialogue with Jesus about your feelings, fears, concerns, desires, etc., about being his disciple, allowing Jesus to respond to you through your writing. How does Jesus affirm or challenge you? How does he invite you into a greater relationship with him? How does he speak of his love for you?

Kathleen Brown

Fourteenth Sunday of the Year [A]

READING I	*Zec 9:9–10*
Responsorial Psalm	*Ps 145:1–2, 8–9, 10–11, 13–14*
READING II	*Rom 8:9, 11–13*
GOSPEL	*Mt 11:25–30*

Reflection on the Readings

Jesus liked children, and they seem to have liked him. The disciples tried to send them away, but Jesus rebuked them. In today's Gospel, Jesus lets us in on a secret. He says that the children understand what the "wise and learned" can't quite grasp.

"Come to me, all you who labor and are burdened, and I will give you rest." A simple message, one that a child would believe. Our Savior will come "riding on an ass," and he will proclaim "peace to the nations." Only a child, or a Christian, would believe that.

Adult solutions to problems are much more complex. Adults go to health spas, they work out, they take stress management classes, they spend years in therapy, they get ulcers and high blood pressure. Children take naps; they play; when something hurts them, they cry. Children have an easier time than adults do admitting that some things are out of their control, and that Jesus can refresh and renew them.

To recognize our Savior, to rejoice and shout for joy, we must be like children. We must give our cares and concerns to the Lord, take up his yoke and shout for joy!

Suggestions for Prayer

1. Where do you find refreshment? How do you relax in the middle of life's tensions? Do you have a sense of humor about yourself?
2. Imagine Jesus sitting on a rock and talking to a group of children. Where are the children sitting? What are they wearing? What are they saying to each other?
3. Watch some children playing, or watch "Sesame Street" or "Mr. Roger's Neighborhood." What is a child's world like? Make a prayer to God, imagining that you are six years old.

Suggestion for Journal Keeping

Write down a good experience you had as a child that was important to you. Did you feel loved? Did this experience change you or affect your life? How does this experience affect your idea of God?

Michael P. Enright

Fourteenth Sunday of the Year
[B]

READING I	*Ez 2:2–5*
Responsorial Psalm	*Ps 123:1–2, 2, 3–4*
READING II	*2 Cor 12:7–10*
GOSPEL	*Mk 6:1–6*

Reflection on the Readings

One of the most painful experiences we can have is rejection. Others reject us or we reject them for a variety of reasons. Rejection can flow from jealousy or envy. Rejection can result when someone feels his security is threatened. Rejection can happen when someone acts contrary to our expectations. Often those who challenge us to live lives that are more virtuous are rejected. Sometimes people who are extraordinarily good or unusually bad are rejected.

The Gospel story today is a story of rejection. When Jesus began his public ministry, he worked many miracles and gave many profound teachings. When Jesus cured the man with the withered hand on the sabbath, the Pharisees and the scribes rejected him. When Jesus gave a profound teaching in the synagogue in Nazareth, his relatives and townspeople rejected him because they believed he was only a carpenter. Some even said Jesus was out of his mind. Their minds were so closed that it prompted Jesus to say, "A prophet is not without honor except in his native place and among his own kin, and in his own house." Because of their closed minds and their rejection of Jesus, they never did find out who he really was, the living Son of God. They rejected the best that God gave them.

There are many people today who, like the people in the days of the historical Jesus, continue to reject Jesus. Rejection is caused by sin and fear, ignorance and insecurity. People with closed minds are easily prone to reject Jesus when he comes to them in new ways.

Suggestions for Prayer

1. Reflect on one or more of the following questions:
   - Have you experienced rejection because of misunderstanding?
   - How do you feel when you have taken a strong faith stance on something you truly believe in and you are rejected and looked down upon?
   - Can you forgive the people who reject you?
2. In your imagination, you are at a meeting. You have just made a motion in favor of some noble cause. The majority votes you down. Jesus is standing beside you. He says, "A prophet is not without honor except in his native place, and among his own kin and in his own house."
3. Pray the responsorial psalm as your evening prayer this week.

Suggestion for Journal Keeping

Write in your journal about an experience in your life where you went out of your way to be gracious to someone for a long time. Then one day this person rejected you. How do you now feel toward this person? How do you feel toward Jesus?

Michael J. Koch

Fourteenth Sunday of the Year
[C]

READING I	*Is 66:10–14c*
Responsorial Psalm	*Ps 66:1–3, 4–5, 6–7, 16, 20*
READING II	*Gal 6:14–18*
GOSPEL	*Lk 10:1–12, 17–20 or 10:1–9*

Reflection on the Readings

In a poetic and exultant way, the prophet Isaiah calls upon the people of Israel to rejoice and be glad, for they will come to know the joy and the fulfillment of the promises of God. Prosperity, peace and comfort are the promises they shall see and come to know. They can hope in the power of God to transform their mourning into joy, for God is the source of new life. In hope they await the reign of God.

In Jesus the reign of God was brought nearer to the people. Through his ministry of teaching, healing and exorcism, Jesus revealed God's power breaking into their world. Jesus also called others to the same ministry, enabling them to be heralds of the coming of the reign of God. Calling first the twelve disciples, Jesus then called seventy-two more to be his disciples. They too went forth, preparing the way for Jesus, like lambs among wolves, announcing the reign of God by their lives, through performing miracles, expelling demons and healing the people in Jesus' name.

Upon return, the disciples reported that in the name of Jesus evil has no power in this world. Through Jesus' empowerment, the disciples experienced first-hand the breaking into their world of God's reign.

Through Paul's example of his life, he reminds the Galatians that what is really important is understanding the relevance of the cross of Jesus Christ for one's life. All else in the world becomes less important in light of the cross.

Suggestions for Prayer

1. As with the disciples mentioned in the Gospel, we too are called and empowered to be disciples of Jesus. In your life how do you hear yourself called and empowered to be a disciple of Jesus? In what area of your life in particular do you see yourself especially sent as a disciple of Jesus?

2. Reflect on your life, family, workplace, city, world. As you do, list all the places and events where you have experienced personally or have seen the power of God active. Throughout the week, become more aware of those places in your life and in the world where God's power is active.

3. The invitation to become a new creation is always given to us through God. Where in yourself do you see the need for new life? Envision what the new life would look like for you. In your imagination come before Jesus and hear him inviting you to his new life.

Suggestion for Journal Keeping

After quieting your mind and relaxing your body, journal your responses to one of the above questions. As you write, enter into dialogue with Jesus about your need for his power of healing, hope and love to come to your life.

Kathleen Brown

Fifteenth Sunday of the Year
[A]

READING I	*Is 55:10–11*
Responsorial Psalm	*Ps 65:10, 11, 12–13, 14*
READING II	*Rom 8:18–23*
GOSPEL	*Mt 13:1–23 or 13:1–9*

Reflection on the Readings

Seeds. Plants. Growing things. Jesus was familiar with these. Many of the images he used to talk about God and the kingdom were taken from the world of plants. He spoke of the grain of wheat dying and becoming more than just a grain of wheat. He spoke of mustard seeds growing to become the largest bushes. He spoke of the vine and the branches, and today he speaks of the sower.

In Jesus' day, farmers weren't as neat as they are today. They spread seed far and wide to ensure a good harvest. They spread extra seed. They even wasted some! Jesus' image of the sower is like Isaiah's image of rain. God's word

falls like rain—everywhere. It will bear fruit in many different ways. It is plentiful. There is even extra rain!

The harvest from God's word will be plentiful. We are showered with love, and this love is powerful. We will become like the valleys and hills. We will rejoice and shout for joy. We will bear fruit one hundred-, sixty-, and thirty-fold. All we need to do is hear the message of Jesus and take it in.

Suggestions for Prayer

1. Read a newspaper or a magazine, or watch the TV news until you find something about hungry people. Pray for them and for the farmers who feed them. Ask the Lord to send them a rich harvest. Ask yourself this question: What do I do for the hungry?

2. Look at a plant. Contemplate it. Look at its leaves. Study its structure. Marvel over its complexity. Wonder how it grows. Spend some time (20 minutes) doing this, then look at your hand. Move your fingers. Thank God for his marvelous craftsmanship.

3. Reread the Gospel. Ask yourself what kind of "soil" you are. What is it in you that limits God's word bearing fruit in your life? Ask God to give you a hand in dealing with this.

Suggestion for Journal Keeping

Remember an experience in your life when you loved someone deeply and your love was not accepted. What happened? How did you feel? How does God feel when we turn away from his love?

Michael P. Enright

Fifteenth Sunday of the Year
[B]

READING I	*Am 7:12–15*
Responsorial Psalm	*Ps 85:9–10, 11–12, 13–14*
READING II	*Eph 1:3–14 or 1:3–10*
GOSPEL	*Mk 6:7–13*

Reflection on the Readings

Most of us have been sent on an errand. A mother sends her son to the store to buy some groceries. A teacher sends a child home with a message. A page in the government delivers a document for an official. Persons doing errands are sent by someone: they do not go in their own name. The one sent carries a message or does a definite thing. It is not the message of the carrier, but the message of the sender that must be delivered. The carrier need not know the details of the message or its consequences. The carrier must have the commitment necessary to get the message delivered, even if it costs.

In the Gospel today, Jesus sends out his twelve on a mission. They are to bring the good news of Jesus to others. Jesus instructs them what to say and do, and he gives them the necessary authority to speak in his name. He instructs them to travel light. All they need is the message. Their creaturely needs will be cared for by the hospitality of those who receive the message. He sends them in pairs for mutual support and to "sacramentalize" the love that they are preaching. They are not to waste their time on those with closed minds and hearts.

Today, Christians by their baptism are mandated to be messengers of the good news. The same criteria apply. We are authorized by Jesus; we are to travel in pairs; we are to travel light. We can expect hospitality from those who accept Christ's message. This is the mission to which you are called and for which you are preparing.

Suggestions for Prayer
1. Reflect on one or more of the following questions:
   - Why did Jesus send out the twelve in pairs?
   - Why is it necessary for the messenger to deliver the message even if he or she doesn't know the content or consequences of the message?
   - Why is it necessary for the apostle or messenger to travel light?
2. In your imagination, Jesus is sending you out to be one of his apostles. With which apostle are you paired? To whom do you go? What is the response of Jesus' message that you bring? What does Jesus say to you when you return?
3. Pray the responsorial psalm as your evening prayer this week.

Suggestion for Journal Keeping
Describe in your journal an event in your life where you were sent on an errand. Did you encounter any opposition? Were you faithful to your commitment even in the face of suffering? How do you feel toward the apostles and Jesus who sent you?

Michael J. Koch

Fifteenth Sunday of the Year
[C]

READING I	Dt 30:10–14
Responsorial Psalm	Ps 69:14, 17, 30–31, 33–34, 36, 37 or 19:8, 9, 10, 11
READING II	Col 1:15–20
GOSPEL	Lk 10:25–37

Reflection on the Readings
The lawyer addressing Jesus knew with certainty the letter of the law, but did he understand the spirit of the law? The spirit of the law calls for a person's total engagement, heart, soul, strength and mind, in responding to the commandment to love God, neighbor and self. To illustrate this and to answer the lawyer's inquiry as to who was his neighbor, Jesus told the parable of the good Samaritan. It was a Samaritan, one looked down upon by Jews as unclean, who chose to help the beaten man. Without doubt, the Samaritan showed the greatest awareness of what it means to live the commandment of love. At the end of the parable, Jesus charged the lawyer to go and do the same.

The knowledge and ability to live out God's command to love was not foreign to the Israelites. As reflected in the first reading, Moses called on the Israelites to adhere to the commandments with all their heart and soul. This knowledge of God's command is already in our mouths and hearts, and all we need to do is to live it out in our lives.

As expressed in Paul's Letter to the Colossians, the perfection of this love is realized in and through Jesus Christ. It is in Christ Jesus that the fullness of what it means to live a selfless love is best exemplified. Through this selfless love, God reconciled everything on earth and in the heavens bringing peace to all.

Suggestions for Prayer

1. Reflect on one or all of the following questions: Where do you see the "beaten ones" in your neighborhood, city or world? Who are the Samaritans that are enabling these defenseless ones to live a fuller life?

2. With whom do you identify in the story: the beaten one, the Levite, the priest, the Samaritan or the lawyer? How do you hear the Lord speaking to you through this reading?

3. Let those people come to your mind who have enabled you or helped you to live your life more fully. Remembering them, thank God for what they have done for you in your life.

Suggestion for Journal Keeping

Recall someone who loves you very much and write that person a letter in your journal, speaking of the meaning and significance of that love for your life, how it enabled you in your journey, how it helped you to get back on the road of life, how it renewed your life, etc. After the letter is written, address Jesus through your writing, giving thanks for this person who has loved you.

Kathleen Brown

Sixteenth Sunday of the Year
[A]

READING I	*Wis 12:13, 16–19*
Responsorial Psalm	*Ps 86:5–6, 9–10, 15–16*
READING II	*Rom 8:26–27*
GOSPEL	*Mt 13:24–43 or 13:24–30*

Reflection on the Readings

The kingdom of God is coming. The kingdom of God is here already. These two statements seem to contradict one another, yet both are true. We know that sometime in the future God's reign will reach its fulfillment, but what about right now? How can it be that we are in the kingdom? We read the papers and see the news on TV and experience in our own lives the effects of evil. Where is the kingdom? If it is already here, why do bad things happen?

In the first parable of today's Gospel, Jesus tells us about the presence of evil. He says that we must be patient and not scandalized about what we see. The weeds, he assures us, will eventually be separated from the wheat.

The second and third parables in today's Gospel reflect another reality of the kingdom. It starts out very small! Mustard seeds and yeast are almost invisible. They grow like mad and make a big difference in their environment. They change things! The kingdom is happening now! The first reading reminds us not to worry. God is "lenient to all," and God, who is just, must be kind.

Although we know all this, sometimes we are still at a loss for words in prayer. We want to ask God why things happen the way they do. We become angry with our own sinfulness and weakness and with what happens around us. At the same time, we want to show our love for God and let God love us back. We come to prayer distracted, or tired, or joyful or empty. We want to enter into communion with God, but can't.

St. Paul knew about this. In writing to the Romans, he tells them to pray as best they can and let the Spirit speak for them. There are times when the best you can do is sit still and let your heart do the talking. That's O.K., St. Paul tells us, because in our weakness God can speak directly to our hearts.

Suggestions for Prayer

1. Have you ever been angry with God for something that happened? What was it? Have you ever "told God off"? Did you feel that this was acceptable or not?

2. Imagine/remember the worst thing that has ever happened to you. Was God present in the situation? How?

3. Pray with your heart. Be still and try to let God touch you on the inside. Don't talk to God—just listen.

Suggestion for Journal Keeping

Write about your prayer life. How do you pray? When? Where? Does your prayer make a difference to you? To God?

Michael P. Enright

Sixteenth Sunday of the Year
[B]

READING I	*Jer 23:1–6*
Responsorial Psalm	*Ps 23:1–3, 3–4, 5, 6*
READING II	*Eph 2:13–18*
GOSPEL	*Mk 6:30–34*

Reflection on the Readings

You have had a very long and grueling day. You are very tired. Nothing appeals to you more than sitting in an easy chair with your feet up and listening to a piece of relaxing music. The telephone rings. You answer. Your neighbor wants you to come over and help move a scaffold behind his house. What are you going to say? What are you going to do?

In the Gospel today, Jesus and the apostles find themselves in a similar situation. The apostles have been out preaching the good news. Their services were in such great demand that they didn't even have time to eat. They returned to Jesus dead tired. Jesus invited them to come with him to a lonely place so that they could rest a while. They took a boat to a secret place. But the people, like sheep without a shepherd, reached the secret place before Jesus and the apostles. When Jesus stepped ashore, he saw a large crowd awaiting him. Jesus, filled with compassion, took pity on them. In his tiredness, he surrendered his own comfort and set about teaching them at length.

Through baptism, Christians today are engaged in the same ministry as the apostles. Being a witness for Jesus and Gospel values can be very exhausting. The Gospel minister needs time to rest. But even while we rest, someone needs help. How will we respond?

Suggestions for Prayer

1. Reflect on one or more of the following questions:
   - What concern does Jesus show toward the apostles after they have worked hard?
   - What is the place of prayer for the apostles when they are on a mission?
   - How does Jesus deal with his own need for rest and the needs of the people who were like sheep without a shepherd?
2. In your imagination, you are sitting in your backyard relaxing after a long day's work. Jesus is standing beside you. He says, "You must come away to a lonely place all by yourselves and rest for a while."
3. Pray the responsorial psalm as your evening prayer this week.

Suggestion for Journal Keeping

Record in your journal an experience in your life where you had worked hard and you needed rest badly. You found yourself in a position of rest. The telephone rang. You answered. A friend was in need. What did you do? How would Jesus have handled this situation?

Michael J. Koch

Sixteenth Sunday of the Year
[C]

READING I	*Gn 18:1–10a*
Responsorial Psalm	*Ps 15:2–3, 3–4, 5*
READING II	*Col 1:24–28*
GOSPEL	*Lk 10:38–42*

Reflection on the Readings

To extend hospitality to friends is a pleasurable task. Extending hospitality to people we do not know, because they are strangers, can be awkward, especially if they arrive unannounced as in the first reading. How many of us would go to as much trouble as Abraham and Sarah to welcome mere strangers? In the Gospel, Martha is concerned about hospitality as well, but not without complaining about Mary's lack of assistance. Both the first reading and the Gospel emphasize the importance of hospitality, but both point to a more important issue.

At the closing of the first reading, the strangers, speaking to Sarah, predict the birth of a child (Isaac) within a year, fulfilling the promise of God to Abraham that he will have a descendant. Through the strangers, God was present to Abraham and Sarah, bringing good news of the fulfillment of the promise. Their openness and presence to the strangers revealed God's presence in their lives.

In the Gospel, Martha complains that Mary is not helping with the hospitality and asks Jesus to do something about it. Jesus does not address what Martha believes to be the problem but instead goes to the heart of the issue. While Martha was anxious and worried, Jesus points out to Martha that Mary has chosen the better part. To welcome, to be present, to keep one's life focused on the Lord, is to come to know the presence of God in all of life. For those who remain in the presence of the Lord there is the promise of a new life, as with Abraham and Sarah.

Suggestions for Prayer

1. Reflect and respond to the following questions: How do you understand Christian hospitality? How do you extend hospitality in your life to friends and to strangers? Recall

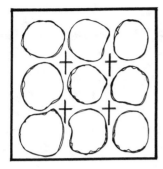

Seventeenth Sunday of the Year
[A]

READING I	*1 Kgs 3:5, 7–12*
Responsorial Psalm	*Ps 119:57, 72, 76–77, 127–128, 129–130*
READING II	*Rom 8:28–30*
GOSPEL	*Mt 13:44–52 or 13:44–46*

a time in your life when hospitality was extended to you as a stranger. How do you hear yourself called to be more hospitable to friends, family and strangers?

2. Have you ever experienced God's presence to you through another person such as a friend, a family member, a stranger, someone at work? Reflect on this experience, the meaning of it for your life, and how it affirmed or challenged your understanding of God's presence in self and others.

3. The Gospel says that Mary had chosen the better part, to be present and to listen to the Lord. Through your imagination, invite Jesus into your home and your daily life. Speak with him about your concerns, hopes, anxieties, worries, joys, etc.; then listen in silence to his response to you.

Suggestion for Journal Keeping

As you listen to the readings, be aware of what touches you, awakens concerns or desires within you about hospitality or about being more present to the Lord in your life. Journal your responses in a dialogue with Jesus, being sure to allow Jesus to respond to you.

Kathleen Brown

Reflection on the Readings

How do you find something you're not looking for? You don't. The man in today's Gospel found the treasure because he was looking for it. The merchant found the fine pearl because he was looking for it. Both men found something they were looking for and did what they had to do to buy it.

Today we might think of an antiques buff who knows Victorian furniture. She looks for original pieces every time she stops at an antique store. One day she sees a table that she recognizes as an original. She asks the price, then races home to get the money she needs. She hurries back, exalted, and snatches up the deal before anyone else can.

Like the men in the Gospel, she sees a valuable thing, recognizes it, and does whatever is necessary to buy the table. The same thing is true for the reign of God. In order to find it, we must be looking for it. We must know what it looks like. We must learn to recognize it. We must, like Solomon, ask the Lord to give us discerning hearts.

Then, when we find evidence of the kingdom, we must do whatever we have to in order to make it our own. We may have to change some of our usual ways of doing things. We may have to give up old prejudices. We may have to let go of patterns in our lives that blind us to God's love and chain us to our pasts. Once we begin looking for the reign of God, we find it, and once we find it, it demands that we change. Our first step on the journey is the same as Solomon's—asking God to give us wisdom.

Suggestions for Prayer
1. Read today's second reading again. Concentrate on the first sentence. Do you think that God makes all things work together? Turn the first sentence over in your mind. Has God pulled things together in your life?
2. Ask God for wisdom. Think of the problems you have. Tell the Lord about them. Ask for some insight into what you should do.
3. Go for a walk around your neighborhood. Look for signs of the reign of God. See if you can spot the hand of God in what you see. If you find something, pause and give thanks to God.

Suggestion for Journal Keeping
Read over your old journal entries. See if you can spot any patterns. What are they? Can you see yourself moving somewhere?

Michael P. Enright

Seventeenth Sunday of the Year
[B]

READING I	2 Kgs 4:42–44
Responsorial Psalm	Ps 145:10–11, 15–16, 17–18
READING II	Eph 4:1–6
GOSPEL	Jn 6:1–15

Reflection on the Readings

Were you ever in a situation where there was not enough food to go around? It may have been a family situation, a social function, a disaster, or a third world country. In the group, there probably were pessimists who complained of the shortage. On the other hand, there may have been optimists present who used their ingenuity to generate alternative ideas. Were there people who tried to hoard?

In the Gospel today, Jesus finds himself, the apostles, and a large crowd of people, numbering some five thousand, in a situation of shortage. The only food they had among them was five barley loaves and two fish. But Jesus was an optimist. He asked the troubled people to sit down. Then he took the loaves, gave thanks, and had them distributed. He did the same with the fish. The hunger of all was satisfied, and there were twelve baskets of scraps left over.

St. John tells this story in a way that reflects the Eucharist. Jesus takes bread, gives thanks, and shares it with the multitude. There is a similarity here to the action of the Last Supper in which Jesus takes bread, blesses it, and shares it with his disciples. The abundance of bread that nourishes the five thousand is both a sign of the abundance of life in the Eucharist, and a call to us, as a eucharistic people, to feed the hungry.

Suggestions for Prayer

1. Reflect on one or more of the following questions:
   - Have you ever found yourself in a situation of shortage?
   - What was the attitude of Philip? What was the attitude of Andrew?
   - How did Jesus deal with the shortage of food?
2. In your imagination, place yourself in the large crowd of hungry people. Jesus is saying to you, "Where can we buy some bread for these people to eat?" What answer are you going to give to Jesus?
3. Pray the responsorial psalm as your morning prayer this week. Bear in mind the graciousness of God.

Suggestion for Journal Keeping

In your journal, write about an incident of scarcity in your life. Did you contemplate hoarding? What did you finally do in that situation? Did the example of Jesus' attitude help you in your decision?

Michael J. Koch

Seventeenth Sunday of the Year
[C]

READING I	*Gn 18:20–32*
Responsorial Psalm	*Ps 138:1–2, 2–3, 6–7, 7–8*
READING II	*Col 2:12–14*
GOSPEL	*Lk 11:1–13*

Reflection on the Readings

Prayer is sometimes nothing more than a conversation with God where we express our hopes, concerns, joys. In the first reading, Abraham is engaged in a conversation with God regarding divine justice for Sodom and Gomorrah. Persistent in his pursuit of justice for the people, Abraham draws God into a dialogue in an attempt to preserve the infamous city from being destroyed. But perhaps the most important aspect of his dialogue has to do with what it reveals about God. Ultimately, this dialogue reveals a God who is just, who says that even ten innocent people are worth saving the rest of the city and who does not destroy or punish at divine whim. Thus, God's great love for the people is revealed through this prayer dialogue with Abraham.

Although all prayer is essentially a conversation with God, some prayer is not as spontaneous as is Abraham's with God. Thus we have received the Lord's Prayer that Jesus gave to his disciples. But all prayer reveals something of the faith of a people and their understanding of who is their God. When the disciples asked Jesus to teach them to pray, he gave them a simple prayer but one that expressed their nascent faith. To believe in and to call for the coming of God's kingdom, to daily come to God with their basic needs as individuals and community, and to pray both to be forgiven and to forgive as they know themselves to be forgiven by God and to not be asked to endure suffering beyond their capacity—this is how the followers of Jesus were to live their lives. Through parables Jesus continued to speak about the disciples' life of prayer. However, the parables pointed more to the relationship between the disciples and God. On the disciples' part, they were to persevere in presenting their needs to God and in their relationship with God. Perseverance in their prayer to God will bear fruit because of who God is.

Suggestions for Prayer

1. Each morning, before beginning the day's activities, slowly and reflectively recite the Lord's Prayer. After each phrase, stop and reflect on the meaning of it for you, your life in your family, work or neighborhood.
2. Review the growth of your prayer life since your childhood. What was your prayer life like as a child? What is it like now? How do you hear yourself called to pray in your life now? Do you have a daily prayer time and do you persevere in it?
3. Reflectively and slowly read the responsorial psalm every day this week.

Suggestion for Journal Keeping

At the end of the day, record the activities of the day, remembering to forgive those who hurt or offended you and to ask forgiveness from those you may have hurt or offended. In your journal writing, include prayer to God expressing your needs and the needs of others.

Kathleen Brown

Eighteenth Sunday of the Year
[A]

READING I	*Is 55:1–3*
Responsorial Psalm	*Ps 145:8–9, 15–16, 17–18*
READING II	*Rom 8:35, 37–39*
GOSPEL	*Mt 14:13–21*

Reflection on the Readings

Being really hungry is a terrible thing! When you're really hungry, little else matters. All you can think of is the growing emptiness in your stomach. You begin to notice the smell of food, to remember eating, to long for something that will take the hunger away. The need we have to eat transforms itself into a consuming desire that absorbs our thoughts and feelings. When we finally eat, we rejoice in the meal we've been waiting for. Sometimes we even eat too much, so strong is our desire to be filled.

In the Gospel today, Jesus feeds the crowd. His action is a response to his being moved with pity. He sees them like sheep without a shepherd and begins to feed them. What he offers them fills them with hope and joy. He meets their need for healing. He touches their emptiness. They stay around until evening, far away from any food. What they've been feeling is stronger than the gnawing in their stomachs.

The disciples come to Jesus and tell him to send them away, since obviously the crowd has to eat. Jesus again makes his love for them concrete. He has already fed their hearts and now he feeds their bodies. The abundant feast mirrors the feast of Isaiah in the first reading. Free food and drink, and lots of it, come from our covenant with God. Life, life in abundance, springs from Yahweh's love. Jesus fulfills that love and brings life to God's people. We only need to listen and the Lord will fill us with the same life.

Suggestions for Prayer

1. Read the second readings from the 15th to the 18th Sunday of the year (or read Romans 8:18–39). Imagine that what you are reading is a letter written to you. Ask yourself these questions:
   - Is there anything that can separate you from the Love of God?

- Is there something that worries you and distracts you from remembering that God loves you? What is it?
2. Imagine Jesus talking to you. Remember your own hurts and need for healing. What could Jesus say to you to heal your deepest wounds? Imagine him saying it to you.
3. Think about your favorite meal of all time. What was your best dining experience? Reread the first reading. Reflect on the promise given. How can you listen to the Lord more carefully?

Suggestion for Journal Keeping

Write down the things that are keeping you from recognizing the love of God in your own life. Can the Lord heal these?

Michael P. Enright

Eighteenth Sunday of the Year
[B]

READING I	*Ex 16:2–4, 12–15*
Responsorial Psalm	*Ps 78:3–4, 23–24, 25, 54*
READING II	*Eph 4:17, 20–24*
GOSPEL	*Jn 6:24–35*

Reflection on the Readings

As we go through life, most of us spend a lot of time, money, energy, and other resources on temporal and passing things. At some point in our life, we may place great value on money, a career, education, a house, becoming a sports champion, or physical pleasure. As we go on in life, these values usually wear out or become meaningless. We outgrow them and replace them with ones that are more meaningful.

In the Gospel today, Jesus challenges his followers to deeper conversion. Jesus has just finished performing the miracle of the loaves and fish. The crowd follows him wherever he goes. They follow him, not because they wish to grow in faith and spirituality, but because they see Jesus as a source of physical bread. Jesus challenges them, "Do not work for food that perishes, but work for food that endures for eternal life." A debate ensues. "What does God expect of us?" they ask. Jesus says, "This is working for God: you must believe in the one he has sent." Show us a sign, they say; work a miracle. Jesus then says it was not Moses who gave the manna, but his Father in heaven. The bread of God is that which gives life to the world. "Give us this bread," they say. Jesus answers, "I am the bread of life."

This struggle of conversion is still going on today. Each one of us is called to conversion and faith. We must give "Jesus, the bread of life," priority over mere physical bread.

Suggestions for Prayer
1. Reflect on one or more of the following questions:
   - What are some of the passing "gods" you have served in your life?
   - Have you outgrown any of these "gods"?
   - Do you believe Jesus is the incarnation of the living God?
2. In your imagination, see yourself in a process of conversion. Much of your life and energy is devoted to a "god" whom you hang onto in the hope of finding a meaningful life. Jesus comes and touches you. He says, "I am the bread of life."

3. Pray the responsorial psalm as your morning prayer this week. It will help in your conversion process.

Suggestion for Journal Keeping

Describe a "god" in your life whom you worked for and loved. Describe your parting and goodbye to this "god" when you finally outgrew it. You then embrace Jesus, the bread of life.

Michael J. Koch

Eighteenth Sunday of the Year
[C]

READING I	*Eccl 1:2; 2:21–23*
Responsorial Psalm	*Ps 90:3–4, 5–6, 12–13, 14, 17*
READING II	*Col 3:1–5, 9–11*
GOSPEL	*Lk 12:13–21*

Reflection on the Readings

"Vanity of vanities" is an often-quoted line. But what does it mean? Qoheleth, the speaker in the first reading, looks about him and, upon seeing the reality of life and death, wisely concludes that to amass wealth is futile, since we cannot take our material fortunes with us after death.

Jesus, addressed by someone in the crowd who wants him to tell his brother to give him his share of the inheritance, instead tells him the parable of the rich man. This rich man had a good harvest and he wanted to store it and save it. He was a fool for amassing such wealth, for upon his death he could not take it

with him. Through the parable, Jesus teaches that possessions and wealth are not bad. Rather, it is one's attitude toward possessions that matters. The danger is that one becomes possessed by possessions, keeping focused on things and wealth, rather than having God as the center of one's life. In other words, the danger is greed. Perhaps it would be better to keep a perspective toward possessions similar to Qoheleth.

Paul in addressing the Colossians invites them as well to refocus their attention. It is through the raising of Christ from the dead for us that we are called to rise above those things of the world that keep us from being Christlike. Setting our hearts and focus on Christ, we will grow rich in God.

Suggestions for Prayer

1. Sit in silence, relaxing your whole body. Closing your eyes, envision your favorite place. See yourself in your favorite place, relaxing. Invite Jesus to come and be with you, sitting quietly. Allow his presence to fill you with peace.
2. Reflect on one or all of the following questions: What is your attitude toward things, possessions, money? Do things, possessions or money ever cause you worry or anxiety? How do the readings affirm or challenge your attitudes toward things, possessions or money?
3. Reflect on what it means for you to grow rich in the sight of God. What do you need for this growth to take place? After reflecting on this, come to the Lord presenting your desires and your hopes.

Suggestion for Journal Keeping

Write a letter to God telling about all the blessings you have in your life and giving thanks for everything in your life at this time. Next, write in your letter what you really need in your life, presenting these to God as well.

Kathleen Brown

Nineteenth Sunday of the Year [A]

READING I	*1 Kgs 19:9a, 11–13a*
Responsorial Psalm	*Ps 85:9, 10, 11–12, 13–14*
READING II	*Rom 9:1–5*
GOSPEL	*Mt 14:22–33*

Reflection on the Readings

Every once in a while, something happens that we can't quiet explain. For some reason, the rules that govern ordinary everyday reality are suspended for a moment and we catch a glimpse of a deeper reality. You've had this experience! It might have been a sunset, or a baby's eyes or the face of your spouse or son or daughter. It might have been a severe storm, or the first snow, or something a stranger did. Sometime, somehow, you've had an experience that lets you see a different reality. What ordinarily you wouldn't notice, suddenly you see. You can tell this has happened because you remember the experience. You remember that sunset, or that glimpse into someone's eyes. Your heart was touched.

In today's first reading, we read of Elijah's experience of God. The Lord God was not present in the earth-shaking "theatrical" ways we might expect. Yahweh was present in a whisper. The special effects were not clues of God's presence. The simplicity of a whisper caused Elijah to hide his face.

The disciples in the boat nearly jumped out of their skins seeing Jesus approach. Peter put this apparition to the test and was himself tested: Why did you falter? Why did you not believe? Peter's faith was strong enough for him to begin the walk, but he was frightened. We too begin the walk toward the Lord but falter. It's then that Jesus reaches down and picks us up.

The presence of the Lord breaks through the mundane and invites us to a deeper way of seeing. Surprised, we find ourselves appreciating the beauty of our world and knowing God's love for us. We respond to the invitation and begin to move closer to the Lord, only to find our knees weakened. Jesus then reaches out and strengthens us for our journey toward the light.

Suggestions for Prayer

1. Watch a sunset. Give thanks to God for the beauty you see there. Listen hard for a "whisper" that will tell you God is present.
2. Imagine that you're Peter. It's dark and you're on a small boat in a storm. You see Jesus and he calls you toward him. Do you go? What happens?
3. Reread the second reading. Why is Paul grieving? Have you ever been saddened watching someone reject love? What happened?

Suggestion for Journal Keeping

Write down the earliest experience you can remember of seeing something beautiful. How old were you? Why do you think you remember this experience? Did it change you?

Michael P. Enright

Nineteenth Sunday of the Year
[B]

READING I	*1 Kgs 19:4–8*
Responsorial Psalm	*Ps 34:2–3, 4–5, 6–7, 8–9*
READING II	*Eph 4:30—5:2*
GOSPEL	*Jn 6:41–51*

Reflection on the Readings

Often at a science fair, there is a section on optical illusions. We are entertained by seeing one thing, but the reality is something else. For example, straight lines appear curved. Often we judge others from mere externals. Internally, people are often not what they appear to be externally. We must remain open to new evidence.

In the Gospel today, some Jews are in a state of illusion. They judge Jesus from mere externals. Jesus says, "I am the bread that came down from heaven." But they say, "You are a mere man, the son of Joseph. We know your family and where you grew up." They see only the externals. Because of their negative feelings toward Jesus, they have closed minds. They have already decided who Jesus is, a mere man. They will not accept Jesus' true identity. Jesus says, "I am the living bread that came down from heaven; whoever eats this bread will live forever; and the bread that I will give is my flesh for the life of the world." To accept Jesus beyond externals requires faith. Faith sees beyond externals.

Throughout the centuries and today, Catholics and other Christians have believed that Jesus is really present in the Eucharist. In a sense, the bread we eat, the wine we drink, is an illusion. Our human eyes see only bread and wine, only externals. Through faith, we go beyond externals and recognize the presence of Jesus in the Eucharist.

Suggestions for Prayer

1. Reflect on one or more of the following questions:
   - Have you ever judged a person from mere externals and later discovered you were not even near to knowing the real person?
   - Why did the Jews in St. John's Gospel have such a hard time with Jesus' true identity?
   - Do you really believe Jesus when he says, "I am the living bread that came down from heaven; whoever eats this bread will live forever"?

2. In your imagination, place yourself at a Sunday eucharistic liturgy after your baptism (or reception into the Church). When the priest holds up the host at the elevation, you acknowledge the presence of Christ in the Eucharist by saying, "My Lord and my God."

3. Pray the responsorial psalm as your evening prayer this week. Delight in the Lord.

Suggestion for Journal Keeping

Record in your journal an experience in your life where you judged a person quite harshly, only to discover later that you saw only externals and that the person was not at all like that. What did you learn from this experience? Does this experience help you to believe in the Real Presence?

Michael J. Koch

Nineteenth Sunday of the Year [C]

READING I	Wis 18:6–9
Responsorial Psalm	Ps 33:1, 12, 18–19, 20–22
READING II	Heb 11:1–2, 8–19 or 11:1–2, 8–12
GOSPEL	Lk 12:32–48 or 12:35–40

Reflection on the Readings

By means of their faith, the Hebrew people knew that God would be faithful to them. They waited for the day when the just would be saved and the enemy destroyed. When, through Moses, the Lord called them out of Egypt, they were ready to go. Their faith and courage in the Lord led the way.

Jesus tells the disciples that they are not to fear. Like the Hebrews, they can put their faith in God. And like the Hebrews, they too are called to be prepared for the Lord's coming at any time. Called to be faith-filled, they are to live a life that speaks of their readiness for the coming of the Son of Man. It is a life of constant faithfulness to God in every activity. Because much has been given to them, much will be asked of the disciples of Jesus.

In the Letter to the Hebrews, faith is defined as having confident assurance concerning what we hope for. To be able to recognize the coming of Christ in our life, we need to be as faithful as our Jewish ancestors were. Sometimes that faith will require belief in God's faithful promises to us, even when we do not see them fulfilled as we would intend. Abraham and Sarah were promised that their names would be famous, that they would have a land of their own and many descendants. They did not see the fullness of these promises, but future generations would come to know that God was faithful. However, throughout their life, Abraham and Sarah remained faithful to God. As followers of Jesus, we are invited to this same faithfulness even in the midst of suffering.

Suggestions for Prayer

1. Reflect on the following questions: In your own life what has it meant for you to be faithful to friends, to family, to yourself, to God? How have you come to believe in God's faithfulness to you? Where in your life do you desire to be more faith-filled?

2. Reflect on the line from the Gospel, "Do not be afraid any longer, little flock, for your Father is pleased to give you the kingdom." What are your fears, your hopes, your expectations, your needs? In silence, present these to God.

3. Read Genesis 12:1–4, then reread the Letter to the Hebrews. As you read, invite the Lord to speak to you through the readings. Listen to the words or phrases that touch you in your life today. What do the readings have to say to you about your own faith?

Suggestion for Journal Keeping

Write the story of the Lord's coming into your life, beginning with your childhood and moving into the present. Conclude by writing a letter to God, expressing your thankfulness, your hopes and your desires for the future.

Kathleen Brown

Twentieth Sunday of the Year
[A]

READING I	*Is 56:1, 6–7*
Responsorial Psalm	*Ps 67:2–3, 5, 6, 8*
READING II	*Rom 11:13–15, 29–32*
GOSPEL	*Mt 15:21–28*

Reflection on the Readings

Whoever you are, rich or poor, there are some places you are not welcome. Whatever your skin color, or age, or sex, there are places where you are not allowed. All of us are victims of discrimination in one way or another. We have all been pre-judged at some time in our lives. We have all been turned away because of our clothes, or our neighborhood, or our family, or our physical characteristics. We know what the Canaanite woman felt.

There is one place, though, where everyone is welcome. There is one place where age, or sex, or sickness, or clothes, or color doesn't make a bit of difference. What does make a difference is our faith. We are all welcome into the house of the Lord. As the first reading tells us, the house of the Lord is a "house of prayer for all peoples." Although it is difficult to live this out in individual parishes, it is true. No one is to be turned away just because we don't like that person. All faithful people are welcome.

This is good news! There is no other place like that on the earth. Even in countries like ours where we are all supposed to be equal, some people are not welcome. At its best, the place where you worship accommodates the whole spectrum of people. It is a sign of the kingdom. The community you want to join opens its arms to you, and to people around the whole earth. You are welcome with all of your strengths, talents and gifts, and with your weaknesses and limits and sinfulness. The only requirement is that your faith is strong.

Suggestions for Prayer

1. Reread the Gospel and imagine the scene. Put yourself into one of the roles: the disciples, the woman, or Jesus. How do you feel? What part did you pick? Why?
2. Remember an experience when you felt prejudice. What happened? How did it affect you? What did you learn from it? Imagine Jesus sitting next to you. Tell him about the experience.

Suggestion for Journal Keeping

Write down the prejudices you have. Think of the kind of people you most dislike. Be honest. Write down why you feel the way you do. Read the list over; then write a prayer for these people and yourself.

Michael P. Enright

Twentieth Sunday of the Year
[B]

READING I	*Prv 9:1–6*
Responsorial Psalm	*Ps 34:2–3, 4–5, 6–7*
READING II	*Eph 5:15–20*
GOSPEL	*Jn 6:51–58*

Reflection on the Readings

No one is an island. It is part of our nature to be in union, in communion with another. Originally, we were part of our parents. As we became individuated, we felt alone, unbonded. There is a desire in each one of us to be one with another. This hunger can only partially be filled by human intimacy. Ultimately, rest and peace come only when we enjoy union, communion, with God. When we enjoy this communion, we experience ourselves as really real, fully alive.

God our Father has always known this. Jesus is our most profound link with God. When we are in communion with Jesus, we are in union with God. Jesus replies to the unbelievers, "Unless you eat the flesh of the Son of Man and drink his blood, you do not have life within you. Whoever eats my flesh and drinks my blood has eternal life. . . . " Jesus adds, "Just as the living Father sent me and I have life because of the Father, so also the one who feeds on me will have life because of me."

Jesus, at the Last Supper, instituted the Eucharist. Throughout Christian history, Jesus has given himself to us in the Eucharist. Through baptism, we become members of the Church, the body of Christ. Through the Eucharist, we are nourished and kept alive in faith. Every time we partake of the Eucharist, we are reminded whose body we are.

Suggestions for Prayer

1. Reflect on one or more of the following questions:
   - Do you believe that Holy Communion is necessary if you wish to grow in your relationship with Jesus?
   - Do you really believe that when you are in communion with Jesus, you are in union with God?
   - Do you believe that anyone who is an island is already in hell?
2. In your imagination, place yourself in a Catholic church during the rite of Communion. As each person returns to the pew, you recognize Jesus within them. Jesus says to you, "Whoever eats my flesh and drinks my blood remains in me and I in him [her]."
3. Pray the responsorial psalm as your evening prayer this week. Continue to delight in the Lord.

Suggestion for Journal Keeping

Report in your journal an experience in which you felt very alone. In your goodness you were grossly misunderstood. Identify with Jesus who gave himself totally and yet was rejected.

Michael J. Koch

Twentieth Sunday of the Year
[C]

READING I	*Jer 38:4–6, 8–10*
Responsorial Psalm	*Ps 40:2, 3, 4, 18*
READING II	*Heb 12:1–4*
GOSPEL	*Lk 12:49–53*

Reflection on the Readings

Jeremiah strongly resisted the call to be a prophet to the king of Israel. He knew that to proclaim the truth and to call Israel to faithfulness would cost him his life. He was not a popular man because he challenged the values and the morals of his day, upsetting important people in high places. But for Jeremiah to be faithful to God was a priority above all else, even above life itself.

In the early Church, many thought being a Christian would mean a life of peace and contentment, a life without pain or struggle. Faithfulness and fidelity to Jesus Christ and the proclamation of the values and morals of God's kingdom revealed that to be a disciple of Christ could bring about division among friends and family. The Gospel of Jesus called for a radical way of life that often stood in contradiction to the popular beliefs of the people. And for those who remained radically faithful to the Gospel, it could mean suffering and death.

Complacency is deadly to the fulfillment of the Gospel. In the Letter to the Hebrews, the reader is challenged to persevere and to keep one's eyes focused on Jesus. To be a follower of Jesus, faithful to the Gospel, causes one's life to be challenged to its core. The values and morals of each generation will inevitably come into conflict with the Gospel of Jesus Christ.

Suggestions for Prayer

1. As you watch TV, what values and morals do you hear being proclaimed? How are these morals and values in agreement or conflict with your own personal morals and values and those of the Gospel? Where do you hear God affirming or challenging you in your own morals and values?

2. Read the psalm slowly, reflecting on its message for you in your life.

3. Reflect silently on what it means for you to be faithful to the Gospel and to be a prophet of God. Where in your life do you experience the call to be prophetic with your family, friends, workplace, neighborhood? In silence, present any fears or concerns that arise to God, asking for strength and courage.

Suggestion for Journal Keeping

Bring to mind someone you consider a modern-day prophet (examples might be Mahatma Gandhi, Dorothy Day, Martin Luther King, Anwar Sadat, etc.). Write a letter to the person, expressing your feelings about him or her, and your own questions and concerns about being a prophet. Through your writing have the person respond to you. At the end of the dialogue, write a prayer that reflects your feelings, your hopes and your concerns about what it means to be a prophet.

Kathleen Brown

Twenty-first Sunday of the Year [A]

READING I	Is 22:19–23
Responsorial Psalm	Ps 138:1–2, 2–3, 6, 8
READING II	Rom 11:33–36
GOSPEL	Mt 16:13–20

Reflection on the Readings

Where does authority come from? To understand today's reading we must first ask that question. Living in a democracy, our answer naturally is "from the people." The biblical answer is different, and can be hard for us to accept.

In today's second reading, Paul talks about the wisdom and knowledge of God. God is the Creator. God needs no counselor. Everything comes from God—everything, including authority.

In the first reading, Isaiah prophesies that Shebna will be pulled down from his position and Eliakim will take his place. Who makes the change? Who will fix Eliakim like a peg in a sure spot? None other than God, who created the world in the first place!

In the Gospel, Jesus asks the disciples a key question, "Who am I?" Simon Peter answers, "The Christ, the Son of the living God." With what authority does Jesus speak then? He then tells Peter that he will be the "rock of the Church" and gives him authority to bind and loose sins. Peter's authority comes from God. The Church's authority comes from God as well. What gives the whole thing a different slant is Jesus' preaching on authority. Authority is for service. Those in power are not to make their importance felt; rather, they are to be the servants of the people. To be a Christian means to be a servant in God's kingdom.

Suggestions for Prayer

1. Think about the people who have power in your life. Reflect on the way they use their power. Pray for them, that they be reflections of God's authority.
2. Imagine yourself as one of the disciples. Imagine Jesus asking you the question: Who do you say that I am? Think of different answers to the question.
3. Baptized people have the right to participate in the sacrament of reconciliation. What sins would you tell the priest in that sacrament? How would you feel, knowing that these could be forgiven? Ask the Lord to help you get ready for that sacrament.

Suggestion for Journal Keeping

Write down a bad experience you've had with authority. What made it bad? Have you ever used your authority badly?

Michael P. Enright

Twenty-first Sunday of the Year [B]

READING I	Jos 24:1–2a 15–17, 18b
Responsorial Psalm	Ps 34:2–3, 16–17, 18–19, 20–21
READING II	Eph 5:21–32 or 5:2a, 25–32
GOSPEL	Jn 6:60–69

Reflection on the Readings

The media seem to be eternally puzzled by the teaching of the Catholic Church. Whenever the Church is in the news, one inevitably hears the media litany that the Church is against this or for that. The media, looking at these issues from a mere secular point of view, from a non-faith point of view, could not possibly understand. "This saying is hard; who can accept it?"

In the Gospel readings for the last few Sundays, Jesus has been saying, "I am the bread of life; if you eat my flesh and drink my blood, you will have eternal life." Many of the followers of Jesus deserted him. "This saying is hard; who can accept it?" They wanted intellectual answers, answers they could understand. Their faith was too shallow. They did not trust Jesus. Jesus addressed the Twelve: "Do you also want to leave?" The apostles were just as puzzled; they did not understand either. But because they loved Jesus, they believed, they accepted him without understanding. Peter says, "Master, to whom shall we go? You have the words of eternal life. We have come to believe and are convinced that you are the Holy One of God."

We cannot really understand how Jesus is present in the Eucharist, how bread and wine can become the body and blood of Jesus. However, when we make our act of faith, we are bonded to the Lord in a loving, life-giving way.

Suggestions for Prayer

1. Reflect on one or more of the following questions:
   - How did you respond when you found yourself in a situation where you couldn't understand something? Did loving or not loving the speaker make any difference?
   - Why did Simon Peter answer: "Master, to whom shall we go? You have the words of eternal life and we believe"?
2. In your imagination, place yourself in the company of Jesus. You hear his teaching. You hear some of Jesus' followers say, "This saying is hard; who can accept it?" Jesus walks up to you and says, "Do you also want to leave?" How do you respond?
3. Pray the responsorial psalm as your evening prayer this week. Note that the verses are different from the previous two weeks.

Suggestion for Journal Keeping

Recall an experience where you did not understand what was going on. You had some insight, but much more evaded you. How much did you accept or reject? How much did your relationship to the speaker affect your decision? Did Peter's response help you?

Michael J. Koch

Twenty-first Sunday of the Year [C]

READING I	*Is 66:18–21*
Responsorial Psalm	*Ps 117:1, 2*
READING II	*Heb 12:5–7, 11–13*
GOSPEL	*Lk 13:22–30*

Reflection on the Readings

The good news, as proclaimed by the prophet Isaiah, is that God intends to gather all the people of the earth. Just as God has saved the Israelites, God will now be the God of all nations. All the peoples of the earth will come to know and see the glory of God.

Although the promise of salvation was offered to all, there were some who rejected it and who in consequence are rejected from the feast of the kingdom of God. In response to a question of whether there would be a lot of people saved, Jesus tells the story of the person who desired to get into the master's house, claiming to know the master, to have even eaten with him and to have heard him teach in the streets. The master of the house would not let him in, denying that he ever knew him. Jesus then raised a caution to those who were gathered. No one receives the kingdom because of ancestry. Rather, one must hear the word of God and live it in one's life in order to gain access to the feast of the kingdom. To do this is to come in through the narrow door. Those who fail to hear the word of the Lord and to respond to it will be turned away from the feast.

The Letter to the Hebrews speaks of a narrow door as well, but in terms of discipline.

Twenty-second Sunday of the Year [A]

READING I	Jer 20:7–9
Responsorial Psalm	Ps 63:2, 3–4, 5–6, 8–9
READING II	Rom 12:1–2
GOSPEL	Mt 16:21–27

Discipline brings forth the fruit of peace and justice in one's life and in the world. The Gospel asks us to be strong, to continue to make straight our lives and to endure our trials. Through our lives lived as disciples of Christ, we will come to know and see the glory of God.

Suggestions for Prayer

1. Reflect on the following questions: How do you hear the word of God addressing you in your own life? In what ways do you hear God offering you salvation?

2. As you reread the second reading, reflect on what it means to be called to bear the fruit of peace and justice in your personal life, in your neighborhood, in your city, in the country.

3. Reflect on the meaning of God gathering nations of every language. What does this mean for world peace, for unity, for future generations? Compose a prayer that expresses your desires and hopes for the future of all God's people.

Suggestion for Journal Keeping

In your journal write what "to be saved" means for you. Describe an event in your life when you have experienced being rescued, protected or saved. In light of this experience, journal what it means for you to be saved by God. Finish by writing a prayer that expresses your needs, your hopes, your thankfulness.

Kathleen Brown

Reflection on the Readings

To be a Christian is difficult. To be a messenger of God means being uncomfortable. It may even mean death. This is Jesus' message to his disciples. Peter didn't like the sound of Jesus' prediction of his own death. Jesus, though, had a radically different set of values and priorities. What seemed foolish to Peter was part of God's plan.

Jeremiah, a messenger from God, could find no comfort. If he spoke the message, he was laughed to scorn. If he tried to hold it in, it became a burning fire in his heart. He agreed to be a prophet and then suffered because of his role.

The Gospel demands that Christians take a stand. It demands that we stand for a different reality. It demands that we not be conformists but that we learn to judge God's will and do it. Does this mean that we all become fanatics? Does this mean that to live your vocation as a Christian you have to stand on street corners and preach against this age? No it does not.

What it means is that you are obligated to take up your cross. It means that you will be uncomfortable with injustice. It means that you learn to pray and judge by God's standards. It means that you follow Jesus, through death to resurrection!

Suggestions for Prayer

1. Look back over your life, and try to remember a time when you picked up the cross. What was your cross? How did you pick it up? Did you feel Jesus' presence as you did what you did?
2. Pray the responsorial psalm from today. Imagine yourself "parched, lifeless and without water." Turn the psalm over in your mind and imagine the right hand of God upholding you.
3. Reflect on the life of one of the martyrs. If you do not know about any, look up Acts 6: 8—7:60. Where do you think martyrs get their courage?

Suggestion for Journal Keeping

Write about a time in your life when you stood up for justice. What happened? Was it difficult? Did you feel God's presence in this experience?

Michael P. Enright

Twenty-second Sunday of the Year [B]

READING I	*Dt 4:1–2, 6–8*
Responsorial Psalm	*Ps 15:2–3, 3–4, 4–5*
READING II	*Jas 1:17–18, 21b–22, 27*
GOSPEL	*Mk 7:1–8, 14–15, 21–23*

Reflection on the Readings

It is interesting to observe people gathered together in a Sunday eucharistic liturgy. Some have been praying all week. They are very close to the Lord. When they participate in the Sunday worship, one can sense integrity in them. Their responses, gestures and song come from the heart. Others who come to the liturgy are quite artificial. Their external behavior has no internal root. Only their external selves are present. They come because of habit, tradition or law. They come late, look around, and leave early. Their hearts are somewhere else.

The Gospel today addresses the question of external practices and internal faith. The Pharisees criticize Jesus and his disciples for not following the Jewish ablution rituals. "Why do your disciples not follow the tradition of the elders, but instead eat a meal with unclean hands?" they ask Jesus. Jesus fires back at the Pharisees and scribes and calls them hypocrites. Jesus quotes Isaiah, "This people honors me with their lips, but their hearts are far from me." Jesus says furthermore, "You disregard God's commandment but cling to human tradition. Nothing that enters one from outside can defile that person; but the things that come out from within are what defile."

Maintaining integrity is a lifelong project. Our external behavior must flow from internal conviction and life if we are to be authentic. Practices that flow only from habit, tradition or law—that is, external criteria—destroy integrity.

Suggestions for Prayer

1. Reflect on one or more of the following questions:
   • Do you believe that external religious practice without internal conviction is worthless?

- Why would the Pharisees and scribes want Jesus and his disciples to "follow the tradition of the elders"?
- What are some of the things that come out of people that makes them unclean?
2. In your imagination, place yourself in a large church. Jesus comes to the pulpit. He says, "You people honor me only with your lips, but your hearts are far from me. In vain do you worship me, teaching as doctrines human precepts." What is the people's reaction? What is your reaction?
3. Pray the responsorial psalm as your evening prayer this week.

Suggestion for Journal Keeping

Record in your journal some incident in your experience where you truly lacked integrity. Your internal self was miles from your external expression. How did you feel during that time? What did your friends say? What impact did you make?

Michael J. Koch

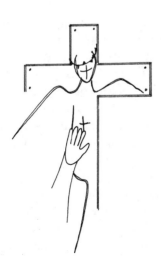

Twenty-second Sunday of the Year [C]

READING I	Sir 3:17–18, 20, 28–29
Responsorial Psalm	Ps 68:4–5, 6–7, 10–11
READING II	Heb 12:18–19, 22–24a
GOSPEL	Lk 14:1, 7–14

Reflection on the Readings

Humility is often misunderstood. Some people believe that to be humble is to put oneself down, to think less of oneself, denying one's giftedness. In the first reading from Sirach, the father advises the son to conduct his affairs with humility, not thinking of himself as greater or less than others. Rather, the better way is to stand in a balance, acknowledging oneself with honesty and as an equal to others. To do so is to appreciate the gift of life from God.

When attending a sabbath meal and seeing everyone trying to get the seats of honor, Jesus told those who were gathered not to attempt to sit in the place of honor. After all, the host could ask them to move when someone with greater dignity arrives. Then, in shame, one would have to take a lower place at the table. It is better to be exalted by the host than to exalt oneself.

Jesus goes on to admonish his host about his invited guests. It is not enough to invite only one's friends; rather the lame, the blind, the poor, those rejected by the society of Jesus' time, should be invited.

The questions of where one is to sit and who is to attend the meal are about the feast of the kingdom of God. The good news is that those who do not think themselves worthy will be welcomed at the feast and the lowly will be exalted. The beggars, the crippled, the lame, the blind, will all be cared for and enjoy God's salvation. For in God's eyes all are equal.

Suggestions for Prayer

1. As a child what was your understanding of humility? How has that understanding changed for you? Listen again to the words of the first reading, silently reflecting on their meaning for your life.
2. Prayerfully reread the psalm and reflect on its significance in your life.
3. Reflect on your own attitude toward the poor, the homeless, the jobless, the illiterate, different races. How does the Gospel enlighten your understanding of God's presence in them? In your imagination, see Jesus come to you and invite you to meet these people. Listen to them speak to you and hear your response.

Suggestion for Journal Keeping

Write in your journal your experiences of being invited to come and to know Jesus. Who are the people that have invited you to come to know you are welcomed and loved by God? Write a letter to God expressing your feelings about this journey toward God and about the people who have invited you onto this road, giving thanks for them in your life.

Kathleen Brown

Twenty-third Sunday of the Year [A]

READING I	Ez 33:7–9
Responsorial Psalm	Ps 95:1–2, 6–7, 8–9
READING II	Rom 13:8–10
GOSPEL	Mt 18:15–20

Reflection on the Readings

What do we do when someone wrongs us? How do we respond? Writing to the Romans, Paul reminds us that the greatest commandment is to love our neighbors as ourselves. Our response should come out of love.

The response outlined in today's Gospel is different from our usual response. Our response to being wronged is often enough to complain to someone else about our hurt feelings (anger, or whatever). The Gospel response calls for a certain amount of courage and is motivated by love.

The first reading also touches on the responsibility we have to correct our brothers and sisters. It is not a responsibility to be taken lightly. What is at stake is important—the health of the individual and of the community.

What if someone does not respond? The Gospel outlines the steps to take, and the final resort is to treat the person as a Gentile or tax collector. To the first Christians, coming from Jewish origins, Gentiles and tax collectors were outcasts. But if we look again to Paul's letter, we find that they too should be treated with love. Love does not mean accepting everything a person does. It does mean accepting the person.

Suggestions for Prayer

1. Remember the last time someone hurt you. What happened? Have you forgiven the person? Pray for him or her.
2. Reread the second reading. Do you love yourself? Do you love your neighbors? Ask God for forgiveness for when you have not.
3. Read the last part of the Gospel. Gather together with one or two other people and pray for what you need. Remember that Christ will be present with you.

Suggestion for Journal Keeping

Write about a time that you tried to correct another person. What happened? Were you motivated by love? Did the person respond? How were things between you later?

Michael P. Enright

Twenty-third Sunday of the Year [B]

READING I	*Is 35:4–7a*
Responsorial Psalm	*Ps 146:7, 8–9, 9–10*
READING II	*Jas 2:1–5*
GOSPEL	*Mk 7:31–37*

Reflection on the Readings

Deafness is a serious handicap. Sooner or later, each one of us meets up with a deaf person. Communication with such a person is very difficult and limited. To save embarrassment, people often just walk away from the deaf person. Being a deaf person can be very lonely. While deaf people cannot hear what others are saying, they also cannot speak well because when you cannot hear correctly, you cannot speak correctly.

In today's Gospel, the compassionate Jesus is met by a deaf man who has an impediment in his speech. The deaf man's friends ask Jesus to lay his hands on him and cure him. Jesus takes the man aside and in private cures him to save him embarrassment. Jesus has a sacramental style in his healing. He uses words, materials and actions. He says, "Ephphatha," which means "Be opened." Ephphatha was retained to emphasize Jesus' mysterious power. He uses spittle. In those days, spittle was believed to have a curative quality. His actions included looking up to heaven and touching the man's ears and tongue. Looking up to heaven implies that healing comes from God. Once the deaf man could hear clearly, he could also speak clearly.

Working with and caring for handicapped persons can help us to learn understanding, compassion and patience. As Jesus cured the physically deaf, so he can also cure the spiritually deaf. Only after we hear the Spirit clearly in our lives can we proclaim the good news of Jesus clearly and emphatically.

Suggestions for Prayer

1. Reflect on one or more of the following questions:
   - Why did Jesus use words, materials and actions to cure the deaf man?
   - Why did Jesus look up to heaven when he prayed for the cure of the deaf man?
   - Why did the deaf man speak clearly after he had been healed from his deafness?
2. In your imagination, see yourself as a deaf person who cannot speak well. Jesus puts his finger in your ears and touches your tongue

with spittle. He says, "Be opened." Describe your new freedom.

3. Pray the responsorial psalm as your evening prayer this week.

Suggestion for Journal Keeping

Describe your journey from spiritual deafness to clearly hearing the word of God. What change has this brought into your life? Describe your journey from spiritual dumbness to joyfully proclaiming God's word. Has this healing made you more mission-conscious?

Michael J. Koch

Twenty-third Sunday of the Year [C]

READING I	*Wis 9:13–18b*
Responsorial Psalm	*Ps 90:3–4, 5–6, 12–13, 14–17*
READING II	*Phlm 9–10, 12–17*
GOSPEL	*Lk 14:25–33*

Reflection on the Readings

Although the first reading stresses the importance of wisdom, it also reminds us that ultimately the secrets of life will elude us. For all of our human wisdom, we cannot understand the ways of God. Wisdom alone knows the mind of God.

In the Gospel, Jesus again speaks about what is necessary to be his disciple. His sayings about building a tower or going into battle emphasize the need for wisdom. Before we do anything in life, we need to know what may be required of us. This is wisdom. Before we decide to be a disciple of Jesus, we need to know that it will involve the cross.

In the New Testament, Jesus is revealed as the wisdom of God. Though we attempt to figure out life, it will continue to elude us. The path that leads to wisdom for us is the path that follows Jesus. But to follow Jesus we must take up the cross, letting go of ourselves and our desire to possess, receiving life with all its mystery as a gift.

Suggestions for Prayer

1. Popular culture furnishes us with many so-called words of wisdom: "Go for the gusto in life," "I did it my way," etc. What are some words of wisdom you have lived by? How do these sayings relate to the Gospel?

2. Imagine yourself walking down a path with Jesus. Tell him what it means for you in your life to take up your cross and follow him. Listen as Jesus responds to you.

Suggestion for Journal Keeping

Discipleship calls us to refocus our lives and our thoughts on Jesus and the Gospel continually. Beginning with your childhood, write a letter to Jesus describing what it has meant for you to be his disciple in the various stages of your life. Then reflect upon how you see your life as his disciple today.

Kathleen Brown

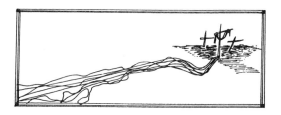

Twenty-fourth Sunday of the Year [A]

READING I	Sir 27:30—28:9
Responsorial Psalm	Ps 103:1–2, 3–4, 9–10, 11–12
READING II	Rom 14:7–9
GOSPEL	Mt 18:21–35

Reflection on the Readings

This week's readings demonstrate the undeniable connection between God's life and our life. Sometimes we experience our relationship with God and we experience our relationship with people, and we view them as two separate relationships, in two separate compartments. Have you ever had a conversation in which someone says, "What Jesus would have done is. . . ." And then someone else chimes in, "Well, Jesus is God. He's not me. I can't do that. I have to live in the real world."

The Scripture readings today tell us that our world and God's world are the same. God the Father throughout history, and ultimately in the person of Jesus, offers us forgiveness. That wonderful, saving reality from "above" only has meaning, only has power, in the ways in which we forgive each other. There is no relationship to God that is lived out apart from our relationship to each other. An abstract love of God, which does not manifest itself in love of neighbor, simply does not exist. An often-quoted Peanuts cartoon sums this up when Linus shouts at Lucy, "I love mankind. It's people I can't stand."

The author of the Book of Sirach bluntly states the theme of this week's readings, "Could anyone nourish anger against another and expect healing from the LORD?" Jesus is equally clear, "Should you not have had pity on your fellow servant, as I had pity on you?" God forgives us that we might live life with the security and generosity that allows us to forgive each other and thereby respond in truth to the gift of God's love. The cycle is complete. As St. Paul writes, "Whether we live or die, we are the Lord's."

Suggestions for Prayer

1. Reflect on one or more of the following questions:
   - Have you ever been forgiven? How did you feel? How did it affect your life?
   - Did you ever forgive another? Could you imagine Jesus doing the same?
   - Have you ever denied forgiveness to another? How did it make you feel? What can you do with those feelings?

2. Is there any past event in your life from which you still feel guilt? If so, imagine yourself in a room with Jesus. Sit quietly for a while with him. Then tell him of the event. In your imagination look into his eyes. What emotion are they expressing? Listen. What does Jesus say to you?

3. Go to a quiet place with a copy of today's Gospel reading from Matthew. Read the story but imagine you are standing next to Peter when Peter asks Jesus his question. Stay with him and imagine you are there as Jesus answers.

Suggestion for Journal Keeping

Describe an event in your life in which you need forgiveness, and an event in which someone needs your forgiveness. At the end write the refrain of today's psalm: "The Lord is kind and merciful, slow to anger and rich in compassion."

Douglas Fisher

Twenty-fourth Sunday of the Year [B]

READING I	*Is 50:5–9a*
Responsorial Psalm	*Ps 116:1–2, 3–4, 5–6, 8–9*
READING II	*Jas 2:14–18*
GOSPEL	*Mk 8:27–35*

Reflection on the Readings

Rejoice! Today Peter, spokesman of the disciples, recognizes who Jesus is—the Messiah! Immediately Peter and the other disciples are challenged to rethink their definition of "Messiah." Jesus is not a military or political savior. He is a suffering, dying and rising Messiah.

What Jesus said was not popular then. Peter tried to get him to tone it down. It has not become any more popular over time. But it is the call of discipleship.

Jesus repeats, even more clearly, to the disciples and the crowd: there is a cost in being a follower. One must be willing to lose oneself and go where Jesus leads—even if that means changing perceptions and beliefs, or suffering injustice, or loss of comforts and complacency.

The prophet Isaiah speaks of the need for open ears, to hear what Jesus is saying and asking. Christians see in Isaiah's words a prediction of what will happen to Jesus. He closes with a prayer that could be said by the suffering Jesus or any persecuted follower of Christ.

James' letter seems to turn the table and puts us in the place of the fortunate watching the unfortunate pass by. When we are in that position, it is our call to let go of our comforts and reach out to the other.

Suggestions for Prayer

1. Recall a time when you felt persecuted unjustly. What emotions, fears and anxieties were involved? Read Psalm 116 and reflect on the promises of freedom from that memory and those hurts.
2. Reflect on the following questions:
   - Who do you say Jesus is?
   - Who is Jesus telling you he is?
   - Are there any conflicts between your answers to these questions?
   - How can you resolve or reconcile the conflicts?
3. Imagine walking along a trail in the snow-covered woods. Jesus is immediately ahead of you and you are walking in his footsteps in the snow. After a while you and he sit down on a bench and you tell him what it felt like to follow in his steps.

Suggestion for Journal Keeping

What are the ways you could provide clothing, food, warmth, shelter or other necessities to someone in need? What are your obstacles to doing such and how can they be overcome?

Kathleen M. Henry

Twenty-fourth Sunday of the Year [C]

READING I	*Ex 32:7–11, 13–14*
Responsorial Psalm	*Ps 51:3–4, 12–13, 17, 19*
READING II	*1 Tm 1:12–17*
GOSPEL	*Lk 15:1–32 or 15:1–10*

Reflection on the Readings

Today's Gospel contains three parables that speak to us of God's love and mercy. Most especially these stories remind us that no matter how far off the chosen path we may stray, God will be waiting and welcoming us. In the Exodus reading the Israelites have built an altar of gold and brought animals to burn as sacrifice. They have turned their backs on the Lord who brought them out of Egypt. Moses pleads on behalf of his people and God relents, keeping his promise to Abraham, Isaac and Jacob. Again, we are reminded that it is in our sinfulness that God comes to us. Like the son who returned to his loving father, we too can celebrate with the Lord out of our weakness. For we walk our closest walk with him when we acknowledge our helplessness and utter dependence on God, our Father.

The Church offers us its welcoming arms, too, through the sacraments of baptism and reconciliation. Celebrating these sacraments is encountering the loving Father as he welcomes us or calls us back to the family of believers. But, like the son, we must acknowledge our sin, turn away, and return to the Father. How often we fail to do this, telling ourselves, "The sin is too great," or "Next time I'll deal with this." We doubt the unlimited mercy of God, and deny the need to have his help in getting back "on track."

Suggestions for Prayer

1. Remember in prayer those individuals "who are lost." Pray that you may be used as the Lord's instrument in helping to bring them home. Use the responsorial psalm as you pray.
2. Pray that this day you may be especially aware of your utter dependence on the Father. Use 2 Corinthians 3:4–5 as you pray.

3. The Lord rejoices over the sinner who is repentant. Rejoice and give thanks with the Lord, remembering that it is in our sinfulness that we are especially loved. Psalm 103:1–5 might be helpful.

Suggestion for Journal Keeping

All of these parables remind us of our importance to God. He loves us as if we were the only person on earth. Write your feelings concerning that. How do you respond to this kind of love and mercy?

Khris S. Ford

Twenty-fifth Sunday of the Year [A]

READING I — *Is 55:6–9*

Responsorial Psalm — *Ps 145:2–3, 8–9, 17–18*

READING II — *Phil 1:20c–24, 27a*

GOSPEL — *Mt 20:1–16a*

Reflection on the Readings

Today's Gospel offers us a powerful insight into the logic of God. We hear Jesus tell his disciples a parable in which people come to work at all different hours of the day but all are paid the same in the end. Any executive would say this is not a good way to run a vineyard. A person should be paid according to the hours worked. But God is not constrained by our logic. God cannot be locked into the way we do things. God may choose to be exceedingly generous—at times and in places we may never have predicted.

The reading from Isaiah adds another dimension to this theme. "Seek the LORD while he may be found, call him while he is near," says the prophet. Where may the Lord be found? Perhaps we think of a church, of quiet mountaintops, or of holy people. But the prophet refuses to let us confine God to the places we expect to find him. God could be anywhere because God's thoughts are not our thoughts and God's ways are not our ways. Seek God where he may be found and that may be in very unlikely places, circumstances and people. What will God be like when we find him? Isaiah tells us: "Our God is generous and forgiving."

Suggestions for Prayer
1. Reflect on one or more of the following questions:
   • Where do you expect to find the presence of God?
   • Have you ever experienced generosity from an unexpected source?
   • What does it mean that God's ways are not our ways? Does that make you feel insecure or hopeful?
2. Imagine yourself there with the disciples when Jesus told this parable. What are your thoughts and feelings? What do you feel when Jesus says, "Thus the last will be first and the first will be last."
3. Read the responsorial psalm slowly to yourself. Substitute "me" for "all" so that you are saying, "The Lord is near to me when I call him."

Suggestion for Journal Keeping
Describe a time in your life when you were depressed, lonely or afraid. How did you come through that time? Could the Lord have been present in the small events, in the people, and in your own heart as you passed through that time?

Douglas Fisher

Twenty-fifth Sunday of the Year [B]

READING I	*Wis 2:12, 17–20*
Responsorial Psalm	*Ps 54:3–4, 5, 6–8*
READING II	*Jas 3:16—4:3*
GOSPEL	*Mk 9:30–37*

Reflection on the Readings
The wisdom necessary to follow Jesus is not the world's. This is an essential lesson any disciple must learn. Jesus is not looking for self-important people or those who strive to be on top at the expense of others. To follow Jesus means to be a servant of others. Being a disciple means welcoming and honoring children, the lowly and unprotected. It means changing our priorities, standards and goals from the world's to Jesus'.

James expounds on the fruits of wisdom that come from God. He contrasts these qualities with those that do not characterize a follower of Jesus and warns of the dangers and consequences of such conduct.

The Book of Wisdom, speaking from the wicked's perspective, gives insight into what Jesus and James are saying. The wicked cannot stand the wise. The just one's ways, by being in conflict with the wicked, reproach and charge them. The gentleness and patience of the wise upset the wicked, who choose hostile and ugly ways to retaliate.

Jesus provides us with a wonderful reassurance and promise: when we welcome the lowly, the outcast, the unclean of our society, we welcome Jesus into our life. And, in welcoming Jesus, God, Father, Son and Spirit, comes to dwell in us.

Suggestions for Prayer

1. Read Psalm 54 and ask yourself these questions:
   - Where have I been confronted or upset by injustice today?
   - Where can I see God's help and sustaining power in the situation?
   - How can I thank and praise God in the situation?
2. Imagine yourself among the disciples when Jesus said that the Son of Man is going to die and then rise in three days. What questions are going through your mind? What questions do you overhear the disciples asking among themselves? Which of the questions would you be willing to ask Jesus?
3. You are the little child Jesus put his arms around. Feel Jesus' arms around you. What parts of yourself are you glad Jesus is embracing? What parts of yourself are you having difficulty letting Jesus embrace?

Suggestion for Journal Keeping

Where are origins of conflict and dispute among your family and close friends? What inner cravings do you have that are in conflict with your body, mind, spirit or emotions? What gifts and riches has our nation received and squandered? As a result of reflecting on today's readings, what can you do in any of the situations you have just outlined?

Kathleen M. Henry

Twenty-fifth Sunday of the Year [C]

READING I	Am 8:4–7
Responsorial Psalm	Ps 113:1–2, 4–6, 7–8
READING II	1 Tm 2:1–8
GOSPEL	Lk 16:1–13 or 16:10–13

Reflection on the Readings

The "good news" in today's readings may strike us as confusing. Is Jesus condoning the shrewd acts of the manager? Is he asking us to act in this way? The confusion may cause us to reflect on our material possessions and our use of them to examine our skills as managers of these gifts. It is in this way that our puzzlement may indeed become "good news." Today we are challenged to look at our management skills, to examine those people and/or things that we have authority over. What kinds of stewards are we? The Gospel calls us to use our gifts of intelligence and perception. It is our privilege and duty to exercise these gifts by keeping ourselves well informed in matters of the world and of our faith. We are promised that we shall be welcomed into an eternal dwelling if we use our gifts to build friendship and to give life in our world.

The reading from Amos calls us to continue to look at our business dealings and all of our dealings with people. Are we honest in these relationships? Are we using our gifts to call forth the best in each situation? If our answer is a consistent "no" and we continue to worship and prepare for initiation into the midst of this kind of living, we scandalize the sacraments. For baptism, confirmation and the Eucharist call us to be more, to be Christ-like in all our doings. Our worship is not authentic if there is no intent to truly give "worth" to God in our life.

Suggestions for Prayer

1. Identify one area of your life where you are not exercising wise use of your gifts. What must you do to change this? What will this cost you? Pray for the courage and the strength to change.

2. Pray that Christ may truly be master of your life, asking for the grace to be honest with yourself and God. What must you do to make him more fully your master?

3. Name those people who have authority over you in various areas of your life. Pray that these individuals will be graced with true wisdom, be guided by God, and be willing to use their gifts for the betterment of the kingdom.

Suggestion for Journal Keeping

Make a list of your gifts (talents, material blessings, etc.). When you are finished take time to look over your list and become more aware of each one as a gift. Remember that these are gifts from God, unearned, undeserved, yet freely given. Write about your feelings when you reflect on this. Take time to respond by writing a prayer on thanksgiving.

Khris S. Ford

Twenty-sixth Sunday of the Year [A]

READING I	*Ez 18:25–28*
Responsorial Psalm	*Ps 25:4–5, 6–7, 8–9*
READING II	*Phil 2:1–11 or 2:1–5*
GOSPEL	*Mt 21:28–32*

Reflection on the Readings

In today's reading from Matthew's Gospel, we hear Jesus tell us of two sons. The one son says he will work for his father but does not. The second son refuses to work but ultimately does. The responses of the two sons reflect two different journeys in faith. Some people experience God's love and say they are going to share it with others, but they never do. Other people resist God's love. They say no to the presence of God in their life. But later they do lead loving lives. They overcome their initial resistance to God's call—and there lies growth, grace and greatness.

Jesus goes on to say that the least likely people, the prostitutes and tax collectors, enter heaven before those who are religious but do not love. This happens because these people need God's love and they know it. They want a Savior. They are open to God coming into their lives and changing them. Sometimes people are in love with being in love with God. They like the security of religion. They like the feeling of being certain they look good and neat. Jesus argues vehemently with people who want the "things" of religion—the ritual, the rules, the secure way of life—more than they want God. The sinners know they need God. And our

God, who needs to be needed because he created us for no other reason than to love us, escorts them into the kingdom of God.

Suggestions for Prayer

1. Reflect on one or more of the following questions:
   - Did you ever say yes to some good and worthy cause and then did not follow through? How did you feel?
   - Do you know anyone personally or in history who led a sinful life and then did something unselfish and loving?
   - Have you ever said no to God's invitation to love and worship him? What led you to consider saying yes?
2. Contact someone you know who works with the poor. Ask him or her what it is like. Ask him or her if it is easier to look for God there.
3. Take the reading from Paul's Letter to the Philippians and read it aloud to yourself. Read it again. What does it feel like to proclaim: "Jesus Christ is Lord"? What kind of Lord is he?

Suggestion for Journal Keeping

Write about a time when you really needed someone—a time you were poor, depressed or abandoned. Now think of that situation with Jesus present. What happens? Write your thoughts.

Douglas Fisher

Twenty-sixth Sunday of the Year [B]

READING I	Nm 11:25–29
Responsorial Psalm	Ps 19:8, 10, 12–13, 14
READING II	Jas 5:1–6
GOSPEL	Mk 9:38–43, 45, 47–48

Reflection on the Readings

God is not limited by our restrictions or shortsightedness. God moves where he wills, bestowing gifts for the good of all. God chooses whom he wills, with criteria frequently different from ours.

When Moses took some of the gift God gave him and passed it on, the elders who were meant to receive the spirit did so whether present in the tent or left behind in the camp. The power to expel demons in Jesus' name was bestowed on one, not of the disciples, who was using Jesus' name. God today has gifts to bestow. We should be vigilant in encouraging such outpourings of God's spirit.

Jesus provides us with guidelines for measuring the purity of our actions and motivations. No one who acts in Jesus' name can speak against Jesus at the same time. If we speak in his name, we can provide wisdom, comfort and healing to those around us.

Jesus warns us against false teachers, and personal failings. The consequences of leading others astray from Jesus' way or of wandering off ourselves are severe. James further expounds on the dangers of putting riches and possessions above God's ways and our fellow human beings.

Suggestions for Prayer

1. What talent would you like to develop that could be used to help others? Spend some time each day this week asking God to give you that gift.

2. If you were one of the elders upon whom Moses bestowed some of the spirit God gave him what would you do with it? How would you want to use the gift for others?

3. Think of some small and ordinary aspect or attribute you have, or a possession you own, or a way you act toward others that moves you or others away from God. How can you remove this from your life? Ask Jesus to help you change.

Suggestion for Journal Keeping

At the end of each day this week, write some small action you did or you received that represented you giving someone a drink of water because he or she belonged to Christ or where you received a drink of water from someone because you represented Christ to him or her.

Kathleen M. Henry

Twenty-sixth Sunday of the Year [C]

READING I	*Am 6:1a, 4–7*
Responsorial Psalm	*Ps 146:7, 8–9, 9–10*
READING II	*1 Tm 6:11–16*
GOSPEL	*Lk 16:19–31*

Reflection on the Readings

The message in today's readings is pointed and perhaps harsh. Lazarus and the rich man are the models of the "have-nots" and the "haves." Could this be a microcosm of what often happens between these two groups in our own society today? Coupled with this story is the reading from Amos that warns us of the attitude that says "we deserve" our blessings.

All we have and are is a gift from God. When we truly understand and believe that, then we can begin to live as one with all men and women. To recognize our complete giftedness is to know that without God we are nothing. In this "nothingness" we can identify with the poor, the sick, the victims of injustice—with all peoples.

As followers of Christ, we are called to recognize and live out a sense of "connectedness" with all humans. When we do this, we model Christ.

Suggestions for Prayer

1. Pray for those who are victims of injustice in our world. Try to identify groups or individuals within your own community. Pray that you may be an instrument of justice in your activities this day and ask the Lord to guide you to respond to those who are oppressed.

2. Reread the Gospel story. Put yourself in the place of Lazarus as he is carried to the door of the rich man to eat the scraps. Pray that you may be sensitive to such victims of injustice.

3. Remembering that all we are and have is a gift from God, focus on one or two of your blessings. Place them in your hands, symbolically. Reflect on them. Then offer them to the Lord's use. Let go of your possession of them.

Suggestion for Journal Keeping

Write about your initial reaction to this Gospel story?

With whom did you identify? Why? Then

write what it would be like to identify with the other character.

Khris S. Ford

Twenty-seventh Sunday of the Year [A]

READING I	*Is 5:1–7*
Responsorial Psalm	*Ps 80:9, 12, 13–14, 15–16, 19–20*
READING II	*Phil 4:6–9*
GOSPEL	*Mt 21:33–43*

Reflection on the Readings

One of the best and most interesting ways to teach is to tell a story. Jesus of Nazareth knew this and used his story-telling skills to challenge us to look at our lives in a new way. Jesus tells a story in today's Gospel that had a specific meaning in his time but still carries a powerful message to us today.

Jesus told the story of the vineyard to explain why he devotes time and energy to the poor and sinners. The chief priests of Judaism, like the tenants in the story, have rejected God's messenger. So Jesus turns to those who will bear fruit, and it is the unlikely sinners who accept the Gospel.

What does this parable have to say to us today? It seems that religious people can be tempted with that same attitude that characterized chief priests and elders: complacency in the underlying belief that we are God's chosen people, that we have the truth, that we have our salvation guaranteed. This complacency shows itself in narrow-mindedness, lack of creativity, lack of passion, and smug self-assurance. The "chosen people" of Jesus' era did not have a monopoly on those qualities. And, as the parable makes clear, if we do not choose to respond, God will find those who will.

Suggestions for Prayer

1. Reflect on one or more of the following questions:
   - Have you ever heard a story, whether from another person, from a book, from a movie, from the news that really moved you? What was that story?
   - Were you ever involved in religion before and then consequently became smug and complacent? How can that be avoided?
   - Why did Jesus spend so much time reaching out to the poor? What is your attitude to the poor?
2. Imagine that Jesus has just had an argument with a smug, complacent religious person. Now he sees you. What does he say?
3. Try to envision what your life might be like for the next few days. Imagine Jesus with you, present as you meet every person, every situation.

Suggestion for Journal Keeping

Think of a time when you might have been narrow-minded and set in your ways. In writing, describe that time. Describe yourself now.

Douglas Fisher

Twenty-seventh Sunday of the Year [B]

READING I	*Gn 2:18–24*
Responsorial Psalm	*Ps 128:1–2, 3, 4–5, 6*
READING II	*Heb 2:9–11*
GOSPEL	*Mk 10:2–16 or 10:2–12*

Reflection on the Readings

Our call from God is a lifelong one, toward perfection. In Genesis, God was creating a new and pure world, a world before the fall, a world of harmony and love. Jesus, by his coming, recalls that perfection created by God. He returns to the indissolubility of marriage and uses children as an example of purity of heart and soul.

Today we still live in an imperfect time. We still have much to learn. But Jesus has come to teach us and set us free, if we are willing. All were welcome around Jesus. Jesus spoke to Pharisees and children alike, he ate with sinners and leaders, he invited rich and poor, men and women to gather around him, he touched the unclean and healed the sick.

Paul speaks further of what Jesus willingly did to begin the reconciliation and return to a time of harmony. Jesus became less than who he was, and by doing so raised us up. Jesus suffered and died for us so that we could live a new life and a new hope.

We must be willing to follow the example of Jesus. People and groups we consider less than ourselves are our equals before God. They are our brothers and sisters. We are called to embrace and bless them as Jesus did.

Suggestions for Prayer

1. We all know people who have been through a divorce. Bring one such person and his or her hurts and worries before Jesus. Tell Jesus your concerns about him or her and ask Jesus to take care of that person. Imagine the person being embraced and blessed by Jesus. Ask Jesus if there is anything he wants you to do for the person.
2. You are the parent who is bringing a child to Jesus. You are scolded by the disciples and you become discouraged. Just then, Jesus invites your child forward and blesses your child. After you return home, you notice differences in your child and yourself. What will you tell Jesus the next time you see him?
3. Take a walk in nature (woods, park, beach, lakeside, etc.). Thank God for each act of creation that comes to mind.

Suggestion for Journal Keeping

Take a group of people you have difficulty believing are your equal (for example: homeless, unemployed, women, homosexuals). List all the reasons why you think or know Jesus loves them. Reread the second reading from Hebrews and see if you can add any more reasons to your list.

Kathleen M. Henry

Twenty-seventh Sunday of the Year [C]

READING I	*Hb 1:2–3; 2:2–4*
Responsorial Psalm	*Ps 95:1–2, 6–7, 8–9*
READING II	*2 Tm 1:6–8, 13–14*
GOSPEL	*Lk 17:5–10*

Reflection on the Readings

The essential ideas in today's Gospel might be "faith" and "duty." At first reading, it may seem that the two have little connection. Jesus responds to the apostles' desire for greater faith by telling them two stories. One story illustrates the power of faith and the other tells us to regard our Christian service as duty, never expecting reward or recognition.

One link between these two stories may be found if we ponder the faith-filled life of someone we know who serves God diligently. Faith grows and is nurtured by service to others. In our service we recognize our helplessness and powerlessness. Thus we rely on God much more and our faith in turn is strengthened. Secondly, one who is truly alive in faith desires to serve in response to this great gift. Just as we have been touched by God, we desire others to experience this new life. We expect no reward and realize that it is a privilege to serve God.

This is what Paul calls Timothy to do in the second reading. As we serve the Lord and prepare for the sacraments of initiation, the Spirit is at work in us, making us "strong, loving, and self-controlled."

Suggestions for Prayer

1. Pray for an increase in your faith. Recognize that as you grow in faith, you may be called to further action. Using the refrain to the responsorial psalm, pray that you will say yes to the Lord.
2. Give thanks for the privilege of serving the Lord. Identify one or two times when you may have been blessed in your service to others. Reflect on the second reading in light of this experience.
3. Faith is a gift. Spend a few moments identifying individuals who may have been "instruments" in your faith growth. Pray for

these people, offering thanks for their faith, asking for courage to be used in this manner.

Suggestion for Journal Keeping

The Gospel uses the phrase "unprofitable servants." How do you feel when you hear that phrase? In what way is it true of you? Why is it only a partial description of you?

Khris S. Ford

Twenty-eighth Sunday of the Year [A]

READING I	*Is 25:6–10a*
Responsorial Psalm	*Ps 23:1–3a, 3b–4, 5, 6*
READING II	*Phil 4:12–14, 19–20*
GOSPEL	*Mt 22:1–14 or 22:1–10*

Reflection on the Readings

What is heaven like? The human mind and imagination have long sought the answer to the question. Children often imagine the answer in terms of playing forever without the imposition of school and homework. The elderly may see it as a time to be reunited with loved ones. Artists and saints may think of mystical union with God. The poor and oppressed hope for a better life with justice, free from suffering. Of course, no one knows exactly what heaven will be like, but that has never stopped us from using our own experience to try to imagine it.

The first reading today from the Book of Isaiah envisions a heavenly banquet in which all sin and suffering will be overcome. Jesus uses this image to talk about his favorite topic: the reign of God. The coming of the reign of God was the central message of Jesus. Jesus was not primarily a teacher of ethics but a person of faith with a distinctly religious perspective. His goal was not simply to get people to act differently, but to change their entire view of life and life's meaning. At the heart of Jesus' message of the kingdom of God was his insistence that the kingdom had already begun. A new way of life reflecting that final banquet was possible now if men and women would turn their hearts to God.

The readings today offer us a vision of heaven as a banquet and feast. The Gospel parable shows us the urgency of the vision. Heaven is not wishful thinking. God's reign has broken through now.

In a society where there is a great distinction between the haves and the have-nots, the image of the heavenly banquet might glare at us like an indictment. All are welcome in the kingdom. The kingdom cannot be confined to our own private vision, but is a life in love with God and neighbor.

Suggestions for Prayer

1. Reflect on one or more of the following questions:
   - How do you envision heaven? What will make it heavenly?
   - Jesus envisions the kingdom as a banquet. What are your family meals like? Are they a sign of community and love? How could you make them that way?
   - How do you feel about the idea of the kingdom beginning now? Is that true in your experience, or is the kingdom for you something in the future?
2. Imagine yourself walking along some back road. Suddenly Jesus appears and invites you to a banquet with him. How do you feel? What do you say to him?
3. Stay with that same scene from suggestion #2. As you walk along with Jesus you come across someone you consider a "bad" person. Jesus invites that person as well. What do you feel about this person? What do you feel toward Jesus?

Suggestion for Journal Keeping

Describe a time you were rejected by someone or some organization. Now imagine Jesus inviting you to the kingdom of God. Write what you feel and what you say to Jesus.

Douglas Fisher

Twenty-eighth Sunday of the Year [B]

READING I	*Wis 7:7–11*
Responsorial Psalm	*Ps 90:12–13, 14–15, 16–17*
READING II	*Heb 4:12–13*
GOSPEL	*Mk 10:17–30 or 10:17–27*

Reflection on the Readings

When Jesus looked at the young man, he spoke only a few words. Those words clearly affected the young man with the power of God's word as described in Hebrews. They penetrated and laid bare the difficulty the man was having with Jesus' call. And the young man went away.

The disciples became very concerned with the apparent impossibility of salvation. Jesus' response was twofold. The invitation is gift, surrounded by love. When Jesus spoke to the young man, Jesus looked at him with love. The call of God's love is strong; once accepted, it becomes so strong that one is willing to give up even family to follow Jesus and the Gospel.

The first reading from Wisdom confirms the pull of God. The author clearly prefers God's wisdom to any earthly possession or physical reality.

But this gift is a two-edged sword. The way of Jesus Christ cuts through the world's ways. And the world objects with violence, ridicule and derision. Jesus, however, promises much good and the greatest gift of all, everlasting life, to those who follow.

Suggestions for Prayer

1. What is the one more thing Jesus is asking of you at this moment in time? Ask for Jesus' help so that it will not become an impossible stumbling block.
2. Pray Psalm 90 daily this week while asking yourself these questions:
   - How have I recognized God's majesty today?
   - How have I felt apart from God today?
   - How have I rejoiced at God's graciousness toward me today?
3. Think of an area in your life where it would help if you had wisdom. Are you willing to pray and plead for the spirit of wisdom? Tell God what the gift would mean to you.

Suggestion for Journal Keeping

Think of a situation where you felt totally overwhelmed and confounded. Write about how it felt. Describe how you felt when the solution was discovered. What assistance does this recalling give you in reflecting on the Gospel?

Kathleen M. Henry

Twenty-eighth Sunday of the Year [C]

READING I	*2 Kgs 5:14–17*
Responsorial Psalm	*Ps 98:1, 2–3, 3–4*
READING II	*2 Tm 2:8–13*
GOSPEL	*Lk 17:11–19*

Reflection on the Readings

Naaman is healed by faith, and comes to profess his belief in the one, true God. The leper is healed through faith and returns to give thanks and to praise God. Both are healed and both deepen in faith as they proclaim their healing and give praise to the source of healing. Though we probably have not experienced such miraculous physical healing, we have experienced God's healing touch in our lives. If we respond in gratitude and praise, we are doubly blessed. Ten lepers came upon Jesus. All of them had enough faith to ask for healing and to follow Jesus' directions. Upon arrival all ten were cured of their leprosy. Yet only one returned to Jesus to give praise and thanksgiving. Only one recognized the true source of the healing, and was thus more fully healed. Only one both was healed and received the gift of salvation.

How often we take for granted the blessings we have been given! It's not so much that we aren't thankful. We just forget to stop and express our gratitude, to recognize and praise the source of all goodness.

Suggestions for Prayer

1. Pray a special prayer of thanksgiving for the gift of life itself. As you pray, be particularly

aware of your heartbeat, a powerful sign of life within us. Take a few moments just to be present to God, the source of that life.

2. As Naaman plunged into the Jordan, he was healed. As you prepare for your own baptismal bath, pray that the Lord may help you to discern what healing you should seek.

3. Pray the responsorial psalm. Read it slowly and deliberately, allowing more time for those words and phrases that seem to express your feelings.

Suggestion for Journal Keeping

Recall a time when you were healed from some sickness, broken relationship, or even a weakened trust in God. Describe the situation, the healing, your response, and your relationship to God afterward. How was your faith deepened as you acknowledged your healing?

Khris S. Ford

Twenty-ninth Sunday of the Year   [A]

READING I	*Is 45:1, 4–6*
Responsorial Psalm	*Ps 96:1, 3, 4–5, 7–8, 9–10*
READING II	*1 Thes 1:1–5b*
GOSPEL	*Mt 22:15–21*

Reflection on the Readings

Jesus' statement in this week's Gospel has been quoted out of context numerous times. "Repay to Caesar what belongs to Caesar and to God what belongs to God." Let's look at this quote in the context of the times and then apply it in its truth to our lives.

The Herodian sympathizers supported the puppet ruler of Israel, Herod Antipas. They would have supported the tax because Herod's power was totally dependent on Rome. The Pharisees, however, being the most devout of all Jews, would have opposed the tax and Roman rule, although they would not have gone as far as the Zealots (anti-Roman insurrectionists) who would have refused to pay the tax. If Jesus says payment is licit, he may be portrayed as a Roman sympathizer. If he says that payment to Rome is not to be obeyed, he is then a subversive.

Jesus refuses to be trapped by the question. By answering as he does, he demonstrates the relative value of all commitments in comparison to the commitment to love God. Everything else will find its meaning in relation to that. Jesus is not giving a definitive teaching on taxes or government. He is saying that love of one's country and allegiance to its leaders have a value, but a relative one. The value of nationalism easily becomes a vice when it is understood in the tribal sense of "us" against "them." Unthinking, uncritical patriotism is simply a form of idolatry. Perhaps St. Thomas More captured the meaning of Jesus' saying in his own life. A man who deeply loved his country, he was convicted of treason for his refusal to acknowledge the king as the supreme head of the Church in England. His words were: "I am the king's good servant, but God's first."

Suggestions for Prayer

1. Reflect on one or more of the following questions:
   • In what ways is being an American an obstacle to being Christian? How is it an aid?

- Can you imagine taking a public stance against a government policy because of your faith?
- In what ways do you think the Church should be involved in the realm of political decision-making?

2. Imagine yourself in the crowd that day when Jesus was confronted by the Pharisees. You hear what he has to say. You go up to him afterward and ask him further questions. What do you ask?
3. Think about an upcoming election. How would a person of faith vote? How will you vote?

Suggestion for Journal Keeping

Describe a time when you were torn as to how to vote. How did you decide? What values were brought into the decision? Are any of these values Christian values?

Douglas Fisher

Twenty-ninth Sunday of the Year [B]

READING I	*Is 53:10–11*
Responsorial Psalm	*Ps 33:4–5, 18–19, 20, 22*
READING II	*Heb 4:14–16*
GOSPEL	*Mk 10:35–45 or 10:42–45*

Reflection on the Readings

Isaiah, the Old Testament prophet, spoke about the Suffering Servant. Isaiah foretold that the Servant would give his life as an offering for our sins. As Christians, we understand that Jesus is the Suffering Servant. The will of God, that we be reconciled to him, is accomplished in Jesus.

Jesus invites us to come and follow him. And, just as James and John did, we shall experience what it means to follow Jesus. We will daily discover opportunities to give our life for others. And we shall feel pain.

Paul offers us hope for such occasions. Jesus sympathizes with our weaknesses. He understands temptation and difficulties. Jesus experienced such things. By living among us Jesus has made God approachable. We can ask for and receive mercy and favor and help in times of need.

But we must not become puffed up and proud because God has chosen us. Rather, we must make it an opportunity to bring others to Jesus. Jesus becomes approachable to others when they see that we are different and do not act in worldly ways. When we practice humility, charity or love, when we serve those in need, when we comfort and stand with the downtrodden, we represent the approachable God who calls all.

Suggestions for Prayer

1. Read Psalm 33 at the end of the day and think of the ways that the psalm has come alive for you throughout the day.
2. Imagine Jesus handing you the cup to drink. What are your reservations about drinking from the cup? Are you willing to ask for Jesus' help in such times of need?
3. Talk with Jesus about the definition of *servant*. What is your definition? What do you hear Jesus offering as his definition? How do they differ? Are you willing to adopt Jesus' definition where it is different from yours?

Suggestion for Journal Keeping

Recall a time when you chose to be humble rather than exalting yourself or letting others honor you. What was the experience like? List the positive and negative feelings it raised. How would being humble be the same or different for Jesus?

Kathleen M. Henry

Twenty-ninth Sunday of the Year [C]

READING I	*Ez 17:8–13*
Responsorial Psalm	*Ps 121:1–2, 3–4, 5–6, 7–8*
READING II	*2 Tm 3:14—4:2*
GOSPEL	*Lk 18:1–8*

Reflection on the Readings

Surely if a dishonest judge would give in to the pleas of this persistent widow, our God will hear our persistent cries. Persistence paid off for the widow, and so will we be rewarded if we persist in our prayers to God. Like the widow, we are asked to stay strong in our faith, even when the going gets difficult. It is easy to persist in the good times, when life is smooth. But, what of our strong faith when we are persecuted or when we just don't feel the presence of God? The Gospel tells us that swift justice is due those who are persistent in calling upon the Lord.

In the second reading, Paul reminds Timothy of the sources of his faith—his family, his teachers and, most importantly, the Scriptures. It is this formation that strengthens Timothy for the task at hand, the preaching of the word. During this time of baptismal preparation, the Scriptures are an essential source to strengthen our faith so that we may be prepared for the tasks that lie ahead.

Suggestions for Prayer

1. Prayer is the work of the Spirit in us, not our own doing. Pray for the grace to be persistent in prayer, especially during those "desert" times.
2. Is there something or someone that you've given up on? Offer this to God again. Consciously pray with confidence in the Father.
3. If this is a particularly good time in your life, bask in the goodness and give thanks in prayer. In doing this, your faith is strengthened for a time when things are more difficult.

Suggestion for Journal Keeping

"But when the Son of Man comes, will he find faith on earth?" Look about you. Reflect on your life situation. What are some signs of faith that help to sustain you?

Khris S. Ford

Thirtieth Sunday of the Year [A]

READING I	*Ex 22:20–26*
Responsorial Psalm	*Ps 18:2–3, 3–4, 47, 51*
READING II	*1 Thes 1:5c–10*
GOSPEL	*Mt 22:34–40*

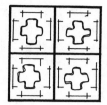

Reflection on the Readings

The key insight of this week's Gospel is Jesus' combination of two commandments as the central meaning of life. This insight, although not unique to Jesus, was one of the abiding principles of his life and teaching: love of God and love of one's neighbor form an inseparable unity. This is evident in not only what Jesus says, but also in how he acts. In Jesus, there is total openness and devotion to the Father. His relationship with the Father is the source of his life. Yet that relationship is not simply a private one. It flows out into the compassion and truth of his relationships with people.

In trying to describe the relationship between love of God and love of one's neighbor, spiritual writers sometimes use the phrases "vertical" (relationship with God) and "horizontal" (relationships with others). It seems that the key is to maintain a healthy and positive relationship between the two and to allow each to enrich the other. A one-sided vertical relationship degenerates into illusion and escapism from the challenges of love. A one-sided horizontal relationship loses sight of the ultimate goal and source of its loving. It collapses under the weight of becoming its own god and has no measure outside itself.

Perhaps there is one more aspect of this commandment that we are ignoring. The law says: Love your neighbor as yourself. It has become commonplace in religious education to say that Jesus is teaching that we must love ourselves as

well. In fact, he is simply assuming it as the condition for loving others. Jesus never explicitly talks about self-love. It is more of a modern concept. However, there is no doubt that Jesus was a champion of the healthy and proper love of oneself. For Jesus this fundamental self-love is very different from many of its contemporary narcissistic manifestations. A person's basic worth is not derived from anything less than God's unconditional love for all of his children and the dignity inherent to that status.

Suggestions for Prayer

1. Reflect on one or more of the following questions:
   - Do you see any aspects of narrow legalism in Christianity?
   - How can you enrich the "vertical" aspect of your spirituality?
   - How do you see the connection between the "vertical" and "horizontal" in your life?
   - How do you understand a healthy love of self?
2. Think of a circumstance in your life where you consistently feel bad about yourself. Imagine Jesus walking into this situation. What happens?
3. Have you ever tried to love someone at a time when you felt bad about yourself? What happened? Reflect on this question and then reread Matthew 22:34–40.

Suggestion for Journal Keeping

Describe a person you know who loves God but does not seem to love people. Describe a person who is generous and unselfish but is not religious. Which person do you identify with? What can you do to integrate the two?

Douglas Fisher

Thirtieth Sunday of the Year

[B]

READING I	*Jer 31:7–9*
Responsorial Psalm	*Ps 126:1–2, 2–3, 4–5, 6*
READING II	*Heb 5:1–6*
GOSPEL	*Mk 10:46–52*

Reflection on the Readings

The blind man is a model for approaching Jesus in faith. He was an active participant in his healing. He persisted in his attempts to attract Jesus' attention, even when others tried to discourage him. He told Jesus what he wanted; he was clear and specific. And he believed in Jesus and his power. The blind man's faith caused his healing.

By the man's willingness to approach Jesus, he revealed his faith in Jesus. That faith was then strengthened by the encounter with Jesus. Thereafter, he followed Jesus up the road.

Jesus met and responded to the man although he was blind. He approaches us even when we are blind. In our encounters with Jesus, we are given the opportunity to express our faith. Consequently, our relationship becomes stronger and it becomes easier to follow Jesus up the road.

Paul reassures us that we can have faith in Jesus. He is our high priest representative before God. Jesus speaks to God on our behalf from the perspective of one who has stood in our shoes. We have nothing to fear in approaching Jesus.

The prophet Jeremiah had foretold an age when God would deliver and gather his people, consoling and leading them. Jesus' coming has inaugurated that time. In Mark's Gospel we see that the blind and lame, women and children, lowly and sinners are welcomed by Jesus. No one is turned away.

Suggestions for Prayer

1. The reading from Jeremiah is a prophecy of comfort in times of distress, a promise of a better future. Think of an area in your life or relationships where you need to know that things will get better. Slowly read and reflect on the reading, savoring its promises.

2. Imagine Jesus as the high priest presenting you to God the Father and the Holy Spirit. Listen to the positive things Jesus says about you.

3. Recall when you were sitting by the roadside and you first decided to approach Jesus. What is it that attracted you to Jesus? Tell Jesus the things that made you decide to find out more about him and caused you to begin exploring the possibility of following him.

Suggestion for Journal Keeping

Write about an area in your life where you have come to realize that you are blind. Imagine Jesus approaching you and asking: "What do you want me to do for you?" Write the stumbling blocks to asking Jesus for sight in that area. Continue with this exercise until, when Jesus approaches and asks the question, you can ask for sight.

Kathleen M. Henry

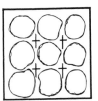

Thirtieth Sunday of the Year [C]

READING I	*Sir 35:12–14, 16–18*
Responsorial Psalm	*Ps 34:2–3, 17–18, 19, 23*
READING II	*2 Tm 4:6–8, 16–18*
GOSPEL	*Lk 18:9–14*

Reflection on the Readings

Today we are given some guidance in how we should pray. We are offered this guidance in the form of a story about two men who pray. One prayed with head held high, listing the many sacrifices he had made for the Lord, and separating himself from the sinners. The other, head and eyes bowed, acknowledged his sinfulness and begged God's mercy. We are told that the second man shall be exalted and the first shall be humbled. Our prayer is to be in humility, raising up God's name in praise, and recognizing our complete dependence on him.

Sirach affirms this in saying that the "prayer of the lowly pierces the clouds." In our lowliness we are joined with all people. We dare not stand in judgment of anyone. Paul too displays this attitude when he forgives those who have betrayed him. He learned how to depend on the Lord alone.

Suggestions for Prayer

1. Pray for the grace of humility. Look at one specific area of your life where you most need this grace.
2. Pray the words: "Jesus Christ, Son of God, Savior of the world, have mercy on me, a sinner." Repeat this several times, saying the words slowly. Emphasize a different word each time. Allow the words to soak into your being.
3. Pray that this day you will judge no man or woman, and that you will seek your identity only in Christ. Use Philippians 2:3–9.

Suggestion for Journal Keeping

With which person did you identify in the Gospel story?

Are you the tax collector or the Pharisee? Why?

Khris S. Ford

Thirty-first Sunday of the Year [A]

READING I	*Mal 1:14b—2:2b, 8–10*
Responsorial Psalm	*Ps 131:1, 2, 3*
READING II	*1 Thes 2:7b–9, 13*
GOSPEL	*Mt 23:1–12*

Reflection on the Readings

"Practice what you preach" is a line all of us have heard many times in many different contexts. In today's Gospel, Jesus addresses it to religious people. When we look at all four Gospels, we see that Jesus is continually frustrated and angered by people who put ornate religious rituals without making the love of God and neighbor part of their everyday living.

Jesus also says that people should not be called "rabbi," "teacher" or "father." The meaning of this passage is very important although the specifics need to be placed in context. The heart of Jesus' message here is that people in leadership positions should not think they are better than everyone else, or that they have the right to demand blind obedience from others. In addition, Jesus does not want people to follow leaders as cult-like figures. We have numerous examples of religious leaders abusing power in our own day. The actual calling of someone "father," "teacher" or "rabbi" is not at the heart of what Jesus is saying and can be interpreted differently in various cultures and historical settings.

We hear many people labeled "great" by our media, but Jesus has a narrow definition of the term. Greatness is determined by service. "The greatest among you must be your servant." Service is given by someone who is humble, that is, as we saw in last week's Gospel, someone who loves himself or herself and therefore can love another knowing that he or she has something wonderful to give.

Suggestions for Prayer

1. Reflect on one or more of the following questions:
   - Have you ever gone to a religious ceremony, knowing that the people attending were not living what they were saying? How did that make you feel?
   - Jesus says that you are great when you serve another. Is there a way open to you now where you could serve?
   - What is the true meaning of "humble"? Could you be a humble person?
2. Take a couple of the prayers from Sunday's liturgy of the word and meditate on them. How could you make them real in your daily living?
3. Think of people who serve others. What are their qualities? Do you think they are great?

Suggestion for Journal Keeping

Describe a time in your life when you were humble and then were exalted. How did it make you feel? How can a person live humbly and what do you believe it will result in?

Douglas Fisher

Thirty-first Sunday of the Year [B]

READING I	Dt 6:2–6
Responsorial Psalm	Ps 18:2–3, 3–4, 47, 51
READING II	Heb 7:23–28
GOSPEL	Mk 12:28b–34

Reflection on the Readings

Moses instructed the people to fear the Lord and to keep his laws so that they would prosper and receive the bounty of God's promises. They were to follow and love God above all else.

When Jesus was asked about the greatest commandment, he began with Moses' admonishment from Deuteronomy. Jesus then coupled it with a second directive whose basis can be found in Leviticus 19:18. Jesus, by story and example, expanded the definition of neighbor. He expands neighbor to include not just our family and friends, but also our enemies as well as those with whom we disagree and those we dislike. Jesus also commands us to love ourselves. Jesus loves us and wants us to love ourselves as we love God and neighbor.

Jesus, by refusing to stop with the first commandment and by joining the two directives, is saying that to follow him is not just to be in relationship with God. We need to also love ourselves and others. Salvation is not just between me and God but is lived out in community, with others and with myself.

Paul reminds us that Jesus is available to us. He is forever ready and willing to stand before the Father on our behalf. Paul sets out a great promise that should not be overlooked or underrated: Jesus is always able to save those who approach God through him.

Suggestions for Prayer
1. Psalm 18 is a wealth of drama and promises fulfilled. Read it this week as follows. Day 1: verses 1–7; Day 2: verses 8–20; Day 3: verses 21–31; Day 4: verses 32–39; Day 5: verses 40–46; Day 6: verses 47–51; Day 7: reread and reflect on the portion that meant the most to you.
2. Reflect on the following:
   • How can I love God with my heart and emotions?
   • How can I love God with my soul and essence?
   • How can I love God with my mind and intellect?
   • How can I love God with my strength and body?
3. We can approach God through Jesus. Jesus has taught us how to pray to the Father. Slowly pray the Our Father, reflecting on the words you are saying. Do you believe and mean what you are saying to God the Father?

Suggestion for Journal Keeping
Draw a picture that represents why you are having a difficult time loving a particular person. The picture can be of how you see the person, the emotions you are feeling in relation to him or her, or the circumstances that are creat-

ing the difficulty. Show the picture to Jesus and write all the things Jesus tells you that he loves about you in the situation.

Kathleen M. Henry

Thirty-first Sunday of the Year [C]

READING I	*Wis 11:22—12:2*
Responsorial Psalm	*Ps 145:1–2, 8–9, 10–11, 13, 14*
READING II	*2 Thes 1:11—2:2*
GOSPEL	*Lk 19:1–10*

Reflection on the Readings
The story in today's Gospel is familiar to many of us. It is the story of Zacchaeus, the chief tax collector, who climbed up a tree to catch a glimpse of Jesus as he was traveling into Jericho. The importance of his public office and his reputation with the people mattered little as this man scurried up the tree. In his desire to get a good look at Jesus, to see him clearly, he forgot everything. How surprised he must have been when Jesus stopped beneath that tree and called up to him, personally. Not only had he seen Jesus, but more importantly Jesus had seen and spoken to him. How often we are caught off guard when we encounter Christ in the events of our daily life. Sometimes we totally miss his presence.

This familiar story ends as Jesus has visited Zacchaeus' home and eaten with him. Zacchaeus is a changed man as he offers to make reparation for those whom he has cheated. Salvation has come to Zacchaeus' house. He was once unable to see Christ clearly; now his vision is restored. He is a new creation.

Suggestions for Prayer

1. Reread the first reading. Let the Lord address these words to you personally. Then respond to God by praying the responsorial psalm.
2. Review the events of the day. Pray for the grace to recognize Christ as he comes to you in the events and people of the day.
3. "Zacchaeus came down quickly and received him with joy." What words of welcome would you offer Jesus? Welcome him into your heart in prayer.

Suggestion for Journal Keeping

Consider an unexpected home visit from Jesus. You've met him in the subway, in the grocery store, or along the corridor of your office. He plans to join you for dinner. Write your thoughts and feelings. Are there some areas of your life that you would want to change immediately? How would you respond to such a visit?

Khris S. Ford

Thirty-second Sunday of the Year [A]

READING I	*Wis 6:12–16*
Responsorial Psalm	*Ps 63:2, 3–4, 5–6, 7–8*
READING II	*1 Thes 4:13–18 or 4:13–14*
GOSPEL	*Mt 25:1–13*

Reflection on the Readings

Part of the human journey through life is the quest for wisdom. Today's first reading is from an Old Testament work called the Book of Wisdom. Wisdom, in this book, is a personified attribute of God, i.e., it is spoken of as a person. It is closely identified with the Spirit of God. Wisdom is, then, not a quality acquired by study and discipline (as for the pagans) but rather a favor to be asked of God. It is not merely an ideal toward which to strive in human life, but the power enabling one to live a meaningful life.

To lead godly lives in a corrupt and temptation-ridden society one needs help, and help is near at hand. God's Wisdom has a radiance that makes her easy to find. Furthermore, while people search for Wisdom, Wisdom actively goes about seeking those worthy of her. The ungodly who seek their own life, their own wisdom, have abandoned God and are headed for destruction. Those, however, who put their trust in the Lord can be confident that in seeking true Wisdom, they will be found by true Wisdom.

The Gospel reading from Matthew tells us more about wisdom. The wise virgins keep a torch lit waiting for the Lord. They look around their world not just with their own eyes, as do the foolish virgins, but they have help to see in the darkness. For us today, the parable seems to say that believers and unbelievers all peer into the darkness. But the Christian can see more when aided by the light of Christ. Believers and unbelievers experience the same world of joy and suffering, life and death, but the believers see more in those events. The believers perceive God's presence.

Suggestions for Prayer

1. Reflect on one or more of the following questions:

- In your life, how have you gone about seeking wisdom?
- In the parable, with whom do you identify? Do you feel as though you are peering into the darkness and seeing nothing, or do you look at the world and see meaning, hope and salvation?
- Reflect on the last line of the Gospel. Have you allowed your heart to grow weary of God's absence in a world of violence and evil?

2. Spend some time praying in a room lit only by a candle. Ask yourself: What is the light in my life? What helps me to see the world in a clearer way?

3. Today's responsorial psalm is often used in the Church's morning prayer. Try to pray it a number of times this week as your own morning prayer.

Suggestion for Journal Keeping

Describe an event in your life in which you gained wisdom. What did you learn? How did it change your life?

Douglas Fisher

Thirty-second Sunday of the Year [B]

READING I	*1 Kgs 17:10–16*
Responsorial Psalm	*Ps 146:7, 8–9, 9–10*
READING II	*Heb 9:24–28*
GOSPEL	*Mk 12:38–44 or 12:41–44*

Reflection on the Readings

Today's Scripture readings present us with two stories of widows with limited resources but generous spirits. In both, the central figure is a second-class citizen, a poor woman, alone, with little resources. Yet both women gave freely out of what they had.

Elijah's widow had a spirit of hospitality for the stranger. She gave and received a year's supply of flour and oil for her generosity.

Jesus' widow had a spirit of humility. Though she did not have much, she did not delay contributing from what she had. She recognized the call to give to God and she did not let the possibility that her gift might appear shabby next to the others deter her. For her effort, she received Jesus' praise and attention.

The contrast with the rich is striking. They gave sizable amounts, but merely from their excess. It cost them little yet it made them appear great. Jesus dug under the surface uncovered the injustice that was the source of their funds, and condemned them. God focuses on the purity of the gift, not on its outward appearance.

The reading from the Letter to the Hebrews continues the theme of Jesus as the perfect high priest standing before God on our behalf. Jesus has removed our sins and moved us from the Mosaic law to the new covenant. It also promises a time in the future when Jesus will come again.

Suggestions for Prayer

1. Imagine yourself as the widow in the story from Kings. You and your son are so poor and there is so little food left that you expect to die soon. You are approached by a stranger who asks you to share. Tell God what your emotions and conflicts are about giving up what little you have for yourself and your child to this stranger.

2. Like the widow in the story, you invite the stranger to share what you have. Wonder of wonders, he promises you a year's supply of staples for you and your son. Reflect on the changes in your attitudes and actions because you know you have a year's supply of food.

3. Read Psalm 146. Praise God for his care of you. Renew your trust in God.

Suggestion for Journal Keeping

Imagine yourself as an observer of the events Mark describes. What do you think the widow's life is like? You hear what Jesus says. Write what you can do for the growing number of elderly and single women with children in your own geographic area who are living on fixed incomes.

Kathleen M. Henry

Thirty-second Sunday of the Year [C]

READING I	*2 Mc 7:1–2, 9–14*
Responsorial Psalm	*Ps 17:1, 5–6, 8, 15*
READING II	*2 Thes 2:16—3:5*
GOSPEL	*Lk 20:27–38 or 20:27, 34–38*

Reflection on the Readings

The Sadducees in today's Gospel provide us with a model of a people without hope. Their cynical question portrays their unbelief in the resurrection of the dead. Thus they live only for today.

As Christians, we may wonder about what life after death will be like. We may try to imag-

ine what heaven will be. Although our faith does not provide us with a picture of heaven, it fills us with hope for an everlasting life of intimacy with God, the source of all love. As we reflect on death, we are rooted in this hope. It gives us cause to live our lives differently. Our God is a God of the living. We are called to live as witnesses of this life.

We do this as we share daily in the paschal mystery. By recognizing in our life the pattern of Jesus' life, death and resurrection, we are filled with hope.

Suggestions for Prayer

1. Christians are called to be a sign of hope for the world. Pray for the grace to respond to that call. Recognize how you are already responding and deepening in that commitment.

2. At the beginning of the second reading, Paul prays that the Thessalonians will be filled with hope. Pray with his words and make them your own.

3. How have you entered into Christ's death and resurrection these past few days? Are you experiencing some kind of dying in your life? Is it a physical dying, giving up a destructive habit, or the letting go of someone or something for the sake of another? Pray that you may accept that death and truly know new life as you come through the experience.

Suggestion for Journal Keeping

Describe your thoughts and feelings as you think about your death.

How are these changing as you grow in relationship with the Lord?

Khris S. Ford

Thirty-third Sunday of the Year [A]

READING I	Prv 31:10–13, 19–20, 30–31
Responsorial Psalm	Ps 128:1–2, 3, 4–5
READING II	1 Thes 5:1–6
GOSPEL	Mt 25:14–30 or 25:14-15, 19–21

Reflection on the Readings

It wasn't too long ago that Catholics spoke of the urgency of "saving one's soul." It usually meant to stay out of trouble, to defend oneself against the snares of the world, the flesh and the devil. It was, for many, a largely negative concept meant to keep a person out of sin. Although well intentioned, it was often sadly self-centered. The focus of life was to save my soul.

How do we think about the meaning of salvation? What relationship do we see between our lives now and the final judgment? To whom does life ultimately belong? The answer in the parable is clear: all that we have is a gift given to us. Life comes from God and ultimately belongs to God. To live solely for oneself is to live an illusion. When we are aware that our lives are part of a bigger reality than ourselves, we can be free to live with a new creativity, seeing our lives as a gift received and a gift given.

Today's Gospel attacks the notion of faith as a security system for heaven. Such a notion is based more on fear than on faith. Like the action of the men in the Gospel who are unafraid to invest their silver pieces, faith for us is a risk, a letting go, a willingness to walk.

Salvation is not "saving one's soul," but generously expanding and donating it. It is finding one's life wrapped up in the concerns of God and freed from petty self-preoccupations.

Understanding ourselves as stewards of God's gifts can drastically affect our lives. Our wives, husbands and children are not "ours" at all. They have been entrusted to us. Our neighbors, our parishes, our country, our planet have all been entrusted to us. In the end, we decide how we will care for these gifts or use them. In deciding that, we decide our very selves and our ultimate destiny.

Suggestions for Prayer

1. Reflect on one or more of the following questions:
   - Do you understand faith as something that encourages creativity or conformity? Why?
   - St. Irenaeus once wrote, "The glory of God is man fully alive." Do you associate holiness with human wholeness? How do you think spiritual and personal growth are related to each other?
   - Of the three men mentioned in the parable, with whom do you identify?
2. List your abilities and talents. How have you used them? Have you used them for personal gain only or have you enriched the lives of others?
3. Have you ever helped someone at great personal risk? What was the result? Did you come away a richer person?

Suggestion for Journal Keeping

Describe a time in your life when you left a "small world" for a larger one. It might be when you went away to college, or started a family, or began a new job. What were your feelings? What were the risks? If you join the Church, what are the risks? Can you imagine it expanding your world? In what way?

Douglas Fisher

Thirty-third Sunday of the Year [B]

READING I	*Dn 12:1–3*
Responsorial Psalm	*Ps 16:5, 8, 9–10, 11*
READING II	*Heb 10:11–14, 18*
GOSPEL	*Mk 13:24–32*

Reflection on the Readings

Jesus and the prophet Daniel speak of a time when the world, as we know it, will end. The physical order we currently rely on will disappear and we will have to look to God for new directions.

Daniel says it will be a time of great distress. Jesus expounds and says that not only will there be many trials, but our own physical surroundings will fail us. Daniel promises a different kind of light to lead us then. The wise shall shine brightly and those who lead others to justice shall be like bright stars.

The descriptions are scary but we should be aware of the promises within them. Jesus' words will not pass away. In times of such turmoil, we can cling to and rely on God's word and the awareness that Jesus is among us. The second reading continues to remind us that, in times of stress and upheaval, we have a spokesman at the right hand of God who loves us and died for us.

Suggestions for Prayer

1. As you say yes to following Jesus, reflect on those areas in your life where you see that the old way of doing things is no longer working. Ask Jesus for the courage to make the necessary changes.
2. Psalm 16 says:

> I set the LORD ever before me;
> with him at my right hand I shall not be
> disturbed.

Begin the day by asking the Lord to be at your right hand. Throughout the day, take moments to sense God's presence. At the end of the day, thank the Lord for being with you throughout the day.

Suggestion for Journal Keeping

From today's readings, it is clear that God's ways are not the world's and will survive the end of the world's order. The world we know today can end in many ways—accident, illness, death, or loss of a job, to name just a few. What are the things in your life that would survive such a change? How precious are those things to you now? Do you need to rethink your priorities?

Kathleen M. Henry

Thirty-third Sunday of the Year [C]

READING I	*Mal 3:19–20a*
Responsorial Psalm	*Ps 98:5–6, 7–8, 9*
READING II	*2 Thes 3:7–12*
GOSPEL	*Lk 21:5–19*

Reflection on the Readings

"Lo, the day is coming," says the prophet Malachi. Jesus too says, "The days will come. . . ." Both Jesus and Malachi use the expression to refer to a time of upheaval, a time of judgment, an apocalyptic time. Although "the day" may sometimes refer to the end of the world, in both these readings it refers to the end of *a* world. It is a time of violent transition, a birth into a new reality.

Malachi describes the twofold effect of "the day." For the proud and the evildoers, it will be like a blazing oven that consumes them. But for those who trust in the Lord, it will be a day of justice and healing.

In the Gospel Jesus uses "the day" to refer to the destruction of the temple. This destruction of the temple in A.D. 70 was indeed a time of upheaval and transition for both Christians and Jews. For the Jews it was a crushing defeat at the hand of the Romans and led to a transition of their focus away from the temple as their spiritual center. For Christians, it marked the emergence of Christianity from Judaism and was followed by the persecutions Jesus goes on to describe in this Gospel. Suffering and persecution were indeed the marks of the early Church and led to the deaths of many believers. Yet in the midst of the tumult, Jesus reminds his followers that they are not alone—the Holy Spirit will give them guidance and by patient endurance, the Church will survive.

Suggestions for Prayer

1. Reflect on the symbol of fire that the prophet Malachi uses to describe the action of God. How has the Lord's love for you been like a "blazing oven"? How has it been like the "healing rays" of the sun?
2. What are the situations in your life that call for "patient endurance"? Reflect on Jesus' pledge to be with his disciples in times of difficulty and renew your trust in him.
3. Paul called the Thessalonians to imitate him, especially in the way he worked to support himself. Reflect on the work you do. How can you be a better worker?

Suggestion for Journal Keeping

The Gospel depicts the sufferings that the first Christians endured. Has your decision to become a Catholic brought about changes in your life, in your relationships with your parents, brothers, sisters, spouse, relatives or friends? How are you dealing with any friction that may have arisen? Is there anything that you would like to work harder on?

Robert M. Hamma

Christist the King [A]

READING I	*Ez 34:11–12, 15–17*
Responsorial Psalm	*Ps 23:1–2, 2–3, 5–6*
READING II	*1 Cor 15:20–26, 28*
GOSPEL	*Mt 25:31–46*

Reflection on the Readings

The title of today's feast is somewhat misleading because in order to understand the kingship of Christ we have to forget our preconceptions about kings. The notion of monarchies and kings usually recalls a social and political system repugnant to democratic American sensibilities.

The notion of the king often conjures up the image of someone who is set apart from the common people. But the lordship of Jesus does not separate him from us; rather it unites us.

In the second reading, Paul tells us that in the resurrection Jesus has destroyed death that separates and divides and has restored life. This reconciliation has come through Jesus' humanity: "Since death came through man, the resurrection of the dead came also through man." It is Jesus' complete and total identification with us that brings us life and unity.

The Gospel today makes the point even more strongly. The last few Sundays we have been focusing on the end-time and the final judgment. Today's Gospel leaves no questions about the prerequisites for entrance into the kingdom: feed the hungry, welcome the stranger, clothe the naked, care for the sick, visit the imprisoned. To love our neighbor (without boundaries) is to love our king. The king is totally identified with the most humble of his subjects: "Whatever you did for one of the least brothers of mine you did for me."

The feast of Christ the King forces us to reevaluate our notions of power and authority. The king is one whose power lies in his love and service, one who seeks out the lost, brings back the stray, binds up the injured and heals the sick (see today's first reading from Ezekiel). In the Gospels, the kingship of Christ is revealed most deeply on the cross: "Jesus of Nazareth, King of the Jews." In his death, the king has become one of us in the darkest moment of our humanity.

Suggestions for Prayer

1. Reflect on one or more of the following questions:
   - How do you use your power and authority?
   - Do you have a commitment to the poor? How is it lived out?
   - How do you imagine a final judgment?
2. Think of a time in your life when you helped someone who was down and out. How did it make you feel? Imagine the event and imagine Jesus witnessing your actions.
3. The responsorial psalm comes from Psalm 23. Sit in a quiet place and read this psalm slowly and thoughtfully.

Suggestion for Journal Keeping

Make a list of the things you worry about in life, leaving a line blank after each item. When you are finished write on the blank lines: "The Lord is my shepherd; I shall not want." Now slowly and prayerfully read what you have written.

Douglas Fisher

Christal the King   [B]

Christ the King   [B]

READING I   *Dn 7:13–14*

Responsorial Psalm   *Ps 93:1, 1–2, 5*

READING II   *Rv 1:5–8*

GOSPEL   *Jn 18:33b–37*

Reflection on the Readings

"My kingdom does not belong to this world." Both the first and second readings tell about the broad reaches of God's kingdom.

Daniel's vision is physically expansive, covering all the earth as well as the heavens. The "Son of Man" receives all dominion and power from God forever. Majesty and power are emphasized.

In the Book of Revelation, Jesus comes on a cloud and is the Almighty, the beginning and the end. Jesus, the faithful witness, has made us a royal nation of priests who serve. The focus is on service.

How difficult it was for the people of Jesus' time to see and understand what Jesus was professing and inviting people to join. The idea of a ruler who serves was as foreign then as it is now. Jesus' kingdom still does not belong to this world. Instead we are called to move from worldly ways and values into God's way.

Because we live in this world as much as Daniel, Pilate or John, we have a limited understanding of what exactly God's reign looks like. However, our entrance is through Jesus. Whoever is committed to knowing the truth hears Jesus and follows his ways of love and service to others.

Suggestions for Prayer

1. Jesus says that those committed to the truth hear him. Place a difficult situation before Jesus and ask to be shown the way.
2. Christ is our King. Think of those areas of your life where Jesus is Lord. Spend time thanking and praising God for his kingship in those areas.
3. Read Psalm 93 and reflect on a time when God saved you from turmoil and distress that seemed to be overpowering you. Tell God how your trust has increased as a result of that experience.

Suggestion for Journal Keeping

Write about what it means to you to be in Jesus' royal nation of priests. How does it feel to be a priest, a leader? How does it feel to be royalty? As a royal priest of the order of Jesus, how are you fulfilling the call to service?

Kathleen M. Henry

Christ the King [C]

READING I	*2 Sm 5:1–3*
Responsorial Psalm	*Ps 122:1–2, 3–4, 4–5*
READING II	*Col 1:12–20*
GOSPEL	*Lk 23:35–43*

Reflection on the Readings

Today we hear the story of the crucifixion of Jesus, how the soldiers threw dice for his clothes, mocked him, and offered him cheap wine. It is in the context of this Gospel reading that we celebrate the solemnity of Christ the King. What a perfect illustration of the paradox that Christ lived!

This is a king like no other we have known, and the contrast is evident as we ponder the scene of his death on the cross. We see his throne to be the cross, no gold-laden vestments, only nakedness before his people, no armored guards on his right and left, only two thieves that share in his painful death. Even more, we see no attitude of revenge or anger. Rather we witness a man who is willing to forgive and offers himself completely for the very men who kill him. He even promises one of the thieves that he will share paradise with him. This is Christ the King whose kingship serves as a model for our living.

Today's Gospel calls us to commit ourselves to be followers of this King and to the building of his kingdom. To do this we must model the King himself.

Suggestions for Prayer

1. Respond to this call to follow Christ the King. Begin your prayer by saying, "Christ, my King. . . ."

2. The cross is the banner or emblem of our King. Begin your prayer with a slow signing of yourself with the cross. Spend some time in silence and reflect on the emblem that you have claimed.

3. Pray with the second reading from Colossians. Read it slowly one time. Then read it again, pausing for prayer after each sentence. Then read it a third time all the way thorough.

Suggestion for Journal Keeping

In Jesus' last moments on the cross, he assured the thief of his place in paradise. Why is that an important part of this story? What does it mean for your personal story?

Khris S. Ford

August 15
The Assumption of the
Blessed Virgin Mary

READING I	*Rv 11:19a; 12:1–6a, 10ab*
Responsorial Psalm	*Ps 45:10, 11, 12, 16*
READING II	*1 Cor 15:20–27*
GOSPEL	Lk 1:39–56

Reflection on the Readings

The feast of the Assumption is a celebration of Mary's sharing in the fullness of God's love in her death. More importantly, though, the feast points to the promised future for all. Mary reminds us of our own desire for completion and union with God. She also reminds us that the fulfillment of that desire can only come when we live lives that are faithful to God's values as proclaimed by Jesus. Mary, because of her obedience to God's ways, now lives in the fullness of life with God: what we all will be in Christ.

The Gospel text today highlights these values of God. Mary's canticle of praise is a proclamation of God's unending love and compassion that calls us to justice, reconciliation, love and community. It is a recognition that in Jesus the reign of God has begun. This reign of God will be fully realized when all creation is drawn up into the fullness of God's embrace, thus experiencing reconciliation, transformation and redemption. We, the followers of Jesus, participate in this reign of God by our witness through our lives of justice and compassion.

Jesus has redeemed us fully. Mary shares in the fullness of this redemption because of her active obedience to God's life in her, the demands of the reign of God. Mary becomes a symbol of hope for our future.

Suggestions for Prayer

1. Reflect on the following: What are my hopes for the future? What are the promises of God for me? What do I need to trust God's promises for life and love?

2. Pray the traditional mantra prayer, the rosary, reflecting on the symbol of the assumption of Mary. Pause between each decade, asking God to help you become more aware of your need to hope in God.

3. Return to the Gospel text for today. Slowly pray the canticle of praise, being aware of the call to lives of justice and mercy contained in the prayer.

Suggestion for Journal Keeping

Recall the opening lines to the canticle of praise in today's Gospel. For what in your life and in our world do you proclaim God's greatness, finding joy in God? How does such awareness call you to be a person of justice and mercy?

Thomas H. Morris

November 1
All Saints

READING I	*Rv 7:2–4, 9–14*
Responsorial Psalm	*Ps 24:1–2, 3–4, 5–6*
READING II	*1 Jn 3:1–3*
GOSPEL	*Mt 5:1–12a*

Reflection on the Readings

The feast of All Saints is a celebration of all those women and men who lived in fidelity to the call of the Gospel: those named by our community as saints and those whose names we do not know. We set them aside, not because they led extraordinary lives, but rather because in their very ordinary lives they believed that the cross of Jesus Christ made all the difference. This feast also reminds us that we are all called to be saints, to be holy.

Today's Gospel invites us to be disciples of Jesus. The beatitudes present a new way of life not centered on personal gain but on self-sacrificing love, a love that witnesses to the gracious and compassionate presence of God that liberates and redeems. Jesus raises up as the way of the holy—the women and men of the reign of God—crucial attitudes toward life and our relationships: being poor, so we know the only source of power is God; the solidarity and compassion of the sorrowing; the gentle who do not

bring violence; the true longing for a holy justice; the plenitude and abundance of mercy; the singleness of heart that acknowledges the one desire that informs all our other desires—to know God; the active stand for restoration, reconciliation and harmony. If we live faithfully these values, then surely we will disrupt the status quo, we will bring upon us the wrath of others, as Jesus did. But we have cause to rejoice, to be glad, for it is in our fidelity to these values of the reign of God that we share in God's very life. Then, as we heard in the text from the Book of Revelation, we will proclaim salvation from our God as one of the saints, the holy women and men of God.

Suggestions for Prayer

1. Remember the women and men in our Christian community who have died and share in the new life of Jesus. Slowly and prayerfully recite or chant their names, recognizing your solidarity with them: "Holy Mary, Mother of God. . . St. Paul. . . St. Mary Magdalene. . . St. Thomas. . . St. Francis. . . " adding names of family, friends and contemporary saints.
2. Bring the needs of your neighborhood to prayer. Who are the women and men who are leading selfless lives, bringing God's love to others? Ask God for the grace to bring holiness to the life of your family and neighborhood.
3. Pray the Gospel text, the beatitudes. Stop between each beatitude, asking God to give you the needed grace to live this value.

Suggestion for Journal Keeping

List for yourself what you consider important and necessary for a happy life. Now reflect on your need for God. What keeps you from recognizing your need for God? How are your "essentials" similar or different from the values of the beatitudes?

Thomas H. Morris

December 8
Immaculate Conception

READING I	*Gn 3:9—15, 20*
Responsorial Psalm	*Ps 98:1, 2–3, 3–4*
READING II	*Eph 1:3–6, 11–12*
GOSPEL	*Lk 1:26–38*

Reflection on the Readings

The feast of the Immaculate Conception is a celebration of Mary's beginnings, of God's free choice to surround Mary from the moment of conception with God's love or grace. Mary reminds us of the possibility of this new life now available to all of us because of Jesus, the Christ. We use many images to say this: freedom from sin, life of grace, God's abiding presence.

Yet the Gospel text points us to the announcement of the conception of Jesus, not of Mary. Why? Because Mary is able to trust God's presence within her (what we call grace), overcoming her own fears and confusions. In the Genesis text, we hear the vivid story of the human community's choice not to live faithfully in relationship with God, thus embracing sin. Mary stands in sharp contrast to this life of sin because of her trust in God's love and presence, and therefore can accept God's invitation to be the mother of Jesus.

Mary is held before us as a model of Christian living: men and women who can trust God present-with-us, and therefore open to the possibilities of life (grace) and not death (sin).

Suggestions for Prayer

1. Take a few moments, quiet down, and gently recall God who is already present with you. Imagine yourself surrounded with God's love. What does this love look like, feel like? Now imagine that same love penetrating you, completely filling you: What does this love look like, feel like? Sit in the recognition of yourself as loved by God.

2. Imagine yourself with Mary at the angel's visitation. Hear the angel turn to you and ask you a special favor from God. What is that favor? Hear your response. What does your response tell you about your relationship with God?

3. Slowly recite the Hail Mary. Be sensitive to Mary's role as advocate and companion with you on your journey of faith.

Suggestion for Journal Keeping

Recall some of the times when you chose to close in on yourself, to not trust, to be afraid, to not have hope. Write images and words that describe the feelings and capture your sense of fear. Now recall times when you believed in your goodness, used your gifts, took important risks. Write images and words to express those feelings. Relate this experience to today's feast of trusting in God's loving presence, the gift of grace.

Thomas H. Morris

Contributors

EMILY J. BESL holds an M.A. in liturgical studies from the University of Notre Dame. Presently she teaches part-time in the theology department at Xavier University in Cincinnati, Ohio, and serves as a consultant to the Archdiocese of Cincinnati Worship Office. A member of the Archdiocesan Worship Commission, she is also a frequent speaker and lecturer.

KATHLEEN BROWN is dean of the School of Theological Studies at Kino Institute, the center for religious studies and lay ministry formation for the Diocese of Phoenix. She serves as an institute coordinator for the North American Forum on the Catechumenate. With Frank Sokol, Kathy edited *Issues in the Christian Initiation of Children: Liturgy and Catechesis* (Liturgy Training Publications, 1991). She received her S.T.B. and Master of Arts degree in theology from St. Paul University, Ottawa, Canada. She has written numerous articles and is an international speaker and consultant on initiation.

JOHN T. BUTLER is president of Archbishop Carroll High School in Washington, D.C., and president/CEO of the Human Resource Learning Center, Inc. For seventeen years, he served as catechumenate director at St. Augustine Parish in Washington, D.C., and continues to serve as an institute speaker and facilitator for the North American Forum on the Catechumenate. He has written on the role of the catechumenate director, lectionary-based catechesis and African American Catholic perspectives on evangelization and initiation. He received his Bachelor of Science degree from St. Michael's College in 1974 and his Master of Education degree from Howard University in 1979.

JOANNA CASE has been directly involved with initiation in the Diocese of Charlotte since 1980. She serves on the board of directors for the North American Forum on the Catechumenate and is a national presenter on the forum team, with special interest in rural ministry. Joanna holds a master's degree in religious education and is retired after nearly forty years of teaching in public and Catholic schools.

CLARE M. COLELLA is director of electronic communications for the Diocese of San Bernardino. She was formerly director of the Office of Sacramental Formation there and continues to serve as a resource person as well as being on her parish catechumenate team. For several years, she served on the board of the North American Forum on the Catechumenate. Mrs. Colella holds a master's degree in religious education from Seattle University.

REV. MICHAEL P. ENRIGHT is pastor of Immaculate Conception parish in Chicago. He has written for *Liturgy 80, The Chicago Catechumenate, Upturn,* and *Crisis.* He has given presentations to the National Association of Directors of Pastoral Education, supervises pastoral education for college seminarians and is a member of the Archdiocesan Commission on Church Art and Architecture in Chicago. Father Enright holds a masters degree and a licentiate in sacred theology from Mundelein Seminary in Chicago.

DOUGLAS FISHER is an Episcopal priest, pastor and college chaplain. He has also directed numerous religious education videos, including the best-selling *Mystery of Faith* and *Questions of the Soul.*

KHRIS S. FORD serves as R.C.I.A. facilitator for the Diocese of Galveston-Houston. A member of the North American Forum on the Catechumenate institutes team, she is also a contributor to *Breaking Open the Word of God,* Cycles A and C (Paulist Press). She holds a master's degree in education.

ROBERT M. HAMMA is the author of numerous books and articles on spirituality and family life. Among his books are *Along Your Desert Journey* (Paulist Press), *Landscapes of the Soul: A Spirituality of Place, Let's Say Grace: Mealtime Prayers for Family Occasions Throughout the Year,* and *Circle of Friends: Encountering the Caring Voices in Your Life,* which he co-

authored with Robert J. Wicks (all from Ave Maria Press). He holds an M.A. in theology from the University of Notre Dame as well as an M.Div. degree.

KATHLEEN M. HENRY has five years of experience in R.C.I.A. Presently she is a parish R.C.I.A. director and a member of the Christian Initiation Committee of the Oakland Diocese. Kathleen is cofounder of Resources for Ministry and Christian Initiation, providing formation and continuing support for parish ministries of initiation. She is a certified spiritual director and has spent eight years in small faith-sharing communities. She is a college lecturer and an attorney in private practice.

REV. MICHAEL J. KOCH is pastor of St. Philip Neri Church in Saskatoon, Canada. He received his education at the University of Saskatchewan and St. Joseph Seminary, Edmonton. He also studied at the University of San Francisco and in Jerusalem. Father Koch is a member of the steering committee of the North American Forum on the Catechumenate, and a contributing author to *Breaking Open the Word of God,* Cycles A, B and C (Paulist Press).

REV. STEVEN M. LANZA is pastor of Notre Dame de Chicago Parish. He has been active in pastoral work in parishes of the archdiocese for eighteen years and serves as a member of the Archdiocesan Catechumenate Board. He is a team member of the North American Forum on the Catechumenate and is a contributing author to the Foundations in Faith series (Resources for Christian Living). He holds an S.T.L. degree from the pontifical faculty of the University of St. Mary of the Lake Seminary.

REV. EUGENE A. LaVERDIERE, S.S.S., is the editor of *Emmanuel* magazine and an associate editor of *The Bible Today*. He holds a doctorate in New Testament and early christian literature from the University of Chicago. Father LaVerdiere is the author of many books as well as audio and videocassettes. His most recent books include *The New Testament in the Life of the Church* and *When We Pray* (both from Ave Maria Press). He was also a contributing author to *Breaking Open the Word of God*, Cycles A, B and C (Paulist Press).

ELIZABETH S. LILLY is a pastoral associate for Sacred Heart Parish in Saratoga, California. Since 1980, she has directed the catechumenate in three parishes in the Diocese of San Jose, where she has also served on the liturgy commission. She continues to serve on the diocesan committees on the catechumenate and on environment and art. She has contributed to several books on the initiation process, including all three cycles of *Breaking Open the Word of God* (Paulist Press). She is a graduate of the University of California, Berkeley, with a master's degree in the history of art.

MARY KAY MEIER is a member of the catechumenate team of St. Irenaeus Parish in Cypress, California. She also serves as a member of the steering committee of the North American Forum on the Catechumenate. Active in spiritual direction and team formation, she holds a B.A. in education from Wisconsin State University.

THOMAS H. MORRIS is a member of the pastoral team at St. Rose of Lima parish, Gaithersburg, Maryland. He is also a team member of the North American Forum on the Catechumenate and instructor in pastoral theology at DeSales School of Theology, Washington, D.C. He holds graduate degrees in theology and spirituality and is a doctoral candidate in Christian spirituality at The Catholic University of America. His publications include contributions to *Breaking Open the Word of God*, Cycles A and B and *The RCIA: Transforming the Church* (Paulist Press).

KATHRYN A. SCHNEIDER is director of St. Margaret's House, a day center for women and children located in South Bend, Indiana. She also serves as director of lay ministry formation for the Master of Divinity Program at the University of Notre Dame. She holds an M.Div. degree from Notre Dame and is coauthor with her husband Robert M. Hamma of *Prayers for a Lifetime Together* (Sorin Books).

JOSEPH P. SINWELL currently serves as diocesan director of religious education for the Diocese of Providence and as codirector of the Rhode Island catechumenate. He is a founding member of the North American Forum on the Catechumenate. His articles have appeared in *Christian Initiation, Resources, Today's Parish, Christian Adulthood* and *Catechist*. He is also the coeditor of *Breaking Open the Word of God*, Cycles A, B, and C (Paulist Press). He holds master's degrees in religious education and agency counseling and is a candidate for a Doctor of Ministry degree at St. Mary's University in Baltimore.